P9-DNW-889

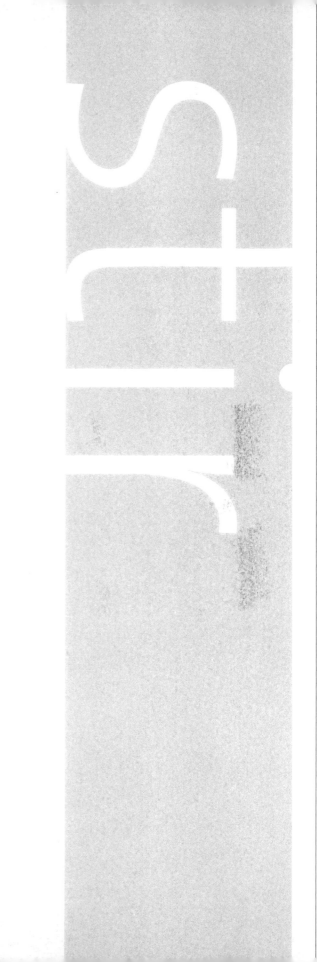

stir

Mixing It Up
In the Italian Tradition

Barbara Lynch with Joanne Smart

photographs by Deborah Jones

HOUGHTON MIFFLIN HARCOURT   BOSTON   NEW YORK   2009

For information about permission to reproduce selections from this book, write to Permissions, Houghton Mifflin Harcourt Publishing Company, 215 Park Avenue South, New York, New York 10003.

www.hmhbooks.com

Library of Congress Cataloging-in-Publication Data

Lynch, Barbara, date.

  Stir : mixing it up in the Italian tradition / Barbara Lynch, with Joanne Smart ; photographs by Deborah Jones.

    p. cm.

  Includes index.

  ISBN 978-0-618-57681-4

  1. Cookery, Italian. I. Smart, Joanne McAllister. II. Title.

  TX723.L87 2009

  641.5945—dc22

2009013281

Book design by i4 Design, Sausalito, CA

Printed in China

SCP 10 9 8 7 6 5 4 3 2 1

TO MARCHESA, THE BEST CARROT PEELER/SOUS-CHEF EVER

ACKNOWLEDGMENTS

Alain Ducasse, Daniel Boulud, Joël Robuchon, and Gualtiero Marchesi are my heroes. When I was learning to cook, I turned to their books for guidance. As a chef, I am still inspired by them.

My restaurant No. 9 Park would not be what it is without Cat Silirie, whose ability to marry my food with incredible wines is nothing short of amazing. Our friendship and collaboration have spanned more than twenty years, and we're still learning as much and laughing as hard as ever. Cat is brilliant and a constant source of insight and motivation. Thank you, thank you, thank you.

Early on, two people made lasting impressions on me and set me on this course. Thank you, Susan Logozzo, for noticing that I had a knack for cooking back in high school home ec and, more important, for teaching me how to believe in myself. Chef Mario Bonello, another early mentor, demonstrated nightly the art of fine cuisine and service. From him I came to understand a chef's most important job: to make people happy. Thank you both for direction and instruction when I needed it most.

My editor, Rux Martin, and my agent, Doe Coover—two hot tickets and the best in the business—challenged me relentlessly. It wasn't always fun (and was sometimes a pain in the ass), but their pushing was all worth it. Thank you both for your endless perseverance, spirit, and support.

Ben Elliott was my right hand throughout this project. Thank you for your tireless recipe development, for your careful recipe testing, and for reading (and rereading) the recipes for accuracy. This book simply would not have happened without you. Thank you for cracking us up regularly, too.

Photographer Deborah Jones immediately "got" my food, and the proof is in her gorgeous photos. I admire her brilliant aesthetic and her respect for simplicity. Thank you for all the listening, tasting, and guiding at our photo shoots. Thanks also to Sandra Cook, who styled the food so beautifully, and to Janet Mumford for her spot-on book design, especially the cover: artistic, modern, but also mouth-watering.

Joanne Smart absolutely nailed my personality and sense of humor, capturing my voice throughout the book. She was also the greatest cheerleader during this process, testing and tasting recipes with gusto and always voicing her excitement and love for a dish. Thank you for your enthusiasm—it is contagious.

The farmers, ranchers, artisans, and winemakers who supply me with wonderful produce, fish, meat, game, cheese, and wine also provide endless education for me and my team. You make it an absolute pleasure to cook, pour, and serve. Thank you.

For providing much of the gorgeous china, flatware, and serving pieces throughout this book and in my restaurants, thank you to Natalie and Curt Carpenter at Lekker.

I also want to thank Colin Lynch, Eli Feldman, Jeff Macklin, Sarah Hearn, Ralph Fiegel, and Caitlin Champagne. Having this great team do what they do best—run my restaurants and make incredible food—made it possible for me to focus on this book.

Also all the cooks, managers, and servers who so fantastically and passionately work each day—you are all an inspiration to me.

And thank you, Charlie. For everything.

contents

INTRODUCTION   x

STARTERS AND SMALL BITES   1

SALADS WITH SUBSTANCE   57

SATISFYING SOUPS   81

A PASSION FOR PASTA   111

FROM THE SEA   175

CHICKEN, DUCK, AND A GOOSE   205

FROM THE BUTCHER: BEEF, PORK, AND LAMB   233

ON THE SIDE   261

SWEET TREATS   289

INDEX   312

SOMETIMES I TRY TO IMAGINE HOW MY LIFE WOULD HAVE TURNED OUT IF I HADN'T DISCOVERED COOKING. It would have been easy for me not to. I was born in 1964 in South Boston, a working-class town bordering Boston proper. My family lived in a four-room apartment in the Mary Ellen McCormack housing project. Like most families in Southie, ours was a big one. And, like most, we were poor, fiercely Irish, and extremely loyal. From what I saw, people hardly ever left the neighborhood. The older boys I knew grew up to be policemen, politicians, and criminals (often a mix of the three), but they stayed right there in Southie. And the girls I knew married them. If I ever had thoughts at all as to what I might be when I grew up, they were modest ones. I might have pictured myself running a bar (in Southie) or maybe opening a sub shop (in Southie). But having a restaurant of my own on Beacon Hill? No way. In fact, if a fortune-teller had told me at fourteen what good things were in store for me, I would have laughed in her face and told her where she could shove such bullshit (even though somewhere deep down I would have hoped that what she said was true). How could I, Barbara Lynch, one of seven kids being raised by a single mother—my dad died a month before I was born—ever hope for something like that?

That my ticket out would involve food was not foreshadowed by the way we were raised. Everything we ate came out of a box, jar, or can. Though my mother eventually remarried, she raised us for the most part alone and worked multiple jobs just to keep us off welfare. Like most of the kids I knew, I didn't give much thought to the food I ate and cared even less about how it was cooked. In good weather we reluctantly headed home to wolf down whatever was put in front of us before heading back out to the streets to play poker on the stoop or drink beer in the underground tunnels that linked the buildings in the project. I can't tell you how many times the police had to chase us out of there. And I can't tell you whose car we "borrowed" one day long before any of us had licenses and drove down the cement steps that led to the project's playground before abandoning it in a rowdy panic. I remember lots of laughs on such wild escapades, but looking back, I marvel that any of us made it out of there without winding up in jail or the morgue. (And plenty of us didn't.)

If my house and the project were crowded and chaotic, high school was worse. Boston was ordered to desegregate its public schools, and we white Southie kids were bused to predominantly black Roxbury while the Roxbury kids went to Southie. I wasn't cut out for high school, and I didn't excel in the overcrowded, tense, and even violent classrooms. I did the minimum to get by and might not even have stayed as long as I did if it were not for the home economics class where I first learned how to cook. Before that time, I had never made anything for anybody. I got hooked on the sense of wonder and accomplishment that I felt after creating something delicious. And so it was there, in Ms. Logozzo's class, that I first got high on that thing that drives all good cooks: the desire to please others by making food they love to eat. I could tell that I had a knack: cooking felt completely natural, as if it were something I was born to do.

During my last year of high school, as one of my three jobs, I worked as a chambermaid at an exclusive private club, where my mother was a waitress. The simple dishes we made in Ms. Logozzo's class were nothing like the fancy French food served here, which was brought with great fanfare into the dining room under shiny silver domes. Though I barely recognized what was on the plate, I loved to watch as the dome was dramatically lifted off and see the delight on the faces of the people being served.

Around the same time, I began to hang out with a girl down the street whose dad was Irish but whose mother was Italian and therefore exotic. On the steps that led to their apartment were huge pots of basil, parsley, and rosemary, none of which I had ever seen fresh. And instead of the Oreos and milk my mother offered to my friends, Mrs. O'Brien plied us with homemade biscotti and tiny cups of espresso from an enormous chrome and gold machine that dominated the room. Eating at her house, you could forget you were in Southie.

EVEN THOUGH I WAS PRETTY SURE I WANTED TO COOK IN SOME CAPACITY, I DIDN'T KNOW WHAT TO DO NEXT. My main job as a secretary at a storage company was boring but steady and uncomplicated. I felt safe tucked away in the little cubicle and might be there still if a friend hadn't literally grabbed me by the hand and pulled me away from my desk, saying I had to get the hell out.

I was hired as an assistant cook on a dinner cruise ship, and the day before the season opened, the head chef quit. Not knowing any better, I took his place and somehow survived. By the time fall came, Ms. Logozzo had gone on to work at the Cambridge School of Culinary Arts. I couldn't afford the classes, but in exchange for washing dishes, she let me audit on the nights she taught. I returned to the men's club, this time to cook, and eventually wound up working for the chef Todd English when he opened Olives in Charlestown.

I loved everything about working in a restaurant kitchen. I would leave for work cranky, tired, and pissed at the world, yet as soon as I stepped into the hot kitchen, my mood shifted. The frantic yet focused energy, the cacophony of sound, the enticing smells coming from the grill, never failed to revive me. My aches, my fatigue, the boyfriend I was thinking of dumping, the overdue rent—all vanished in the tasks at hand.

Even though I worked hard, it was painfully obvious that I lacked the experience and knowledge of other cooks. The louder the chef yelled at me, the more resolute I became. I worked all night and studied cookbooks all day. I read Waverley Root's *The Food of Italy* cover to cover three times in a row.

ULTIMATELY, IT WAS A TRIP TO ITALY THAT HELPED ME FIND MY OWN VOICE IN THE KITCHEN. At a small farm in Tuscany, under the tutelage of a farmer and his wife, I learned Italian cuisine at the source. I refined my pasta-making technique, striving to make each batch even more delicate than the last. I learned the value of seasonal cooking and local products, all of which came in handy when, back in Boston, I took over the kitchen of Galleria Italiana as executive chef and transformed a tiny, casual, cafeteria-style establishment into a hip place that got national attention. At Galleria I found my stride. Not only was the press positive, but I also met my future husband, Charlie, while working there. Cat Silirie, my friend and wine director at No. 9, and I had a great time running Galleria, but the thought kept occurring to me that it was time to have complete control and to open my own restaurant, where I could do everything the way I wanted.

It's amazing how quickly things can change. Within five months of leaving Galleria, I not only found the perfect spot for my restaurant but also married Charlie. On a walk one night, the two of us came upon the space for what was to become No. 9 Park: a former card shop in an elegant townhouse just steps away from the gold-domed state house. Charlie and I signed the lease for the restaurant one day and got married the next.

Before opening No. 9, Charlie and I took a trip to France. I was not on vacation—I was on a mission. I had read cookbooks by the French masters, and now I wanted to experience their cooking firsthand. Charlie and I dined at eight different Michelin starred restaurants, including Taillevent, Alain Ducasse, and L'Arpège. It was a marathon of phenomenal food and discovery.

By the time I actually opened No. 9, in 1998, I had learned to trust my instincts and follow my palate, and I had developed my own cooking style: Italian inspired, French influenced, with a heavy Boston accent from our native ingredients—lobster, clams, scallops, and local fruits and vegetables. In Italy I learned to love pure, simple flavors, exquisite fresh pastas, and homey braises. My trip to France gave me an appreciation of traditional technique, deeply flavored sauces, and classics like consommé and duck confit. New England practicality keeps my food honest.

DESPITE MY SUCCESSES, I REMEMBER HOW STARVED I WAS FOR INFORMATION AS AN ASPIRING CHEF, WHICH IS WHY I DECIDED TO FINALLY WRITE MY OWN COOKBOOK. You'll note that the title is a verb. That's because I want to inspire you to get moving. I want you to read my recipes, try them, and make them again. Some, like Gorgonzola Fondue (page 37), are so incredibly easy and quick to make that it's almost embarrassing. Others, such as my Prune-Stuffed Gnocchi with Foie Gras Sauce (page 159), should be saved for special occasions. Most are for those days when you have the time to slow down and prepare something with care to share with others. Whichever recipes you choose, the following advice will help you achieve delicious results.

START WITH THE BEST INGREDIENTS. Part of me, the part that remembers what it was like to have no money, wishes this weren't so, but how well a dish turns out depends on the goodness of its ingredients. You can't make a delicious raw tomato salad with winter tomatoes flown halfway across the world to your supermarket.

GET TO KNOW YOUR STOVE AND OVEN. Every stove and every oven cooks food differently. Regard cooking times as broad guides only. Rely more on the descriptions of doneness in the recipes, and trust yourself to know when something looks deeply browned or feels tender.

SEASON WELL AND KEEP TASTING. Your tomatoes may be sweeter than mine, your vinegar sharper, your olive oil fruitier. Most home cooks don't salt their food enough. Without a good amount of salt, the flavors of the dish stay muted. The kind of salt is important: use kosher, not table salt. Not only does kosher salt taste better, but the crystals are easier to see when you're salting a piece of meat, fish, or poultry. Table salt contains unpleasant-tasting additives, and its fine grain does little to enhance food. Acidic ingredients like lemon can also serve to brighten the overall flavor of a dish.

BREAK RULES ONCE IN A WHILE. Maybe it's the Southie rebel in me, but as soon as you tell me I can't do something, I have to try it for myself. Traditional Italian cooks say never serve fish with cheese, but I love Parmigiano and clams. I also let my potatoes cool before making them into gnocchi—a big no-no in some Italian kitchens, but it works better. As you cook from this book, you may want to break my "rules." For instance, I don't let my chefs use tongs (see why on page 183), but if you like them, go for it.

FIND PLEASURE IN THE PROCESS OF COOKING. Set aside a chunk of time, put on some comfortable shoes, play your favorite music, and give yourself over to the tasks at hand. Have a glass of wine, if that helps, and relax into the feeling that what you make will bring happiness to your family, your friends, and, most important, you.

starters and small bites

BAKED CHEESE AND TOMATOES WITH BLACK OLIVE CRISPS   5

HAM AND CHEESE PUFF-PASTRY BITES WITH HONEY MUSTARD   7

FIG, RICOTTA, AND PROSCIUTTO TARTINES   10

SPICED PRUNES   12

PICKLED ONIONS   13

YELLOW AND RED BELL PEPPER AGRODOLCE   14

QUICK CHICKEN LIVER PÂTÉ   15

BUTCHER SHOP BEEF TARTARE   18

CAULIFLOWER CHAUD-FROID   22

TOMATO TARTE TATIN   26

RICOTTA-STUFFED HEIRLOOM TOMATOES WITH BLACK OLIVE
VINAIGRETTE AND SAFFRON CROUTONS   30

GORGONZOLA FONDUE   37

SLOW-ROASTED CLAMS WITH SPICY TOMATO SAUCE   38

OYSTERS ON THE HALF SHELL WITH SPARKLING MIGNONETTE   39

CITRUS-CURED SALMON   41

CLASSIC SHRIMP COCKTAIL   43

FRIED CALAMARI WITH SPICY LEMON AÏOLI   45

BRIOCHE PIZZA WITH FRIED PISTACHIOS AND HONEY   50

BRIOCHE PIZZA WITH BLACK OLIVES AND FRESH RICOTTA   51

BRIOCHE PIZZA WITH ROASTED POTATOES AND ROSEMARY   52

BRIOCHE PIZZA DOUGH   54

I'm a big believer in first impressions. For instance, when I met my husband, Charlie, I knew right off that he was the one for me. A lot of people say that about their spouse. But if you had known me at the time—a young, somewhat brash, hardworking chef who could drink and swear with the best of them (little has changed)—and you had known Charlie, then a recent widower and quite a bit older than me, you would have been as surprised as everyone else when we became a couple. Yet that first time we met, we connected. His calm and assured demeanor, his wit, and (he'll kill me if I don't say this) his good looks all made a favorable first impression. I was smitten.

I think a lot about first impressions when I'm creating first-course dishes for my restaurants. A lot rides on these small plates. For people new to my restaurants, appetizers are the first impression of my cooking—and, by extension, of me—and I want people to feel nothing less than love at first bite. I want them to swoon, to sigh, to say to the person next to them, "This is *so* f'ing good." For my regulars, an appetizer is the first taste of what a particular night has in store; I want to excite them— *especially* them—with something fabulous.

Fabulous doesn't have to mean complicated or difficult to make. In the summer, perfectly ripe heirloom tomatoes sliced thickly, drizzled with the best olive oil, and sprinkled with fleur de sel rival all else as the best way to kick off a meal. And when I have such great seasonal produce, I tend to treat it simply, which makes my job easy. Yet I also enjoy creating more elaborate starters, playing with textures and flavors to offer a taste of something new. Because I have mined recipes for this chapter from all of my restaurants, the dishes reflect various styles and moods; some are elegant and refined, while others are much more casual.

CAULIFLOWER CHAUD-FROID (PAGE 22)

Baked Cheese and Tomatoes with Black Olive Crisps

SERVES 4

Baked whole tomatoes engulfed by soft baked cheese; you spread some black olive paste on thin slices of toasted bread and use them to scoop up the delicious, melty goodness. Be warned, though: guests can't stop eating this, even when they know there's a lot of food ahead.

I love fresh goat cheese here because it melts well, but just about whatever cheese you have on hand will work, including a mix of cheeses. In fact, I always make this after a party to use up all those bits left over on the cheese board. (It's also great hangover food.) The tomatoes are more pleasant to eat if peeled, but you can leave the skins on if you're feeling lazy. If there are pretty green vines on the tomatoes, I like to leave them attached, especially if they are connecting a few of the tomatoes. The vines add height and color to the dish and just look cool rising up from the cheese. Serve the tomatoes from a single baking dish as a dip to share, or divide the cheese and tomatoes among smaller, individual baking dishes for a first course. Though I give amounts, this recipe doesn't really need such precision.

12	medium tomatoes, preferably heirloom, or 48 Campari or cherry tomatoes, preferably with some of their vines still attached, peeled if you like (see page 6)
3	tablespoons extra-virgin olive oil, plus more for making the crisps
	Kosher salt and freshly ground black pepper
	Pinch sugar, if needed
9	ounces cheese (see headnote), cut into pieces
2–3	tablespoons heavy cream, if needed
	Fleur de sel
½	loaf ciabatta or other rustic bread, sliced as thin as possible
2–3	tablespoons Black Olive Paste (recipe follows) or good purchased tapenade

Heat the oven to 325°F. Put the tomatoes on a small baking sheet. Drizzle the olive oil over the tomatoes and season with salt, pepper, and a pinch of sugar if the tomatoes are not very sweet. Bake until the tomatoes begin to soften, about 12 minutes for medium tomatoes and 8 minutes for cherry tomatoes. Remove from the oven.

Meanwhile, crumble the cheese into an 8- or 9-inch square baking dish or divide it among four individual baking dishes. If using mostly hard cheese, add the cream. Put the tomatoes on top of the cheese and bake until the cheese melts, 5 to 8 minutes. Sprinkle the tomatoes with a little fleur de sel and some pepper.

Increase the oven temperature to 375°F. Brush the bread slices with a little olive oil and bake on a baking sheet, turning once, until crisp and golden brown on both sides,

6 to 8 minutes total (check early). Let cool briefly, spread on some black olive paste, and serve with the warm baked tomatoes.

MAKE AHEAD: *You can assemble the dish up to a day ahead. Cover it with plastic wrap and refrigerate it. Then all you have left to do is pop it in the oven to melt the cheese.*

Black Olive Paste

MAKES 1 CUP

I constantly find myself reaching for black olive paste in the kitchen. Delicious on its own as a spread for bruschetta, it's also tasty rubbed on lamb (page 37), spread on pizza or sandwiches, or added to a vinaigrette or sauce. You can buy good prepared versions of it, or even substitute jarred tapenade (which often includes garlic and other ingredients, too). However, I prefer the fresher taste I get when making it myself. It really couldn't be easier: two ingredients and a whir in the food processor and you're done.

1 cup pitted black olives, such as Kalamata or Niçoise
¼ cup extra-virgin olive oil

Combine the olives and olive oil in a food processor or a blender. Process on high until pureed, 1 to 2 minutes.

MAKE AHEAD: *I always have some of this hanging around; it will keep for a month at least, refrigerated in a plastic container with a lid, with a thin layer of oil on top.*

Peeling Tomatoes

To peel tomatoes, cut an X into the bottom of each one with a small paring knife. Bring a saucepan of salted water to a boil and have a bowl of ice water nearby. Put the tomatoes in the boiling water for about 30 seconds, or until the skins begin to pucker, then immediately plunge them into the ice water. The skins should peel off easily. If not, use the paring knife to help them along.

Because I am trained not to let any food go to waste, I sometimes fry the tomato peels in a little hot oil to use for a garnish. Give it a try if you're feeling fancy.

Ham and Cheese Puff-Pastry Bites with Honey Mustard

Think of the best grilled cheese you've ever had. This is way better. With its layers of salty ham, honey mustard, and melted cheese nestled between crisp, buttery puff pastry, it's the perfect finger food to offer at a cocktail party.

I make my own honey mustard (a simple endeavor) because I am a control freak. I can taste and add more or less honey depending on how sweet I want it to be. You don't have to, but I find that it has a fresher flavor than purchased mustards do. This recipe is so easy and so cocktail-friendly that you simply have to make it for your next party; people will go crazy for it.

FOR THE HONEY MUSTARD

- 2 tablespoons extra-virgin olive oil
- 1 large Spanish onion, thinly sliced
- 3 tablespoons honey
- 3 tablespoons full-flavored Dijon mustard (I like Edmond Fallot)
  Kosher salt and freshly ground black pepper

FOR THE HAM AND CHEESE BITES

- 2 sheets frozen puff pastry, preferably all-butter, thawed as the package directs
- 1/2 pound thinly sliced ham, preferably Tuscan
- 1/2 pound thinly sliced (or grated) Gruyère
- 1 large egg, beaten
  Fleur de sel

TO MAKE THE HONEY MUSTARD: Heat the oil in a medium skillet over low heat. Add the onion and cook, stirring occasionally, until onion is very tender, 20 minutes. Add the honey and the mustard and cook, stirring occasionally, for another 5 minutes. If the mixture begins to stick to the pan before the onion is fully cooked, you can add up to 1/4 cup water. Let cool a bit and then transfer the mixture to a blender or food processor, using a flexible spatula to get it all, and puree until smooth. Season to taste with salt and pepper. You should have about 3/4 cup honey mustard.

TO MAKE THE HAM AND CHEESE BITES: Heat the oven to 375°F. Line a baking sheet with parchment paper. Roll the puff pastry to a thickness of about 1/8 inch, if necessary. Lay one sheet of puff pastry on the baking sheet. Spread all of the honey mustard over the pastry, leaving a 3/4-inch border around the edge of the puff pastry sheet. Lay all of the ham and then the cheese over the mustard, overlapping where necessary. Brush the 3/4-inch border with some of the beaten egg and then place the other sheet of puff pastry on top. Seal the edges together by pressing down firmly all the way around the sides of the rectangle. Brush the top sheet with the remaining beaten egg and sprinkle with about 1/2 teaspoon fleur de sel. Lay a sheet of parchment paper over the top and then place a baking sheet over that to keep the puff pastry from puffing up too much during baking.

Bake for 20 minutes. Remove the top baking sheet and the top sheet of parchment and continue baking until the pastry is a beautiful golden brown all over, another 10 to 20 minutes. Let cool for at least 10 minutes before slicing into squares. For a neat cut, use a large, sharp chef's knife. Put the tip of the knife down first and then use quite a bit of force on the blade as you slice down to make a clean cut. Serve warm.

MAKE AHEAD:

▎ *The honey mustard will keep for up to a week, covered and refrigerated. It's so good that you may want to double the recipe so you can use half for this recipe and the rest on your favorite sandwiches.*

▎ *You can assemble the pastry, up to the point of brushing the top with egg wash, a day ahead of baking it. Loosely cover it with plastic wrap and keep it refrigerated. Just before baking, brush the top with the egg wash and sprinkle it with the fleur de sel. If it's cold going into the oven, it may take a few more minutes to bake.*

All-Butter Puff Pastry from a Box: Easy and Delicious

I make fresh pasta all the time at home. Gnocchi, too. But I rarely make my own puff pastry from scratch (though my pastry chefs do). Dufour is an excellent all-butter puff pastry that's as good as anything I can make. More and more food markets seem to be carrying it these days. It *is* expensive (all that butter), and unlike, say, a box of Pepperidge Farm Puff Pastry, which comes with two sheets per package, a retail box of Dufour contains just one sheet. If you can only get puff pastry that is not all-butter, the results won't be quite as rich and the puff won't be quite as dramatic, but the dish will still be great and your wallet will be a little heavier.

Fig, Ricotta, and Prosciutto Tartines

Tartine—isn't that an awesome word? Very elegant and very French, it's an open-faced sandwich that's often served warm and usually features a rich spread of some kind. My tartines start with a large round loaf of country bread, which gives you long, raftlike slices of bread on which to build. I brush these with olive oil, season them with salt and pepper, and toast them lightly. As with bruschetta and pizza, the options for what can go on top of the toast are endless. Sweet, salty, and creamy, this one is my favorite.

6   very thin (about $3/8$-inch) slices country bread, preferably from a round loaf,
      or a baguette cut on the diagonal to yield 6 slices 6–8 inches long
    About $1/2$ cup extra-virgin olive oil
    Kosher salt and freshly ground black pepper
$1^1/2$ cups fresh ricotta (see page 34)
6   thin slices good-quality prosciutto, about 8 ounces
6   ripe Black Mission figs, at room temperature
6   fresh mint leaves
$1/4$ cup honey

Heat the oven to 350°F. Brush the slices of bread on both sides with olive oil. Sprinkle with a little salt and a couple grinds of fresh pepper and toast on a baking sheet in the oven, turning once, until golden on both sides, 6 to 8 minutes (begin checking early).

Lower the oven temperature to 325°F. Spread each slice of toast with the ricotta. Top each with a layer of prosciutto, overlapping to cover the entire slice. Return the toast to the oven and bake for 5 to 10 minutes to warm the cheese and lightly crisp the prosciutto.

While the tartines bake, cut the figs into quarters. Stack the mint leaves and use a very sharp knife to slice them very thinly into confetti-like strips. Distribute the fig quarters evenly, cut side up, over the warm tartines. Drizzle more olive oil over the figs and season with additional salt and pepper. Transfer the tartines to serving plates, shower them with the mint, and pour a drizzle of honey over all.

Antipasti

When I was a kid, our family parties revolved mostly around Catholic rites of passage, as the Lynches celebrated baptisms, first communions, and confirmations. As compensation for having to wear a dress and suffer wet kisses from relatives I barely knew, I could count on a huge platter of cold cuts, the slices rolled up like tubes and arrayed so that the whole thing looked like a giant fleshy flower. Nearby stood stacks of cheese—American for sure, and possibly some Swiss. A jar of mustard, mayonnaise, and a pile of soft rolls rounded out the offerings.

When I have a party, I put out an antipasto spread. Though it showcases thinly sliced meats, cheese, condiments, and bread, it's light-years away from my mother's platter. Literally translated "before the meal," an antipasto is a collection of nibbles made ahead of time. It's a typical Italian invention—no fretting involved, because everything is at room temperature and guests help themselves.

Must-haves for my antipasti include smooth, sweet slices of melt-in-your-mouth prosciutto di Parma arranged flat on the plate or platter. I include a couple of *salumi,* hard dried sausages of different styles: one that's hot, such as a spicy soppressata, and one that's more sweet, such as Genoa salami. They may be large, thin slices or small, thicker rounds. Mortadella, the tender smoked sausage from Bologna studded with garlic, pork fat, and pistachios, is large, so I fold that in half and in half again before arranging it on the platter. While those four items are enough, I might also put out some chicken liver paté (page 15) or jazz up the mix with something unexpected: perhaps some duck prosciutto or bresaola (air-dried beef tenderloin), which you can find at specialty food markets. Chunks of Parmigiano-Reggiano are always on my platter, and slices (or tiny balls) of fresh mozzarella are also welcome, to eat with the cured meats or as a break from them. In lieu of rolls, my guests get crostini, little toasts brushed with olive oil.

Now for the fun part: the condiments. I like to add a few spreads or relishes so people can create their own taste sensations. Three of my favorites are silken spiced prunes, tangy, crunchy marinated onions, and tender sweet-and-sour bell peppers (recipes follow). All are simple to make and can be prepared well ahead of serving. Paired with prosciutto, the prunes emphasize the meat's sweetness; try them with something spicy, and you get a whole different sensation, a coolness that's a welcome contrast. If you don't feel like making all three, go ahead and complement the offering with top-quality purchased items; a *mostarda* (preserved Italian whole fruits and spices) is a good choice, as is a jarred pepper relish or even a chutney. In the summer, I might include Tomato Jam (page 284) as part of the offering or put some ripe fresh figs on the plate. Just hold the mayo, please.

Spiced Prunes

**MAKES ABOUT
1½ CUPS**

Smooth and deeply flavored, these prunes become spreadable once softened. Delicious with all kinds of cured meats, they also go well on top of a seared duck breast (page 222) or served with crispy duck confit (page 225).

1	cup pitted prunes
1	cinnamon stick
5	cardamom pods
1	teaspoon coriander seeds
1	teaspoon black peppercorns
1	star anise
1	1-inch-wide strip orange zest
2	cups dry red wine
¼	cup sugar

Put the prunes in a small bowl. Tie the cinnamon, cardamom, coriander, peppercorns, star anise, and orange zest in a cheesecloth sachet (see page 224). Combine the wine, sugar, and sachet in a saucepan and cook over medium heat until the wine has reduced by about half. Pour everything, including the sachet, over the prunes and let them steep at room temperature until cool. If the prunes have not softened nicely, return everything to the saucepan and gently cook over medium-low heat until the prunes are soft.

Refrigerate the cooled prunes until ready to use. Let them warm up at room temperature for 30 minutes or so before serving.

MAKE AHEAD: *The prunes will keep for a week, covered and refrigerated.*

Pickled Onions

These tangy onions are a staple at my house. Their crunch and acidity pair wonderfully well with all kinds of pâtés, dried sausage, and salami. When you're done with the onions, you can strain the flavored vinegar and use it to make a kick-ass vinaigrette.

1	large red onion, very thinly sliced
¾	cup white wine vinegar
½	teaspoon kosher salt
¼	teaspoon sugar
1	fresh thyme sprig
6	black peppercorns
6	coriander seeds

Put the onion in a heatproof container. Combine the vinegar, salt, and sugar in a small saucepan. Tie the thyme, peppercorns, and coriander in a cheesecloth sachet (see page 224) and add that to the pan as well. Bring to a boil and pour everything over the sliced onion. Let sit at room temperature to cool, then cover and refrigerate until ready to use. Remove the sachet before serving the onions.

MAKE AHEAD: *The onions, which add a crunchy burst of flavor to green salads and sandwiches as well as a charcuterie plate, will last for a couple of weeks covered in the refrigerator. In fact, you may want to double the recipe.*

Yellow and Red Bell Pepper Agrodolce

Agrodolce in Italian means "sour-sweet," and that's what this condiment is. The sour comes from the sherry vinegar and the sweetness from golden raisins. It makes a good accompaniment to roasted or grilled chicken.

2   red bell peppers

2   yellow bell peppers

¼   cup extra-virgin olive oil

1   medium onion, cut in half and thinly sliced

1   cup golden raisins

1   tablespoon sugar

¼   cup sherry vinegar

Kosher salt and freshly ground black pepper

¼   cup finely chopped fresh parsley

Stem and seed the peppers. Cut each into 2 or 3 segments, remove the ribs by running a paring knife along the flesh, and cut the sections crosswise into thin strips.

Heat the olive oil in a large skillet over medium heat. Add the peppers, onion, raisins, sugar, and vinegar and cook until soft, stirring occasionally, about 30 minutes. If the vinegar evaporates before the peppers are tender, add a little water (up to ¼ cup) as they cook to keep them from browning. Season to taste with salt and pepper. Sprinkle with the chopped parsley.

MAKE AHEAD: *You can make this 2 days ahead of serving and keep in the refrigerator, covered with plastic, though the parsley will darken a bit.*

Quick Chicken Liver Pâté

Many of my pâtés require more work than most home cooks are game for. But my chicken liver pâté is super-quick and extremely easy. The shallot and port give it a wonderfully deep flavor, while the cream cheese makes the texture both rich and light. If you don't have port on hand, you can substitute just about any good fortified wine (not the cooking wine from the supermarket), such as sherry, Marsala, or Madeira. (See the photo on page 16.)

1	tablespoon grapeseed or canola oil
1	shallot, sliced
8	ounces chicken livers, trimmed and patted dry
	Kosher salt and freshly ground black pepper
½	cup port (see headnote)
1	tablespoon cream cheese

ACCOMPANIMENTS

Toasted country bread, Dijon mustard, cornichons, fleur de sel

Heat the oil in a large skillet over medium-high heat. Add the shallot and cook, stirring, for about 2 minutes. Add the livers, season with salt and pepper, and cook undisturbed on one side for about 1 minute. Turn the livers over and cook the other side for about 1 minute, too. The idea is to get a little color on each side but keep the livers rare to medium-rare. Transfer the livers to a plate. If there is a lot of fat in the pan, pour it off. Add the port to the pan and cook over medium-high heat until reduced to about 2 tablespoons.

Combine the livers and port reduction in a blender or food processor and pulse to puree. Add the cream cheese and pulse. Pass the mixture through a fine-mesh strainer (this is easier than it sounds) to make it very smooth. Season to taste with salt and pepper.

Put the pâté in a serving crock and chill it for an hour before serving. Serve with toasted country bread, mustard, cornichons, and fleur de sel.

MAKE AHEAD: *This will keep for 2 to 3 days covered and refrigerated, but it will lose its nice pink color as it oxidizes.*

QUICK CHICKEN LIVER PÂTÉ (PAGE 15)

Butcher Shop Beef Tartare

My version of steak tartare, with its bold yet balanced flavor, looks gorgeous, gets made in minutes, and goes perfectly with a gin martini. What more could you want? When you make it, keep in mind that your capers, mustard, and cornichons may taste different from mine; start with the given amounts and then trust your own palate. If you taste too much mustard, add a little more of the pickles. Not sharp enough? Add more capers. There's no real right or wrong here as long as *you* like the results. Want even more flavor? Spread Truffle Aïoli on the brioche before topping it with the tartare.

1 pound top-quality beef tenderloin, trimmed of all fat and sinew
4 large egg yolks, lightly beaten
1 heaping tablespoon finely chopped shallot
1 heaping tablespoon finely chopped cornichons
1 heaping tablespoon finely chopped capers
1 heaping tablespoon whole-grain mustard
1 tablespoon Tomato Syrup (recipe follows) or 2 teaspoons ketchup
   mixed with 1 teaspoon Tabasco
   Kosher salt and freshly ground black pepper
   Toasted slices of brioche or other fine-grained white bread
   Truffle Aïoli (optional; page 20)

If you have some time, freeze the tenderloin for a couple of hours; this will firm it up and make slicing it easier. (Once chopped, it will defrost quickly and may then be mixed with the rest of the ingredients.) With a very sharp knife, cut the beef into $1/8$-inch cubes. If you go slowly and slice with care (and check a ruler to see just how small $1/8$ inch is), your tartare will look as great as it tastes.

To serve, gently combine the beef with the egg yolks, shallot, cornichons, capers, mustard, and tomato syrup and season with salt and pepper to taste. Serve with the toasted bread and truffle aïoli, if using.

MAKE AHEAD: *You can chop all but the beef well ahead of time, but once everything is combined, it's best to serve the tartare immediately. If prepared ahead, the meat oxidizes and loses its beautiful red color.*

NOTE: If consuming raw eggs is a health issue for you, look for pasteurized eggs, which are becoming more common at the supermarket and are sold by the dozen just like regular eggs.

Tomato Syrup
MAKES ¾ CUP

This makes a lot more than you need for the beef tartare on page 18, but it's an awesome condiment. Think of it as fancy ketchup and use it on burgers and eggs.

1	tablespoon extra-virgin olive oil
¼	cup thinly sliced white onion (about ½ small onion)
1	small garlic clove, chopped
1	cup canned crushed tomatoes
¼	teaspoon crushed red pepper flakes, plus more to taste
1	small bay leaf
2	black peppercorns
3	fresh basil leaves
1	tablespoon sugar
1	teaspoon kosher salt

Heat the olive oil over medium heat in a small saucepan. Add the onion and garlic and cook until just tender, about 5 minutes. Add the remaining ingredients and simmer over medium heat until slightly reduced, 10 to 15 minutes. Puree in a blender until smooth and pass through a fine-mesh strainer. Taste, adjust the seasoning, and chill.

MAKE AHEAD: *This will keep for at least a couple of weeks covered in the refrigerator, and I've used some that was much older and lived to tell the tale. You can also freeze it indefinitely. If frozen flat in a zip-top bag, it needs only a quick run under hot water to defrost.*

Truffle Aïoli

MAKES 1 CUP

I like to serve a little of this with beef tartare (page 18). Though the tartare is fantastic on its own, when paired with this creamy, musky, and earthy condiment, the result becomes fall-off-your-chair delicious. However, that's only if you use an excellent truffle oil, so don't cheap out when you buy it. Use any leftover aïoli to transform a steak sandwich into something amazing or as a sumptuous dip for the French fries on page 280.

1	large egg yolk
3	tablespoons very finely grated Parmigiano-Reggiano; use a rasp-style (Microplane) grater
2	teaspoons whole-grain mustard
	Kosher salt and freshly ground black pepper
1	tablespoon white wine vinegar, preferably Chardonnay
1	tablespoon truffle oil (see headnote)
3/4	cup vegetable oil, preferably grapeseed oil

In a bowl, whisk together the egg yolk, Parmesan, mustard, 1 teaspoon salt, 1/2 teaspoon pepper, the vinegar, and the truffle oil. Very slowly drizzle in the vegetable oil while whisking nonstop to create an emulsion. (If you add the oil too fast, especially at the beginning, the mixture can separate.) Continue adding oil, whisking until the mixture has thickened to the consistency of mayonnaise. (Alternatively, make the aïoli in a food processor, combining all the ingredients except the vegetable oil. With the motor running, slowly add the vegetable oil, processing until thickened.) Season to taste with additional salt and pepper and keep cold until ready to serve.

MAKE AHEAD: *The aïoli will keep, covered in plastic wrap and refrigerated, for up to 3 days.*

NOTE: If consuming raw eggs is a health issue for you, look for pasteurized eggs, which are becoming more common at the supermarket and are sold by the dozen just like regular eggs.

A Great Grater

One of the best tools to hit the kitchen in recent years is the Microplane grater. Modeled after a rasp for woodworking, it grates hard cheeses very finely, quickly creating mounds of exceedingly light and fluffy flakes that mix beautifully in sauces and melt quickly and evenly into risotto. The Microplane also makes quick work of zesting citrus, easily stripping just the zest and not the white pith below. You can use a Microplane for grating chocolate, garlic, fresh ginger, and nutmeg. Though there are now other makers of this style of grater, I prefer the original. Look for the grater at your favorite home-goods store.

Cauliflower Chaud-Froid

Rich and silky but also light and cold with a briny hit, this savory cauliflower custard makes the perfect first course: it stimulates the eye, the palate, and, usually, the conversation (as your guests have likely never had anything quite like it). I call the dish *chaud-froid* (show-FRWAH), not only because it's fun to say but also because the French phrase signals that this is dressy food, something you'd serve for a special dinner party. All it means, however, is that a food that was prepared hot (*chaud*) is served cold (*froid*). In this recipe, what essentially starts out as a cauliflower soup is molded, chilled, and then topped with a raw oyster or caviar, or both if you're going all out, as I like to do. For a sit-down dinner, use silicone cupcake molds or small ramekins to make a first course that takes a few bites to finish. For a larger gathering, use mini-muffin tins to make one-bite hors d'oeuvres. Though the dish feels quite fancy and looks spectacular, the elements are all prepared ahead of time, which makes it convenient for serious entertaining. The cauliflower puree, before the gelatin is added, also makes a delicious soup on its own; serve it hot or cold.

2	tablespoons unsalted butter
1	shallot, sliced
	Kosher salt
½	pound cauliflower, trimmed and chopped (from about ¼ head)
1¼	cups heavy cream
4	tablespoons freshly grated horseradish or 2 tablespoons strained prepared horseradish
⅛	teaspoon finely ground white pepper, plus more if needed
¼	teaspoon fresh lemon juice, plus more to taste
2¼	teaspoons (1 packet) powdered gelatin
12–30	oysters, rinsed and shucked (see page 40), and/or caviar, as much as you can afford
	Celery Emulsion (optional; recipe follows)
	Small celery leaves (from the celery for the Celery Emulsion) for garnish
	Fleur de sel

In a medium saucepan, melt the butter over medium heat. Add the shallot and 1 teaspoon salt and cook, stirring occasionally and being careful not to let the shallot brown, until the shallot is tender, about 7 minutes. Add the cauliflower and sauté for 1 minute. Add the cream and 1 cup water and simmer until the cauliflower is just tender, about 20 minutes. Puree the cauliflower with the liquid in a blender. Add the horseradish, 1 teaspoon salt, and the white pepper. Strain through a fine-mesh strainer, pressing hard on the solids

with a ladle, and cool to warm. Discard the solids. Add the lemon juice, then taste and season with additional salt, pepper, and lemon juice, if needed. However, if you plan on serving the *chaud-froid* with oysters or caviar, go easy on the salt, bearing in mind that they add their own salty flavor.

Sprinkle the gelatin over $^1/_4$ cup cold water in a small saucepan and let it sit for 5 minutes to "bloom." Heat over low heat until it becomes a clear liquid; whisk this into the warm cauliflower mixture and strain again.

While the mixture is still warm, divide it among the flexible silicone cupcake molds or mini-muffin tins (these are available at most kitchen stores). Use the cupcake molds to make 12 large servings or the mini-muffin tins to make 30 bite-sized ones. (Regular muffin tins or ramekins also work, but you may need to run a knife around the edge and dip them in warm water before removing the *chaud-froid*.) Alternatively, make and serve the *chaud-froid* in the ramekins. Place the molds in the freezer to chill and set, which will take about $1^1/_2$ hours. (Freezing the cauliflower mixture makes the *chaud-froid* much easier to remove from the molds.)

Pop the *chaud-froid* out of the molds and invert onto small serving plates. Allow to defrost in the refrigerator for at least 30 minutes and up to 1 day before serving. Top each *chaud-froid* with a single shucked oyster and some caviar, if using. Spoon 1 to 2 tablespoons of the celery emulsion, if using, around each *chaud-froid* and finish the plate with a sprinkling of celery leaves and a tiny pinch of fleur de sel.

MAKE AHEAD:

I *You can make the cauliflower puree (without adding the gelatin) up to 2 days before finishing the* chaud-froid *and refrigerate it, covered with plastic wrap. Before adding the gelatin, reheat the puree until just warm. (Combining the gelatin with a mixture that's too cold produces an unpleasant stringy texture; too hot, and the gelatin won't set.)*

I *The unmolded* chaud-froid *can be refrigerated, covered with plastic wrap, for 1 to 2 days before serving.*

Celery Emulsion

MAKES 1 CUP

This may make more than you need for the cauliflower chaud-froid, but that's fine because you can enjoy it (unfrothed) as a soup.

9	ounces celery (5–6 stalks)
2	tablespoons unsalted butter
1	cup whole milk
1	teaspoon kosher salt

Remove the small leaves from the celery and save them to garnish the *chaud-froid*. Give the celery a rinse and use a vegetable peeler to peel away the tough strings. Chop the celery to yield 3 cups.

Melt the butter in a small saucepan over medium-high heat. When hot and bubbling, add the celery and sauté it briefly to brighten its color, about 1 minute. Add the milk, bring to a simmer, and cook until the celery is just tender, 1 to 2 minutes. Do not cook too long or you will lose the bright green color. Puree in a blender until smooth. Season with the salt and pass through a fine-mesh strainer. Just before serving, use a hand blender to buzz the warm celery mixture to incorporate air and create froth. If you don't have a hand blender, a whisk and a strong arm can create froth, too. A handheld cappuccino frother also works.

MAKE AHEAD: *You can puree the celery a day or two ahead and refrigerate it, covered with plastic wrap. Just before serving, warm it gently and then froth it.*

Save Your Celery Leaves

I use celery leaves all the time in my cooking. They're beautiful, with all the flavor of celery without being stringy. It's a shame that this undervalued part of the plant gets tossed out by so many cooks. I add them to dishes as I would any delicate herb, generally toward the end of cooking or as a flavorful garnish. Harvest the tiny, pretty inner leaves, which look and taste better than the larger outer leaves.

Tomato Tarte Tatin

With layers of sweet roasted tomatoes, caramelized onions, and buttery puff pastry, this pretty dish is a play on tarte Tatin, the famous French dessert made by covering caramelized apples with pastry and then inverting the pan to show off the glistening fruit.

This makes six individual tarts, each about 4 inches across. You can make them in tartlet pans, ramekins, or even muffin tins. Or you can make one 9- or 10-inch tart and cut slices from it, though the larger tart can be a challenge to invert. Either way, this is a perfect first course or even a light lunch when paired with a green salad. If you have tiny tartlet molds, you can opt to make bite-sized tarts to serve as hors d'oeuvres; simply divide the ingredients among the smaller molds and bake them for less time.

Frying basil leaves is easy, and that familiar summertime flavor delivered in a crisp bite is novel. I don't recommend skipping that step, but if you must, you can garnish the tart with fresh basil leaves. Note that you need to make the Tomato Confit before you can assemble the tarts.

2	tablespoons extra-virgin olive oil
2	large yellow onions, halved and thinly sliced
1	garlic clove, thinly sliced
2	teaspoons Dijon mustard, preferably whole-grain
8–14	fresh basil leaves (the number depends on how many servings you plan to make), 2 leaves chopped
	Kosher salt and freshly ground black pepper
	All-purpose flour for dusting
1	sheet frozen all-butter puff pastry, thawed
1½–2	tablespoons honey
	Tomato Confit (recipe follows)
1	large egg
½	cup vegetable oil (for optional garnish)
3	tablespoons mascarpone cheese or ricotta, preferably fresh (see page 34)

Heat the olive oil over medium heat in a large skillet. Add the onions and garlic, reduce the heat to low, and cook, stirring occasionally, until the onions turn an even dark brown, 45 minutes to an hour. Be patient; if you crank the heat and brown them too early, they won't get the sweet caramelized flavor and soft texture you're after. If the skillet dries out, add a tablespoon or two of water as needed. When the onions are nicely caramelized, take the skillet off the heat and stir in the mustard and chopped basil. Season with $^1/_2$ teaspoon salt and a few grinds of pepper.

Lightly flour your work surface and roll out the puff pastry until $^1/_8$ inch thick. Invert a tart pan over the pastry sheet. Trace around the pan with a sharp paring knife; do this multiple times if using smaller tart pans or molds. Transfer the cut-out dough to a very lightly floured baking sheet and refrigerate while you assemble the rest of the tart.

Heat the oven to 375°F. Use a finger to spread the honey on the bottom of the tart pan, dividing it as necessary among multiple molds if you're going that route. Place a single layer of tomato confit, skin side down, in the tart pan or pans, overlapping as needed to cover the bottom completely. (A very small tart mold may need just a single piece of tomato.) Distribute the caramelized onions over the tomatoes, dividing them evenly among multiple pans as needed and gently spreading them to disperse them evenly.

Remove the cut dough from the refrigerator and place it directly over the onions. Lightly beat the egg and brush the top of the tart or tarts with the beaten egg. Sprinkle each lightly with kosher salt. Bake until the pastry is puffed and a deep, golden brown, 10 to 30 minutes, depending on size. Allow the tart or tarts to cool for about 10 minutes before unmolding, but unmold the tarts while they are still warm, because there's less chance they will stick. To unmold them, run a small knife around the edge of each tart to loosen it. Place a serving plate a little larger than the tart pan directly over the top and invert the tart onto the plate. If the tarts have cooled too much and the tomatoes are sticking, place the tart pans in a warm oven for a minute or two to melt the honey. If a tomato piece sticks, just carefully remove it from the pan and arrange it on the tart.

If you want to fry some basil leaves for the garnish, heat the vegetable oil in a small saucepan until a basil leaf dipped into it sizzles. Place the remaining leaves in the oil and fry, turning them once, until crispy, 30 seconds to 1 minute. Drain on paper towels.

If you have made one large tart, slice it into 6 servings; serve the tiny tarts whole. Garnish each serving with a small dollop of mascarpone and a fried or fresh basil leaf.

MAKE AHEAD:

▌ *You can cook the onions up to 3 days ahead. Keep them covered and refrigerated.*

▌ *You can arrange the onions and tomatoes in the tart pan early in the day, keep them at room temperature, and then top them with the cut dough right before baking.*

Tomato Confit
MAKES ABOUT 4 CUPS

When you make tomato confit, you get two gifts: intensely flavored, silky-soft tomatoes that you can store for almost a week and use in salads or on sandwiches, plus a garlicky oil that's delicious on grilled bread, on pasta, or whisked into a vinaigrette.

3½	pounds plum tomatoes (12–14 tomatoes)
4	garlic cloves, thinly sliced
1	tablespoon sugar, if needed
2	teaspoons kosher salt
	Freshly ground black pepper
1	cup olive oil
6	fresh thyme sprigs

Cut the tomatoes into quarters lengthwise and seed and core them.

Heat the oven to 300°F. Divide the garlic slices between two baking dishes or two baking sheets, each about 9 × 13 inches, spreading them out on the bottom. Lay the tomato pieces cut side up in the pans. If the tomatoes are not very sweet, sprinkle them with the sugar; otherwise, omit it (the tomatoes will sweeten as they bake). Sprinkle the salt over the tomatoes and season generously with pepper. Divide the olive oil between the two dishes, pouring it over the tomatoes, and top the tomatoes with the thyme. Bake until the tomatoes are soft and wrinkled but still retain their shape, 25 to 30 minutes.

Cool the tomatoes completely in the pans before transferring them with a slotted spoon to a serving plate or storage container. Discard the thyme and reserve the oil for another use. Keep both the tomatoes and the oil covered and refrigerated.

MAKE AHEAD: *Tomato confit is something I like to have on hand; it's a good thing a batch will keep for 5 days covered and refrigerated.*

Ricotta-Stuffed Heirloom Tomatoes with Black Olive Vinaigrette and Saffron Croutons

SERVES 6 This is an absolutely stunning dish. Every bite excites with a different mingling of textures and flavors—creamy ricotta, tender tomato, sweet raisins, briny olives, crunchy croutons, crisp, peppery radishes. You place the stuffed tomato upside down on the plate, concealing the elegant surprise of the ricotta within. Serve during the height of tomato season—it's spectacular made with Green Zebra tomatoes—when you want a dish that will make people say, "Wow!"

6	ripe medium tomatoes, preferably pretty heirloom tomatoes, peeled (see page 6)
1½	cups fresh ricotta (see page 34)
1	teaspoon kosher salt
½	teaspoon freshly ground black pepper
6	marinated white anchovy fillets (optional; don't substitute regular anchovies)
	Saffron Croutons (recipe follows)
2–3	small radishes, sliced paper-thin (about ¼ cup)
¼	cup celery heart leaves
¼	cup very thinly sliced scallions
¼	cup torn basil leaves
	Black Olive Vinaigrette (page 33)
	Fleur de sel

With a sharp paring knife, hollow out each tomato. Start by cutting a hole about the size of a quarter at its stem end and removing the core. Next, use the knife to cut out the membranes on the wall of the tomato and discard those. Seed the tomato by using the handle end of a spoon to flick out the seeds. Place the tomatoes on paper towels cut side down to allow any excess juice to drain off.

Season the ricotta with the salt and pepper and mix it with a fork. Fill each tomato with ricotta. (A piping bag or a zip-top bag with a corner snipped off is the quickest and neatest way to go, but you can spoon in the filling as well.)

Set each filled tomato cut side down in the center of a dinner plate. Cut each anchovy, if using, not quite all the way through lengthwise and place one, opened to look like a wide V, in front of each tomato. Next, ring each tomato with croutons (about a dozen per plate), radish slices, celery leaves, scallions, and basil. Take your time with these

garnishes and think of the plate as a canvas; you want to distribute the various colors and shapes in a way that's pleasing to the eye. Spoon a little—about 2 tablespoons per tomato—of the vinaigrette on the plate in a ring around the tomato, being sure that some raisins and olives are dispersed there, too. Sprinkle each tomato with a smidge of fleur de sel and serve.

MAKE AHEAD: *These are great for entertaining because you can fill the tomatoes ahead. They can sit at room temperature for an hour, covered with plastic wrap, and can be refrigerated, covered with plastic wrap, for a few hours without any loss of flavor. Do take them out of the fridge at least half an hour before serving, as the cold mutes the flavor.*

Saffron Croutons

MAKES 1 CUP

Saffron adds an aromatic, slightly exotic flavor to croutons, and the jagged bright red threads against the bread look jaunty. I love brioche for croutons because it slices evenly, has a nice tight crumb, and browns beautifully. You know what has similar attributes? Pepperidge Farm White Sandwich Bread. Seriously.

3   thin slices bread, preferably brioche, crusts removed

2   tablespoons extra-virgin olive oil

2   pinches saffron threads (about ¼ teaspoon)

2   pinches kosher salt

Heat the oven to 325°F. Cut the slices of bread into ¼-inch cubes to yield about 1 cup. Heat the olive oil in a skillet over low heat. Add the saffron and gently cook for about 1 minute to infuse the oil with the flavor and color of the saffron. Add the bread cubes, season with the salt, and toss to coat with the flavored oil. Spread out on a baking sheet and toast in the oven, tossing occasionally, until golden and crunchy, 10 to 15 minutes.

MAKE AHEAD: *After the croutons have cooled completely, you can store them in an airtight container at room temperature for a couple of days.*

Black Olive Vinaigrette

MAKES ABOUT ¾ CUP

This vinaigrette rocks. It's amazing not only with stuffed tomatoes but drizzled over grilled striped bass, slices of juicy, ripe tomatoes, lamb, and eggplant.

2	tablespoons golden raisins
¼	cup Niçoise olives, pitted and chopped
1	tablespoon finely chopped shallot
½	cup grapeseed oil or mild olive oil
1	tablespoon sherry vinegar
1	teaspoon fresh lemon juice
¼	teaspoon kosher salt
	Freshly ground black pepper
1	tablespoon finely chopped fresh parsley

Soak the raisins in hot water for 15 minutes to plump them, then drain. In a small bowl, combine the raisins, olives, shallot, oil, vinegar, and lemon juice. Season with the salt and a few grinds of pepper. Just before serving, whisk in the parsley.

MAKE AHEAD: *You can make the vinaigrette without the parsley a couple of days ahead. Refrigerate it, covered with plastic wrap, but bring it to room temperature before using. Whisk in the parsley just before serving.*

Fresh Ricotta

I call for fresh ricotta in my recipes because I want you to seek out the real deal and not settle for the soupy mass-produced stuff. Imported Italian ricotta, which you can find at Italian specialty markets, is my first choice. A by-product of cheesemaking, it's traditionally made by heating the leftover liquid whey until delicate curds are created. (*Ricotta* is Italian for "recooked.") Usually made from sheep or water buffalo milk whey, Italian ricotta has a mildly sweet, slightly nutty flavor that I love. And though its curd is creamy, it's dry enough that it can be sold wrapped in paper. Imported Italian ricotta is not so easy to find, however. (If you have an Italian neighborhood near where you live—I have Boston's North End, for example—try there.)

Ricotta from here in the United States is usually made with cow's milk, tastes sweeter, and is considerably more moist. Calabro, which you can find at Whole Foods Markets and other supermarkets, is a great domestic ricotta. My favorite, which I often use at my restaurants, is Calabro's hand-dipped ricotta, which comes in a metal container with tiny holes for drainage. The ricotta the company sells in a plastic tub, which is much more widely available, is still leaps and bounds better than most, because it contains no fillers or artificial preservatives and has a lovely soft but not overly wet curd. If you can't find it, look at the ingredient list on the ricotta that is available to you and avoid those with additives.

Finally, you can use the recipe that follows to make your own ricotta using just whole milk, vinegar, and salt. The resulting curds can be as wet or dry as you like, and the flavor is fresh and delicious. I usually get my daughter, Marchesa, involved when I make this at home. Kids love it because the creation of the curds seems so miraculous.

Easy Homemade Ricotta

MAKES 2 CUPS

Aside from milk, vinegar, and salt, you'll need some cheesecloth and a cooking thermometer (both of which you can find at most supermarkets). Then it's just a matter of heating, stirring, and straining.

1	gallon whole milk
³⁄₄	cup distilled white vinegar
1	tablespoon kosher salt

Line a footed colander with a double layer of cheesecloth and set it in a clean sink. In a large saucepan, combine the ingredients over low heat. Clip a cooking thermometer to the pot and, stirring constantly with a wooden spoon or rubber spatula, heat the liquid to 140°F, about 10 minutes. Stop stirring and let the temperature of the liquid climb to 175°F. This will take another 8 to 10 minutes, but stay close by; it's important not to let the liquid exceed 180°F, or the cheese will be overcooked and become grainy. As soon as it hits 180°F, remove it from the heat and gently ladle the separated curds out of the saucepan and into the cheesecloth-lined footed colander (you need some height for the liquid to drain away). Alternatively, tie the curds in the cheesecloth with ample string and then tie the cheesecloth package to a cabinet knob, positioning it over a bowl to catch the liquid that drains from it. Allow the curds to drain for about an hour, until the ricotta is soft and spreadable but no longer wet. (The longer it drains, the firmer the cheese becomes.) Transfer the ricotta to a bowl, cover, and refrigerate if not using immediately.

MAKE AHEAD: *The ricotta will keep for a week, covered and refrigerated.*

Gorgonzola Fondue

SERVES 4   Picture skewering pieces of beautifully seared, tender lamb and golden cubes of toasted bread and dipping them into a warm, creamy, tangy Gorgonzola sauce. If you've never tried making fondue at home, you should. It's a blast. You don't have to invest money or cabinet space in a fancy fondue kit, either. In fact, I serve this fondue, both at home and at No. 9 Park, where it's always on the bar menu, in a simple white porcelain pot that is little more than a votive candle set under a bowl. I got it at Crate & Barrel for something like $12.

1	pound boneless lamb loin, trimmed of any fat and sinew and cut into 4 pieces
1/4	cup good-quality purchased tapenade or Black Olive Paste (page 6)
	About 2 tablespoons unsalted butter
4	thick slices brioche or other fine-grained white bread, cut into 1-inch cubes
2	tablespoons extra-virgin olive oil
1/2	pound Gorgonzola, crumbled
1/2	cup heavy cream
1/4	teaspoon freshly ground black pepper
	Fleur de sel

Rub the lamb with the black olive paste, coating the surface completely. Set aside.

Melt 1 tablespoon of the butter in a large skillet over medium heat. Add as many brioche cubes as will fit in a single layer and cook without moving them until golden brown on one side, about 2 minutes. Flip the cubes over and toast the other sides, adding more butter, if needed, until golden. Drain the croutons on paper towels. You may need to do this in batches.

Heat the olive oil in a medium skillet over medium-high heat. Sear the lamb, flipping it once, and cook to rare (120° to 125°F), 4 to 6 minutes, depending on thickness. Remove the pan from the heat and allow the meat to rest for 6 to 8 minutes.

While the meat is resting, combine the cheese, heavy cream, and pepper in a saucepan over low heat. Cook, whisking, until the cheese melts. Pour the cheese into a fondue pot and light the heat source beneath the pot.

Slice the lamb into bite-sized pieces. Arrange the meat and the croutons around the fondue pot. Sprinkle the lamb with a tiny bit of fleur de sel. Serve with skewers or fondue forks for dipping.

Slow-Roasted Clams with Spicy Tomato Sauce

SERVES 4   This recipe, inspired by a dish served at Al Forno restaurant in Rhode Island, is so easy: all you have to do is lay some clams down on crushed tomatoes, olive oil, garlic, and onion and cook it in the oven for about half an hour. As the clams slowly steam open and become perfectly tender, the rest of the ingredients soften and exchange flavors for an effortless sauce. Very simple, very rustic. You'll find yourself turning to this method again and again. Served with grilled bread, it's practically a meal.

1	28-ounce can crushed tomatoes
¼	cup dry white wine
1	medium onion, halved and very thinly sliced
4	garlic cloves, 3 thinly sliced and 1 left whole
1½	teaspoons crushed red pepper flakes, plus more to taste
	About ½ cup extra-virgin olive oil
	Kosher salt and freshly ground black pepper
36	littleneck clams, well scrubbed
	Slices of ciabatta, country, or Italian bread for serving
½	cup sliced scallions

Heat the oven to 400°F. On a baking sheet, toss together the tomatoes, wine, onion, sliced garlic, red pepper flakes, and about 3 tablespoons olive oil. Season with a pinch of salt (remember that the clams and possibly the tomatoes are salty) and a few grinds of pepper. Add the clams in a single layer and roast them uncovered until they have opened, 25 to 35 minutes (begin checking at 25 minutes), discarding any unopened ones. Remove the clams from the oven and heat the broiler to toast the bread.

Brush the slices of bread with a little olive oil and season with a little salt and pepper. Toast the bread on both sides under the broiler. (The bread is also excellent grilled, a good choice in the summer.) Rub the toasted bread with the reserved whole garlic clove.

Drizzle 2 to 3 tablespoons olive oil over the clams and divide the clams and sauce among four deep bowls. Sprinkle the scallions over them and serve with the bread.

MAKE AHEAD:

❚ *The prep for this recipe is minimal, but you can have all the ingredients ready on the baking sheet and refrigerated, covered loosely with plastic wrap, ahead of roasting them; just keep in mind that the clams will take longer to steam open if very cold.*

❚ *You can grill or toast the bread ahead and serve it at room temperature.*

Oysters on the Half Shell with Sparkling Mignonette

Oysters are something people expect to get only at a raw bar, which is why I like to serve them icy cold and on the half shell at home, especially for a dinner party. Their bracing, briny flavor starts off the meal with a refreshing bang, and all that slurping and sighing puts everyone in a congenial, conspiratorial mood, particularly when those oysters are paired with a beautiful Grand Cru Chablis.

I'm partial to East Coast oysters; the farther north they're from, the better. But I'm no purist when it comes to eating them. I love to have a few plain to appreciate their flavor, and then I go to town dousing them with a squeeze of lemon juice, the bubbly, peppery mignonette in this recipe, or even some cocktail sauce (page 44). Then I sit back and enjoy the explosion of flavors. You can shuck them yourself or have them shucked by your fishmonger ahead of time. Just be sure the oysters are opened as close to serving as possible and kept on ice.

2	tablespoons freshly ground black pepper
2	shallots, very finely chopped (about 1/2 cup)
1/2	cup Prosecco or other dry sparkling wine
1/2	cup white wine vinegar, preferably Chardonnay
1	teaspoon kosher salt
	As many of your favorite oysters as you and your friends want to eat, rinsed and shucked (see following page)

Using a fine-mesh strainer, sift the ground pepper and reserve only the coarsely ground pepper left behind in the strainer. (If you include the finely ground pepper, the mignonette sauce will be too hot.)

In a medium bowl, combine all the ingredients except the oysters. Taste and correct the seasoning if necessary and keep chilled. Put just a few drops of the mignonette on each oyster just before serving.

MAKE AHEAD: *The mignonette lasts for 2 days, covered and refrigerated, but the bubbles from the Prosecco will dissipate.*

How to Shuck an Oyster

The only way to get really good at shucking is to shuck a lot of oysters. The first half-dozen may feel like a struggle. As you gain experience, you'll more easily find the oyster's sweet spot—the perfect place to slip the blade—then twist, and hear that wonderful popping sound that signals success.

A good oyster knife is the key to shucking well; the best ones are squat, with a fat and comfortable handle and a short, thick blade. To start, hold the oyster with its cup side down, with a towel or glove in front of your hand to protect it from a slip of the knife. Look for a tiny slit near the hinge. Slip the tip of the blade between the top and bottom shell; if you've found the right spot, the knife should go in pretty easily. Once the knife has been inserted, twist the blade to open the hinge. Sometimes oysters can be quite stubborn, or the blade of the knife just can't seem to find a way in. In these cases, be Zen-like. When you meet resistance, don't struggle; put the oyster aside and come back to it later. With oysters, the harder you try, the harder they resist.

Once you've got the oyster open, keep it level to preserve those delicious juices inside the shell. Slide the knife flat against the top shell to cut off the connective tissue, then twist off the top shell, taking care not to spill. Slide the knife flat against the bottom shell, under the meat, to disconnect the muscle that attaches it to that shell.

Arrange the shucked oysters on a bed of salted crushed ice, again keeping them level. They're best served immediately.

Citrus-Cured Salmon

I'm not a big fan of smoked salmon. Too often, all you taste is the smoke, and it can feel greasy. On the other hand, I love gravlax, which is salmon that's been cured with sugar and salt but not smoked. Though the texture is similar, the flavor of gravlax, especially this one, loaded with citrus, is much brighter. I serve thin slices of it with such traditional accompaniments as capers, diced red onion, and hard-boiled eggs. It's also excellent as a first course on top of diced roasted beets that have been dressed with a little lemon juice and olive oil and seasoned with finely grated fresh horseradish.

1	cup coriander seeds
1/2	cup juniper berries
1/2	cup black peppercorns
6	bay leaves
2	cups kosher salt
2	cups sugar
	Zest from 6 lemons, chopped
	Zest from 8 limes, chopped
	Zest from 6 oranges, chopped
2	pounds skin-on salmon fillet (in 1 piece), preferably center-cut, pinbones removed

In a spice grinder or a coffee grinder dedicated to spices, grind the coriander, juniper, peppercorns, and bay leaves together. In a large bowl, toss the ground spices with the salt, sugar, and zests until well combined.

Put the salmon skin side up on a cutting board. Slash the salmon on an angle perpendicular to its length 8 to 10 times with a very sharp knife to help the cure penetrate the fish. Each incision should be 3 to 4 inches long and 1/4 inch deep, just barely cutting into the flesh.

Spread half of the curing mixture on a baking sheet, or a platter large enough to hold the salmon, over an area just a bit larger than the salmon. (The salmon will give off a lot of liquid as it cures.) Lay the salmon skin side down on the baking sheet on top of the curing mixture and then cover it with the rest of the curing mixture, gently patting the mixture down to make sure the salmon is well covered. Cover the dish with plastic wrap and refrigerate for 48 hours.

Rinse the cure off the salmon under cold running water (some will remain) and gently pat the salmon dry with paper towels or a clean kitchen towel. The salmon will have become slightly translucent in appearance and firmer to the touch. Wrap it in plastic wrap and refrigerate it until ready to serve.

To slice the salmon neatly, lay it on a cutting board with the thinner tail end at your right side (if you're right-handed). Begin slicing at the thicker head end, slicing away from you, toward the left. Be sure to slice against the grain of the fish. If you slice with the grain, your nice thin slices will fall apart.

MAKE AHEAD: *Once cured, the salmon will keep for at least a week and likely longer, well wrapped in plastic wrap and refrigerated.*

Classic Shrimp Cocktail

Everybody loves shrimp cocktail. For all my innovation with other dishes, I want my shrimp served with the traditional cocktail sauce, and It has to be made with Heinz ketchup. Too often the shrimp is overcooked. To solve that, I barely boil it and then let the shrimp finish poaching off the heat. My husband, who likes his shrimp curled up and dry as can be, says I undercook it, and we fight about this all the time. But everyone else loves my shrimp, so I know I'm right.

1	cup dry white wine
1/2	cup chopped peeled carrot
1/2	cup chopped onion
1/2	cup chopped celery
2	garlic cloves, crushed
3	bay leaves
1	tablespoon black peppercorns
1	tablespoon coriander seeds
1	teaspoon crushed red pepper flakes
2	teaspoons kosher salt
4	fresh parsley sprigs
2	lemons, one juiced and one cut into wedges for serving
1	pound jumbo (16–20 count) shrimp, unpeeled
	Cocktail Sauce (recipe follows)

In a large saucepan, combine the wine with 3 cups water. Add all of the other ingredients except the lemon wedges, shrimp, and cocktail sauce and bring to a boil. Reduce to a robust simmer and cook for 6 minutes to infuse the flavors and cook off the raw taste of the wine. Strain the liquid into a clean saucepan or pot and bring it back to a boil. Add the shrimp. As soon as the liquid is barely boiling, move the pan off the burner and let the shrimp finish poaching in the hot liquid for 3 to 4 minutes. Drain the shrimp and let them cool for about 15 minutes before peeling. Devein the shrimp by making a shallow slit along the back and pulling out the dark vein. Chill, covered, for at least 2 hours before serving with cocktail sauce and wedges of lemon.

MAKE AHEAD: *Shrimp cocktail should be served nice and cold, so you want to poach the shrimp at least a couple of hours ahead of serving them. They'll stay fresh-tasting for at least 24 hours covered with plastic wrap and refrigerated.*

Cocktail Sauce

MAKES ABOUT 1 CUP

Cocktail sauce is one of those flavor memories I don't mess with, so I buy prepared horseradish and happily use a lot of it.

1	cup ketchup, preferably Heinz
¼	cup prepared horseradish, plus more to taste
1	teaspoon fresh lemon juice
½	teaspoon kosher salt
¼	teaspoon freshly ground black pepper

Combine all the ingredients. Adjust the seasoning if necessary. Chill before serving.

MAKE AHEAD: *Cocktail sauce keeps like a dream; any left over will keep for weeks covered in plastic wrap in the refrigerator.*

Fried Calamari with Spicy Lemon Aïoli

A soak in buttermilk not only helps the flour coating stick but also tenderizes the squid. Mixing some semolina with all-purpose flour gives the coating a little crunch. You can also serve this with Odd Fellow Marinara (page 120) in place of or in addition to the aïoli.

If you're afraid of frying, see my tips on the following page.

2 pounds small squid, cleaned
2 cups buttermilk
About 4 cups peanut or canola oil for frying
1 cup all-purpose flour
¼ cup semolina (available in health-food stores and large supermarkets)
1 tablespoon kosher salt
¼ teaspoon freshly ground white pepper
Fleur de sel
Celery leaves for garnish (optional)
1 lemon, cut into 4 or 6 wedges
Spicy Lemon Aïoli (recipe follows)

Slice the squid bodies crosswise into ½-inch-thick rings. Unless very large, leave the tentacles whole. Rinse both the rings and the tentacles under cold water, then soak them in the buttermilk for at least 1 hour before frying.

Fill a medium saucepan halfway with the oil and heat until it reaches 350°F.

Meanwhile, combine the flour, semolina, salt, and white pepper in a medium bowl. Drain the squid and dredge them in the flour mixture to coat. Using a Chinese skimmer or other slotted spoon, submerge a few of the coated squid (do not crowd) in the hot oil and fry until golden and crisp, 2 to 3 minutes. Drain on paper towels and sprinkle with the fleur de sel. Fry the remaining squid. Serve immediately, garnished with celery leaves, if you like, and lemon wedges, and with the aïoli on the side.

MAKE AHEAD:

❚ *You can soak the squid in the buttermilk in the refrigerator for up to 24 hours.*

❚ *Frying is an of-the-moment kind of cooking. Instead of trying to keep the fried calamari warm in the oven, gather people near the stove and serve the calamari hot from the pot.*

Try Deep-Frying

Everybody loves fried food, so it's too bad that so few people fry at home. It's actually easy, and I guarantee you'll be lavished with praise along the lines of "I can't believe you did this!"

If you have a fear of frying, you probably think it will be messy. But the truth is that pan-frying, which most home cooks do without a second thought, is more likely to spread grease around the kitchen than deep-frying, because the oil in the shallow frying pan sputters and sprays. The oil for deep-frying, however, remains within the confines of the pot (so long as you fill the pot only halfway with the oil). You will have to deal with the oil left over after frying, which can be a drag. My solution is to use less oil than is called for in many conventional recipes. A medium saucepan will do the trick, because for the best results, you have to fry in batches, and there's no point in heating up a huge pot of oil if you're only going to throw in a few fritters or a handful of squid rings at a time. To get rid of the oil, simply funnel it back into its container—after it has cooled—and discard it.

The other reason people don't fry at home is they are nervous about the hot oil. And while you do need to be careful around it, if you fill the pot only halfway and cook in batches, you can avoid any messy and dangerous overflow. Use a candy or frying thermometer to keep an eye on the temperature of the oil, and use a Chinese skimmer (available at kitchen stores) or spider (a large, flat wire spoon used in most restaurant kitchens) to retrieve the hot food easily and safely from the oil.

So be a hero and consider deep-frying next time you have friends over.

Lemon Aïoli

MAKES ABOUT 1 CUP

Aside from making a great dip for calamari (and just about anything else fried), this spicy, lemony spread is really good on sandwiches. I use it in place of mayonnaise in my lobster roll (page 200), and I especially like it on a BLT. If you don't feel like making a proper aïoli or freak out over eating something made with raw eggs, you can simply whisk together ¾ cup mayonnaise (I like Hellmann's), 2 teaspoons fresh lemon juice (and 2 teaspoons harissa for spicy), and salt and pepper to taste. It won't be quite as good, but it will be close.

2	large egg yolks
1	teaspoon harissa or sriracha (optional; for Spicy Lemon Aïoli)
1	tablespoon fresh lemon juice
	Kosher salt and freshly ground black pepper
¾	cup grapeseed oil or mild-tasting olive oil

In a medium bowl, whisk the egg yolks, harissa (if using), 1 teaspoon of the lemon juice, 1 teaspoon salt, and ½ teaspoon pepper until combined. Slowly drizzle in the oil while whisking nonstop until the mixture begins to emulsify. As the mixture thickens, whisk in the remaining 2 teaspoons lemon juice and continue to whisk in the oil until the mixture has achieved a thick, mayonnaise-like consistency. (Alternatively, make the aïoli in a food processor, combining all the ingredients except the oil and 2 teaspoons lemon juice. With the motor running, slowly add the oil and lemon juice, processing until thickened.) Taste and adjust the seasonings.

MAKE AHEAD: *Aïoli will keep, covered in plastic wrap and refrigerated, for up to 3 days.*

NOTE: If consuming raw eggs is a health issue for you, look for pasteurized eggs, which are becoming more common and are sold by the dozen just like regular eggs.

STARTERS AND SMALL BITES

STIR

Brioche Pizza

With these pizzas, I take a purely French creation—insanely rich and buttery brioche—and marry it to Italy's most famous food export: pizza. I would be lying if I said I developed brioche pizza after much deliberation and experimentation. As delicious as it is, it came about on the fly when I was way behind at the restaurant and still had to make the staff's preservice meal. I was planning on pizza but had neglected to make the dough. That's when I spied brioche dough, which was in the fridge waiting to be shaped into loaves for the next day's bread. "What the hell!" I thought. I rolled out balls of the buttery dough and went to town. The pizzas became an instant hit with the staff and then, quickly thereafter, with our customers.

Pizza crusts made with brioche dough turn out sweet, buttery, and crackerlike. The rich flavor and crisp texture of the crust combined with unique toppings make these pizzas perfect as appetizers.

Here's why you want to make brioche pizzas at home. Although brioche dough may sound intimidating, it's actually quite easy to make if you have a stand mixer with a dough hook. The dough can accommodate your schedule: while it needs to proof (rest) to develop more flavor, that time can be a matter of a few hours or up to 2 days. You can also portion out pieces of dough, wrap them well, and freeze them. Let them thaw in the refrigerator for a day before rolling them out. This dough is also really easy to roll out, and the pizza is baked right on a baking sheet, so you don't have to haul out your pizza stone.

BRIOCHE PIZZA WITH FRIED PISTACHIOS AND HONEY (PAGE 50)

Brioche Pizza with Fried Pistachios and Honey

Pistachio pizza? Sounds weird, but it's so good. I like to cut this thin flatbread pizza into small slices to serve with aperitifs. (See the photo on page 49.)

1   cup extra-virgin olive oil

⅓   cup shelled unsalted pistachios

2   garlic cloves, thinly sliced

1   teaspoon crushed red pepper flakes

     All-purpose flour for rolling the dough

2   4-ounce balls (about ½ rounded cup) Brioche Pizza Dough (page 54), refrigerated for at least 4 hours and used straight from the fridge

1½   cups fresh ricotta (see page 34)

     Kosher salt and freshly ground black pepper

4   teaspoons honey

     Fleur de sel

Heat the olive oil in a medium saucepan over medium-high heat until hot; a pistachio dropped in will sizzle immediately. Add the pistachios and fry them until lightly browned in spots, 30 seconds to 1 minute. Use a slotted spoon to transfer them to a paper-towel-lined plate. Remove the oil from the heat and let it cool down a bit, then add the garlic and red pepper flakes to it. Once the pistachios are cool, chop them coarsely.

Heat the oven to 375°F. On a generously floured surface with a floured rolling pin, roll out a ball of brioche dough into a thin oval or rectangle measuring about 9 × 12 inches (a little smaller than the baking sheet it will bake on). Don't worry about making it look perfect; these pizzas are meant to be rustic, and oblong is just fine. Transfer the dough to a baking sheet. Repeat with the other ball of dough.

Drizzle some of the reserved flavored oil over the dough, being very generous with it (save the rest to use in vinaigrette or for dipping bread). Sprinkle each pizza with pistachios, dividing them equally, and dot with spoonfuls of ricotta. Season with salt and pepper and bake until the crust looks golden brown and crisp, about 10 minutes.

Let the pizzas sit briefly before moving them to a cutting board. Drizzle each with 2 teaspoons of the honey, sprinkle with a pinch of fleur de sel, slice, and serve.

MAKE AHEAD: *The pizzas are best served hot; as they sit, the crust will soften. But you can make them a few hours ahead. Keep at room temperature on the baking sheet and reheat to serve.*

Brioche Pizza with Black Olives and Fresh Ricotta

MAKES 2
(9-x-12-INCH)
PIZZAS; SERVES
6 TO 8 AS
AN APPETIZER

I love the interplay of flavor, texture, and temperature in this pizza. Cool, creamy ricotta is spread on crisp, hot pizza crust made wonderfully savory and salty by smearing on a black olive paste before baking.

All-purpose flour for rolling the dough

2 4-ounce balls (about ½ rounded cup) Brioche Pizza Dough (page 54), refrigerated for at least 4 hours and used straight from the fridge

3–4 tablespoons extra-virgin olive oil

1 cup Black Olive Paste (page 6) or good-quality purchased tapenade
   Kosher salt and freshly ground black pepper

1 cup fresh ricotta (see page 34)

2 tablespoons chopped scallions

Heat the oven to 375°F. On a generously floured surface with a floured rolling pin, roll out a ball of brioche dough into a thin oval or rectangle measuring about 9 × 12 inches (a little smaller than the baking sheet it will bake on). Don't worry about making it look perfect; these pizzas are meant to be rustic, and oblong is just fine. Transfer the dough to a baking sheet. Repeat with the other ball of dough.

Brush both doughs with the olive oil and spread the olive paste over them. Season with salt and pepper and bake until golden brown, 8 to 10 minutes.

Season the fresh ricotta well with salt and pepper and put dollops of it over the hot pizzas. Sprinkle the scallions over the pizzas, slice, and serve.

MAKE AHEAD: *These pizzas are best served hot; as they sit, the crust will soften. But you can make them a few hours ahead. Keep at room temperature on the baking sheet and reheat to serve.*

Brioche Pizza with Roasted Potatoes and Rosemary

MAKES 2
(9-x-12-INCH)
PIZZAS; SERVES
6 TO 8 AS
AN APPETIZER

Lightly caramelized onions and tender roasted potatoes make a satisfying topping for this thin-crusted and crispy pizza. With its scent of rosemary, this may be my favorite pizza topping of all. Larger slices, served with a salad, make a great light supper.

2	medium red-skinned potatoes, sliced about 3/8 inch thick (leave skins on)
3–3 1/2	tablespoons extra-virgin olive oil
1/2	large red onion, thinly sliced
2	garlic cloves, finely chopped
	All-purpose flour for rolling the dough
2	4-ounce balls (about 1/2 rounded cup) Brioche Pizza Dough (page 54), refrigerated for at least 4 hours and used straight from the fridge
1	tablespoon finely chopped fresh rosemary
1/4	teaspoon crushed red pepper flakes
	Fleur de sel
	Freshly ground black pepper
	About 2-ounce wedge Parmigiano-Reggiano for shaving over pizza (large enough to drag a vegetable peeler over; you won't use all of it)
1/4	cup crème fraîche

Heat the oven to 375°F. Toss the potatoes with enough oil to coat them well (1 1/2 to 2 tablespoons) and spread them in a single layer on a small baking sheet or in an ovenproof skillet. Roast until just tender when pierced with a skewer, 4 to 6 minutes. Remove the potatoes from the oven and increase the oven temperature to 425°F.

Heat 1 1/2 tablespoons olive oil in a medium skillet over medium heat. Add the onion and cook, stirring, for a few minutes. Add the garlic and cook, stirring, until the onion is tender and lightly browned, about 10 minutes.

On a generously floured surface with a floured rolling pin, roll out a ball of brioche dough into a thin oval or rectangle measuring about 9 × 12 inches (a little smaller than the baking sheet it will bake on). Don't worry about making it look perfect; these pizzas are meant to be rustic, and oblong is just fine. Transfer the dough to a baking sheet. Repeat with the other ball of dough.

Spread the onion and garlic over each pizza, leaving a little bit of a border. Top with the potatoes in a single layer. Sprinkle with the rosemary, crushed red pepper, a little fleur de sel, and a few grinds of black pepper. With a vegetable peeler, shave the Parmesan thinly over the pizzas in a single layer. Bake until the crust looks golden brown and crisp, about 8 minutes.

Let the pizzas sit briefly before moving them to a cutting board. Garnish with tiny dollops of crème fraîche, slice, and serve.

MAKE AHEAD:

▌ *You can roast the potatoes and cook the onion and garlic well ahead of assembling the pizzas.*

▌ *These pizzas are best served hot; as they sit, the crust will soften. But you can make them a few hours ahead. Keep at room temperature on the baking sheet and reheat to serve.*

Brioche Pizza Dough

MAKES 1¾ POUNDS
BRIOCHE DOUGH,
ENOUGH FOR 7
(9-x-12-INCH) PIZZAS

Bread baking intimidates me. But I do make buttery brioche dough a lot. Everything, including kneading the very sticky dough, is done in the bowl of a stand mixer fitted with a dough hook. Make the dough up to 2 days ahead so it has time to rest and develop its sweet, yeasty, buttery flavor. You can make awesome rolls with this dough (see opposite page). Or double the recipe and bake it in a rectangular pan (no tricky shaping required) to get a loaf of sweet, buttery, fine-grained bread perfect for making into croutons, toasting and serving with steak tartare (page 18), and using in bread pudding (page 292).

1	tablespoon active dry yeast
¼	cup plus ¼ teaspoon sugar
2¾	cups unbleached all-purpose flour, plus up to ½ cup more for kneading
2	teaspoons kosher salt
3	large eggs
16	tablespoons (2 sticks) unsalted butter, at room temperature

Stir together the yeast, ¼ teaspoon sugar, and a scant ¼ cup warm water. Let stand for 5 to 10 minutes to dissolve and activate the yeast.

Combine the flour, the remaining ¼ cup sugar, and the salt in the bowl of a stand mixer fitted with a dough hook.

Whisk the eggs and then combine them with the dissolved yeast. With the mixer on low speed, add the egg-yeast mixture to the flour. Mix, scraping the bowl and the dough hook once or twice during mixing, until you have a stiff dough that clings to the dough hook, 6 to 8 minutes. Turn the mixer off and push the dough off the hook and into the bowl.

Turn the mixer back on low and add about a tablespoon of butter at a time. Mix each piece until incorporated, stopping occasionally to scrape the bowl and pull the dough off the dough hook. It will take 12 to 15 minutes to knead in all the butter. At this point the dough will be quite loose and very sticky, which is as it should be. Transfer the dough to a lightly floured surface. Sprinkle with some flour and knead by hand to finish incorporating any butter, adding more flour as needed to create a supple dough. Lightly oil another bowl. Gather the brioche dough into one mass, scraping the sides and bottom of the bowl. Transfer the dough to the greased bowl, cover loosely with plastic wrap, and refrigerate for at least 4 hours and up to 2 days. (The dough will not rise dramatically, but it will get easier to handle as it chills.)

To make brioche pizzas, portion the dough into 4-ounce balls (about ½ rounded cup) and follow the directions for shaping in the pizza recipes beginning on page 50.

MAKE AHEAD: *If you don't plan to use the full batch of dough right away, portion it after it's been refrigerated (it's much easier to handle when cold) and freeze each portion in a zip-top bag for up to 3 weeks. Let it thaw in the refrigerator for a day before using it.*

VARIATIONS

BRIOCHE ROLLS: *Roll 2½- to 3-ounce pieces (about ¼ cup) of the cold dough into balls and set them on a baking sheet. Cover with plastic wrap and leave them at room temperature to proof for 2 to 3 hours. You'll know the dough has risen enough when it pops back a little after you press it with one finger; it will still seem soft, however. Brush the rolls with a beaten egg and bake in a 375°F oven until golden, 12 to 15 minutes. Let cool a little before serving. Makes 10 to 12 rolls.*

BRIOCHE BREAD: *Lightly butter a loaf pan. Roll a piece of dough that will roughly fill the pan about three-quarters full into a cylinder shape and place it in the pan. Cover with plastic wrap and proof in a warm place until it has risen some and the dough feels softer to the touch, 2 to 3 hours. Bake in a 375°F oven for 30 to 45 minutes, or until the top is deeply golden and the loaf sounds hollow when you tap it on the bottom. Makes 1 loaf.*

salads with substance

MIXED GREENS WITH FRESH HERBS 60

BIBB LETTUCE WITH CREAMY PARMESAN DRESSING
AND CHEESE CRISPS 62

ICEBERG WEDGES WITH BLUE CHEESE DRESSING AND
BACON 65

BEET AND FRISÉE SALAD WITH BLUE CHEESE 66

HARVEST SALAD 69

TOASTED BREAD SALAD WITH TOMATOES AND CUCUMBER 71

FENNEL, CUCUMBER, AND GREEN BEAN SALAD WITH ROASTED
POTATOES AND CREAMY YOGURT 72

ROASTED EGGPLANT WITH GOLDEN RAISIN–PINE NUT
VINAIGRETTE AND FETA 75

GREEN BEAN AND SEARED SHRIMP SALAD WITH SPICY CURRY
VINAIGRETTE 77

I am *so* over mesclun. A decade or so ago, these mixed greens were novel, but mesclun's popularity gave rise to so many bad renditions—bowl after boring bowl of stale-tasting, lackluster greens—that I almost never order a lettuce salad when I eat out.

My favorite salads feature vegetables, all kinds of them—crisp, paper-thin slices of celery, fennel, and red onion; roasted baby eggplant or diced sweet beets; blanched green beans and peppery radish coins. There may be some leaves in these salads, but the greens act more as a garnish than as the main attraction. Such salads make a great start to a meal, and they can also be served as a side along with the main course. You can change them with the seasons, they are more nutritious than green salads, and they can usually be almost completely made ahead. But the main reason I prefer them is that, with their widely varied flavors and textures, they are a hell of a lot more exciting to eat than lettuce.

When I do make a green salad, I think back to the days when *mesclun* actually meant something special: a mix of truly wild greens, baby lettuces, and tender herbs, carefully proportioned so that each bite delivered a different experience. I avoid the mixed lettuces sold in sealed plastic at the supermarket. Most are actually made up of torn mature plants and have a flavor that ranges from bland at best to inedible, especially when the leaves on the bottom of the bag are smashed and blackened. And so I seek out tender young greens with varied textures and personalities and mix them myself, adding whole-leaf herbs to boost the flavor. The *only* place I buy premixed lettuces is at the farmers' market, where the greens have been recently picked and packed by hand with care. Because the bags are not sealed, you can smell to double-check for freshness. Most farmers will even encourage you to have a taste. And if you can't find greens that wow you, grab some fennel, celery, and beets and make a different kind of salad for a change.

Mixed Greens with Fresh Herbs

To make a great salad, you need to start with excellent greens. If you have a garden, I'm jealous. If you buy them, choose what looks best and combine them yourself, or buy premixed greens at the farmers' market, where you can see, smell, and taste what you're getting. Wash them well and, just as important, dry them gently but thoroughly. Add fresh herbs to the mix, leaves whole if small or coarsely chopped if large.

Make your vinaigrette from scratch; this one takes about 1 minute. The maple adds a touch of sweetness without tasting too maple-y. Be really stingy with the dressing, adding just enough to make the leaves shine. (An overdressed salad is among the worst food offenses committed by home and professional cooks alike.) Finally, finish with a pinch of fleur de sel, which brings out all the flavors of the greens, herbs, and dressing.

1	large shallot, finely chopped
1/3	cup sherry vinegar
1	tablespoon Dijon mustard, preferably whole-grain
2	teaspoons real maple syrup
1	cup grapeseed oil or mild olive oil
	Kosher salt and freshly ground black pepper
8–10	ounces mixed tender-leaf greens, well washed and dried
1/2	cup mixed fresh tender herbs, such as parsley, tarragon,
	chervil (my favorite), basil, and chives
	Fleur de sel

In a small bowl, combine the shallot, vinegar, mustard, and maple syrup. Whisk in the oil and season with about 1/2 teaspoon salt and a few grinds of pepper. In a large bowl, toss the greens with the herbs and just enough of the dressing to lightly coat the leaves (you will not use all the dressing). Sprinkle each serving with a pinch of fleur de sel.

MAKE AHEAD:

▌ *You can combine the greens and herbs in a bowl, cover with a damp paper towel, and refrigerate them for up to 1 day. Never, ever toss a salad with its dressing until just before serving.*

▌ *The vinaigrette makes about twice as much as you need for the salad, and it keeps, covered and refrigerated, for a week to 10 days.*

Washing Greens

When it comes to salad greens, you want to wash them thoroughly but with care so as not to bruise the leaves. To do so, swish them around in a large bowl filled with cool water. Use both hands to lift the greens from the water. If there is grit left in the water bowl, you'll need to rinse the bowl and repeat, soaking them in fresh water until the bowl looks clean when the greens are lifted from it. Most greens will need just a single rinse, but spinach, escarole, and herbs like cilantro often need a few baths to get rid of the clinging sand. Dry the leaves well. A salad spinner works quickly and efficiently, and I highly recommend getting one if you don't have one already. You can gently pat the leaves dry, but this takes up a lot of counter space, not to mention time. Be sure to dry them, or your salad will feel limp and its dressing will taste watery. For weeknight salad-making, it's handy to have your greens already washed and dried, so consider doing that soon after you get them home from the market. Store them in an airtight container or plastic bag lined with a paper towel.

Bibb Lettuce with Creamy Parmesan Dressing and Cheese Crisps

This salad—soft, buttery Bibb lettuce coated in a creamy, mustardy dressing and topped with a crisp cheese garnish—is irresistible. Have you ever made a grilled cheese sandwich only to find that the tastiest bit is the cheese that oozed out into the pan and browned? If you love to scrape up that stuff and eat it, you will love these cheese crisps. In Italy they're called *frico,* and they're made by frying a layer of grated cheese to create a crisp round that's thin and lacy but still holds together. Instead of frying the cheese, I bake it in the oven, which is faster and easier. To prevent the wafers from sticking to the baking sheet, I strongly recommend using a Silpat, a thick, silicone, reusable pan liner that's available in most kitchen stores (see page 64). Coated parchment paper also works, but the Silpat releases the fragile *frico* so easily that even I don't swear when making these.

1   large egg yolk
1   tablespoon whole-grain mustard
    Juice of ¹/₂ lemon
1   tablespoon white wine vinegar, preferably Chardonnay
1   cup grapeseed oil or mild olive oil
3¹/₂   cups finely grated Parmigiano-Reggiano
    Kosher salt and freshly ground black pepper
1¹/₂   tablespoons extra-virgin olive oil
3   small heads Bibb lettuce, cores removed, leaves well washed, dried, and torn into pieces
¹/₂   cup whole almonds, toasted and finely chopped
    Fresh fines herbes (page 254) for garnish (optional)

In a medium bowl, whisk the egg yolk, mustard, lemon juice, and vinegar until well combined. Slowly add the grapeseed oil in a thin, steady drizzle until the oil is completely incorporated and the dressing looks emulsified. Whisk in 2 cups of the grated cheese. Season to taste with a little salt and pepper. Thin with a teaspoon of cold water if very thick.

Heat the oven to 350°F. Line a baking sheet with a Silpat liner. In a small bowl, combine the remaining 1¹/₂ cups cheese with the extra-virgin olive oil. Make little mounds of cheese on the Silpat, using a heaping tablespoon of cheese per mound and leaving about 2 inches between them. Gently flatten the mounds with an offset spatula or the palm of your hand to spread the cheese mixture evenly into a very thin circle. You need to make at least 12 crisps for the salads; if you have any cheese left, however, make more, as you'll want to snack on them. Garnish with fines herbes if you like.

Bake until golden brown and bubbly, 10 to 12 minutes. Let the crisps cool on the baking sheet before carefully removing them with a thin spatula.

Divide half of the lettuce among six dinner plates. Drizzle about a tablespoon of the dressing over each pile of greens. Top each with a cheese crisp. Divide the rest of the greens among the plates, piling them on top of the cheese crisp. Drizzle a tablespoon or so more dressing over the greens (you will have leftover dressing) and top with a second crisp. Sprinkle the toasted almonds over all and serve.

MAKE AHEAD:

▌ *The leftover dressing will keep for a couple of days covered with plastic wrap in the refrigerator. Use it as a dip for vegetables or on a Caesar-inspired salad of romaine, anchovies, and hard-boiled egg.*

▌ *On dry days, the crisps stay crispy for about 2 days in an airtight container, but on a hot August day all bets are off; then I make them as close to serving as is manageable.*

NOTE: If consuming raw eggs is a health issue for you, look for pasteurized eggs, which are becoming more common and are sold by the dozen just like regular eggs.

Silpats: No Longer a Secret

Time was when Silpats—thick, reusable, heatproof baking-sheet liners loved by pastry chefs around the world—were not readily available to the home cook. But as silicone has taken over in the kitchen, used in everything from muffin tins to pot holders, this French import, made of silicone-coated fiberglass and available in a variety of sizes, has gained in popularity outside the restaurant world. Now, instead of having to visit a restaurant supply store to get one, you can buy a Silpat at houseware stores, your local Bed Bath & Beyond, and even some supermarkets. These flexible mats conveniently roll up for easy storage.

Iceberg Wedges with Blue Cheese Dressing and Bacon

SERVES 4   Food snobs say they don't like it. But I love iceberg lettuce. Its refreshing crunch is perfect on a sandwich or tossed into a vegetable salad. Next to smoky-salty bacon and pungent blue cheese, a cold wedge of iceberg is like an oasis. I change up this steakhouse favorite a little by adding some Tomato Confit for color and sweetness. The leftover dressing makes a terrific dip.

8   slices bacon, preferably thick-cut and applewood-smoked
(I like Niman Ranch's)

6   ounces blue cheese, crumbled

1   cup buttermilk

1/2   teaspoon kosher salt
Freshly ground black pepper

1   medium head iceberg lettuce
Tomato Confit (page 28)

Heat the oven to 350°F. Lay the strips of bacon on a parchment-lined baking sheet. Bake in the oven until golden and crisp, about 20 minutes. (Alternatively, fry the bacon in a skillet.) Transfer the bacon to a plate lined with paper towels.

If you would like a smooth blue cheese dressing, combine the cheese, buttermilk, salt, and a few grinds of pepper in a food processor or blender and blend until smooth. If you prefer a little more texture, combine the same ingredients in a bowl and whisk by hand until creamy but still chunky. Keep the dressing chilled.

Meanwhile, remove the outer leaves of lettuce if they are discolored or bruised. Cut the head into 4 equal wedges through the core and keep refrigerated until ready to serve.

To serve, divide the wedges of lettuce among four plates. Put a few pieces of tomato confit next to the wedges. Drizzle 3 to 4 tablespoons of the dressing over the lettuce and lay a couple of slices of bacon on top. Season with a few grinds of black pepper.

MAKE AHEAD:

▌ *You can cook the bacon a few hours ahead and keep it at room temperature, though it may be hard to keep from eating it. If you would like the bacon warm, reheat it briefly in the oven or a skillet.*

▌ *The blue cheese dressing will keep for a couple of days, covered, in the refrigerator.*

Beet and Frisée Salad with Blue Cheese

Creamy and tangy blue cheese offsets the sweetness of the beets in this earthy yet beautiful salad. For contrast, I also add crunchy croutons flavored with a little olive paste.

I like Great Hill Blue Cheese for this salad. Made from the milk of Guernsey cows that graze at a farm overlooking Buzzards Bay on nearby Cape Cod, the cheese has a sharp flavor that works exceptionally well in the salad. When I first created this salad, I made the cheese creamier by whirring it in a food processor with a tablespoon of heavy cream. If you don't mind one more thing to clean, you may want to do the same.

2	pounds beets, stems trimmed to ½ inch (leaving a little stem helps preserve nutrients and color during cooking)
	Kosher salt and freshly ground black pepper
4	tablespoons plus 1 teaspoon extra-virgin olive oil
1	tablespoon plus 1 teaspoon fresh lemon juice, plus more if needed
1–2	slices day-old brioche or other good-quality white sandwich bread, crusts removed, cut into ½-inch cubes (¾ cup)
1	tablespoon Black Olive Paste (page 6) or good purchased tapenade
1	bunch frisée, core and tough outer leaves trimmed away, cut into 1-inch pieces
3	tablespoons finely chopped fresh chives
½	pound robust blue cheese, at room temperature

Heat the oven to 400°F. Scrub the beets and put them in a small ovenproof pan with a little bit of water on the bottom. Season the beets with salt and pepper and cover the pan with aluminum foil. Bake until the beets are tender when pierced with a paring knife, 40 to 50 minutes or more, depending on size. Remove from the oven and reduce the oven temperature to 350°F.

When the beets are cool enough to handle, peel them and cut them into small dice to yield about 4 cups. Toss them with 3 tablespoons of the olive oil and 1 tablespoon of the lemon juice and then season to taste with salt and pepper.

Meanwhile, toss the bread cubes with the olive paste and 1 teaspoon of the olive oil. Spread the cubes on a baking sheet and bake until crisp and browned, about 10 minutes. Drain on paper towels and set aside.

To serve, combine the remaining 1 tablespoon olive oil with the remaining 1 teaspoon lemon juice in a medium bowl. Toss the frisée with just enough of this vinaigrette to moisten slightly and season with a little salt and pepper. Add the chives to the beets and toss. Reserve about one fourth of the cheese. Divide the rest among six plates, crumbling it. Top with the beets, frisée, and then the croutons. Crumble the reserved cheese over the salads and serve.

MAKE AHEAD: *I like to keep cooked beets on hand to toss in a green salad. Left whole with their skin on, cooked beets will keep in the refrigerator, covered, for at least a week. You can also dice them ahead and keep them refrigerated for a couple of days, but add the chives close to serving time.*

Harvest Salad

An explosion of color, this crisp, refreshing salad features from the farmers' market—tender baby fennel, sweet red and golden beets, tiny earthy turnips—all sliced paper-thin and topped with a warm, just-set soft-boiled egg. I love how the bright yellow-orange yolk oozes and mingles with the vegetables, adding its own contrasting warmth and color. To take away the last-minute stress of cooking and peeling the eggs, I parcook them and peel them so that once the salad is ready, I only need to reheat the already shelled eggs. A mandoline, even one of those cheap Japanese models, makes preparing this salad a breeze. If you don't have one, be sure your knife is very sharp.

Don't feel you have to include all these vegetables. For a nice mix of colors and flavors, I like to serve the salad with a slice of toasted baguette slathered with truffle butter or Fresh Herb Butter (page 239).

	Kosher salt
4–6	large eggs
	About 1 tablespoon unsalted butter
4	small red beets, peeled and very thinly sliced
4	small golden beets, peeled and very thinly sliced
4	small fennel bulbs, trimmed and very thinly sliced lengthwise
8	small carrots, peeled and very thinly sliced
8	small radishes, very thinly sliced
4	small white turnips, peeled and very thinly sliced
2	celery stalks, peeled and very thinly sliced (reserve the inner celery leaves for the garnish)
3	tablespoons extra-virgin olive oil
3	tablespoons white balsamic vinegar
	Freshly ground black pepper
	Fleur de sel

In a medium saucepan, combine 6 cups water with $^1/_2$ cup salt. (Using a lot of salt makes the eggs easier to peel.) Bring the water to a rolling boil. Meanwhile, fill a large bowl with ice water and set it near the stove. Reduce the heat to a low boil. Place 4 eggs (plus a couple extra in case of any mishaps) in the water and boil for 6 minutes. Remove the eggs immediately with a slotted spoon and transfer them to the ice water to cool quickly. After 10 minutes, remove an egg, tap its shell lightly with a spoon or a knife to crack it, and very gently peel the shell away; keep in mind that if you break into an egg, the yolk will flow out.

When all of the eggs are peeled, place each one on a piece of plastic wrap large enough to fit around it and place a small pat of butter next to the egg. (The butter will prevent the plastic wrap from sticking when the eggs are reheated.) Bring the sides of the plastic wrap around the egg and butter to form a sack. Tie the top securely with a piece of string (or a piece of twisted plastic wrap) so the egg is completely sealed. Refrigerate until ready to use.

Line a baking sheet with parchment paper. Put the vegetables in different piles on the baking sheet (to prevent the color of the beets from bleeding into the rest of the vegetables). Drizzle the oil and vinegar over the vegetables and season them with a few pinches of salt. Allow the vegetables to "pickle" for at least 15 minutes and up to an hour.

To serve, bring a medium saucepan of fresh water to a boil.

Toss the vegetables together. Season with additional salt, if needed, and pepper. Divide the vegetables among four large plates.

Meanwhile, reduce the boiling water to a simmer. Submerge the wrapped eggs in the simmering water and cook for 2 minutes (the plastic will not melt). Remove the eggs, gently unwrap, and place 1 on top of or alongside each salad. Sprinkle each salad with reserved celery leaves and a pinch of fleur de sel and serve immediately.

MAKE AHEAD: *I love soft-boiled eggs and use them all the time on all kinds of salads. You can cook them 2 days ahead and pull them out when you need them. Simmer them in their plastic wrap for 2 minutes.*

Toasted Bread Salad with Tomatoes and Cucumber

SERVES 4   This is my version of panzanella, the classic Italian bread salad, usually made by tearing bread into chunks and tossing it with tomatoes, onions, olives, basil, olive oil, and vinegar. I pile the salad fixings on a toasted brick of bread (easily made by trimming a baguette) rubbed with olive paste. The refined result is drop-dead gorgeous.

1	small red onion, cut through the root into 1/2-inch wedges
2–3	tablespoons extra-virgin olive oil
1	teaspoon balsamic vinegar, plus more to taste
	Kosher salt and freshly ground black pepper
1	baguette
1/4	cup Black Olive Paste (page 6)
1	pint tiny tomatoes, preferably a mix of colors and shapes, sliced in half
1	small fennel bulb, cut in half lengthwise and sliced 1/8 inch thick
1/2	small cucumber, seeded and cut into small dice (about 1 cup)
	Fleur de sel
2	teaspoons baby basil leaves or larger leaves torn into pieces

Heat the oven to 350°F. Line a small baking sheet with parchment paper. Toss the onion wedges with enough olive oil to coat them lightly and put them on the baking sheet. Drizzle with 1 teaspoon balsamic vinegar and 1 teaspoon water. Season with salt and pepper and roast for 30 to 40 minutes, until nicely browned and tender.

Meanwhile, trim the ends off the baguette. Cut two 6- to 7-inch lengths from the baguette. Trim off all the crusts and, in the process, shape each length of bread into a rectangle. Cut each rectangle in half lengthwise so you have 4 rectangles. Spread the olive paste over the bread, thinly coating both sides. Use the back of a spoon for spreading, and don't worry if you flatten the bread a little in the process. Transfer the bread to a baking sheet, drizzle with olive oil, and toast in the oven, turning once, until golden brown on both sides, about 15 minutes.

Toss the tomatoes, fennel, and cucumber with 1 tablespoon olive oil, a good pinch of salt, and a few grinds of black pepper.

To assemble, center each piece of bread on a dinner plate. Separate the onion wedges a bit and arrange along the top of the bread (they don't have to cover it completely). Pile the tomatoes, fennel, and cucumber on the bread, allowing the vegetables to fall on the plate. Sprinkle a few drops of balsamic vinegar and olive oil over the panzanella and around the plate. Finish with a pinch of fleur de sel and a few basil leaves.

Fennel, Cucumber, and Green Bean Salad
with Roasted Potatoes and Creamy Yogurt

SERVES 6 Once you experience the cool crunch of fennel, cucumber, and yogurt combined with the homey goodness of roasted potatoes, you'll want to eat this salad all the time. (I do.) Delicious on its own and a great way to start a meal, it also works well as a side dish, especially when paired with rich meats and game. I like to serve it alongside the rack of lamb on page 252.

1	pound potatoes, preferably fingerlings or other small potatoes
¼	cup extra-virgin olive oil
	Kosher salt and freshly ground black pepper
½	pound green beans or a mix of green beans and wax beans, trimmed
1	cup plain whole-milk Greek-style yogurt, such as Fage Total brand
1	tablespoon chopped fresh parsley
4	celery stalks, trimmed, peeled, and very thinly sliced on the diagonal, with a few leaves reserved for garnish
1	fennel bulb, trimmed, cut in half, core removed, and very thinly sliced
1	English cucumber, peeled, cut in half, seeds removed, and very thinly sliced on the diagonal
	About 1 teaspoon fresh lemon juice

Heat the oven to 350°F. Cut large potatoes into 1- to 2-inch pieces, but leave small potatoes whole.

On a small baking sheet, toss the potatoes with 1 tablespoon of the oil and season with salt and pepper. Roast until tender when pierced with a paring knife, about 30 minutes. Cool and reserve; you can serve the potatoes hot, warm, or completely cooled in this salad.

Meanwhile, blanch the green beans in lightly salted boiling water until just tender. Cool rapidly by plunging them into a bowl of ice water, then drain well. Leave whole or slice in half on the diagonal.

Combine the yogurt and parsley and season well with salt and pepper; keep chilled until ready to serve.

Combine all the vegetables in a bowl and toss with the remaining 3 tablespoons olive oil and a squeeze (about a teaspoon) of lemon juice. Add a good amount of salt and a few grinds of pepper and toss again.

Divide the yogurt among six plates, putting a spoonful of it toward the center of the plate, and top the dressing with the salad and some celery leaves.

MAKE AHEAD:

▌ *You can prepare the vegetables a few hours ahead of serving. Combine all but the potatoes in a bowl, cover them with a damp paper towel, and refrigerate.*

▌ *The dressing takes only about two seconds to whip together, but you can make it ahead and refrigerate it, covered, for at least a day or two.*

Roasted Eggplant with Golden Raisin–Pine Nut Vinaigrette and Feta

SERVES 6 You can make this with any kind of eggplant, though I created it for Fairy Tale eggplants, available in summer. Streaked white and light purple, they're just a few inches long when harvested young. Standing up on the plate, anchored in feta cream, with their caps intact, the eggplants do, indeed, look like something straight out of a fairy tale. If you can't find Fairy Tale eggplants or similar-sized baby eggplants at your farmers' market, you can still make a delectable (and more rustic-looking) salad by roasting slices of eggplant, preferably small rounds from a Japanese eggplant, until tender.

Don't be tempted to leave the anchovy out of the vinaigrette; it adds a deep, slightly salty (but not fishy) undertone that perfectly balances the sweetness of the raisins and the toasty flavor of the pine nuts. The versatile vinaigrette is also delicious with hearty greens. Thick and somewhat chunky, it can even be served as a relish with roasted leg of lamb.

1	pound eggplants (see headnote), cut into 1-inch pieces if large, left whole if tiny
³/₄	cup extra-virgin olive oil
	Kosher salt
¹/₂	cup golden raisins
¹/₂	cup heavy cream
6	ounces feta cheese, crumbled
	Freshly ground black pepper
1	shallot, finely chopped
1	garlic clove, finely chopped
1	anchovy fillet, rinsed, patted dry, and finely chopped
¹/₂	cup pine nuts, toasted in a dry skillet or in the oven until golden brown
1	tablespoon plus 1 teaspoon sherry vinegar
	Fleur de sel
	Parsley leaves for garnish (optional)

Heat the oven to 350°F. Toss the eggplants with 2 to 3 tablespoons of the olive oil, season with salt, and roast until just tender but still holding their shape, 20 to 25 minutes; time will vary depending on the size of the eggplant pieces.

Meanwhile, plump the raisins in hot water until soft, 5 to 10 minutes.

In a small saucepan, bring the cream to a simmer. Whisk in the cheese and cook gently, stirring, until there are no lumps, about 6 minutes. (For a completely smooth mixture, pass it through a fine-mesh strainer.) Season to taste with salt and pepper and set aside.

Heat 1 tablespoon of the olive oil in a small skillet over medium heat. Add the shallot, garlic, and anchovy and cook, stirring, until the shallot is tender, about 5 minutes. Transfer to a small bowl and reserve.

Drain the raisins and add them to the bowl with the anchovy mixture. Add the pine nuts and vinegar and whisk in the remaining $\frac{1}{2}$ cup olive oil. Season to taste with salt and pepper.

Gently reheat the feta cream. Divide it among six plates, spooning it in the center. Stand whole eggplants up in the cream (you may need to take a little off the bottom to get them to stand upright) or lay roasted eggplant rounds or chunks on top of the cream. Drizzle a couple of spoonfuls of the vinaigrette over all (you may not use all of it) and sprinkle with a little fleur de sel and parsley, if you like.

MAKE AHEAD: *The vinaigrette will keep, covered and refrigerated, for up to a week. Serve leftover vinaigrette with lamb, shrimp, or chicken.*

Green Bean and Seared Shrimp Salad
with Spicy Curry Vinaigrette

This is the kind of salad I could eat every day and never tire of. The heat of the curry, the sweetness of the shrimp, the crisp green beans, the fresh cilantro, and the toasty crunch of the hazelnuts all work together, and it's really pretty. This salad, which is easily doubled, makes a great main dish or summertime side dish. It's perfect to take along to a picnic or cookout because the beans hold up really well even after they are dressed. (If I'm serving it that way, I sometimes leave out the shrimp, depending on how long it will be sitting out, and toss the cilantro right in with everything.)

Thai red curry paste and crème fraîche are available at most supermarkets.

1½	tablespoons finely chopped shallot
1½	tablespoons white wine vinegar
1½	teaspoons Thai red curry paste, plus more to taste
½	cup grapeseed or canola oil
¼	cup crème fraîche
1	teaspoon fresh lemon juice
	Kosher salt
1	pound green beans (haricots verts or a mix of beans), trimmed
½	cup whole hazelnuts
1	tablespoon extra-virgin olive oil
½	pound shrimp, shelled, deveined, and cut into 2 or 3 pieces each
	Freshly ground black pepper
2–3	small radishes, very thinly sliced
1	bunch fresh cilantro, well washed and dried, tough stems removed

In a medium bowl, combine the shallot, vinegar, and curry paste. Slowly whisk in the grapeseed oil, crème fraîche, and lemon juice. Season well with salt and add additional curry paste to taste.

Heat the oven to 350°F. Bring a medium saucepan of salted water to a boil and boil the green beans until just crisp-tender, 3 to 4 minutes (the best way to judge texture is by tasting one after a few minutes). Cool them rapidly by plunging them into a bowl of ice water.

Put the hazelnuts on a small baking sheet or in an ovenproof skillet and toast them in the oven until fragrant and lightly browned, 7 to 10 minutes. Let cool. If using skin-on hazelnuts, rub them against each other in paper towels or a clean dish towel to remove their papery skins (don't worry if some remains). Chop and set aside.

In a large nonstick skillet, heat the olive oil over medium-high heat. Cook the shrimp, stirring occasionally, until pink and just cooked through, 1 to 2 minutes. Don't overcook them. Season to taste with salt and pepper. Take the shrimp off the heat; they can be served warm or at room temperature.

To serve, toss the green beans, nuts, shrimp, and radishes together in a large bowl. Toss well with the dressing. Pile the salad onto the center of the plates and garnish each plate with a good handful of cilantro.

MAKE AHEAD:

▌ *You can store the vinaigrette for a few days, covered in the refrigerator; just give it a whisk before using.*

▌ *You can blanch the green beans up to a day ahead; keep refrigerated and covered with plastic wrap until about half an hour before using.*

▌ *The cooled, toasted nuts can be kept in a sealed container for up to a week.*

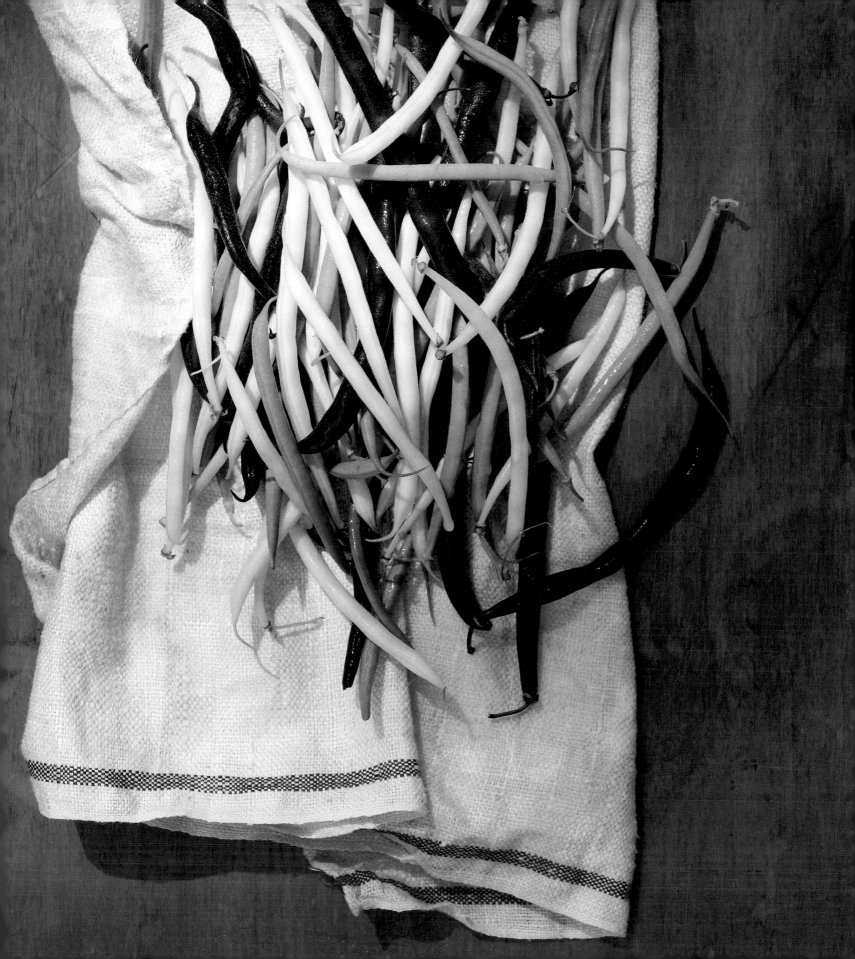

satisfying soups

ASPARAGUS SOUP WITH SAFFRON CROUTONS   84

CHILLED TOMATO CONSOMMÉ   86

COOL CORN SOUP WITH MUSHROOMS, SCALLION, AND LEMON   88

SPICY TOMATO SOUP WITH CRISPY GRILLED CHEESE   91

CREAMY LEEK AND POTATO SOUP WITH BAY SCALLOPS   93

CREAMY CHESTNUT BISQUE   96

WHITE BEAN SOUP WITH SAGE AND HAZELNUTS   98

CHICKEN CONSOMMÉ   101

CHICKEN AND VEGETABLE SOUP WITH CARAWAY GNOCCHI   104

ROASTED CHICKEN STOCK   108

In homes across Italy, whether an apartment in Rome or a villa in Tuscany, you can follow your nose to the kitchen, where chances are, you'll find a pot of soup simmering away on the stove and the room filled with its wonderful fragrance. That's a scene repeated in plenty of other countries, too. Here? Not so much.

Maybe we've all been raised to think that soup comes from a can. (I, for one, ate only Campbell's as a kid.) Or now that we're grown up and busy, we think we don't have the time to make soup. But both of these are misconceptions. When you have homemade soup, you immediately recognize the inferiority of canned. (Sorry, Ma.) Making soup also doesn't have to take a lot of time. Some, like Creamy Leek and Potato Soup with Bay Scallops, are made from start to finish in about half an hour. Those that do need a long simmer, like my favorite bean soup, on page 98, don't need to be babysat constantly, meaning you can do all those other important things you need to do while it cooks.

I got into the habit of making soup at home for a few reasons. For one thing, I am always trying to eat more healthily. Soups, especially ones chock-full of vegetables, are a delicious way to do so. Even on nights when I'm working (which is, admittedly, most nights), I make my family a home-cooked meal. So around 4:00 on a Sunday, I'll get started on a soup, maybe Chicken and Vegetable Soup or Spicy Tomato Soup. The chopping of vegetables can take a little time, but I'm in no hurry; Charlie's keeping me company on a stool at the table, and there's some good music on the stereo. Once the soup has simmered for a while, Charlie, our daughter, Marchesa, and I will have some of it for supper. The rest is put in the fridge to heat up through the week. It's a great routine, particularly in winter, when nothing beats a bowl of hot soup on a frigid night.

In the summer, I switch gears and make soups to be served cold, often as a first course. For big parties outside on our deck, I pass around glasses of Chilled Tomato Consommé, which is gorgeous, refreshing, and a fun way to start off the night. At the height of summer, when native corn is at its best, I make a silky corn soup garnished with kernels right off the cob. All soups, but especially pureed ones, benefit from an accompaniment or garnish for added texture and flavor, which is why I include one with all of my recipes. You don't *have* to make the accompaniment, but the soup will feel much more complete if you do.

COOL CORN SOUP WITH MUSHROOMS, SCALLION, AND LEMON (PAGE 88)

Asparagus Soup with Saffron Croutons

This soup celebrates spring with its gorgeous green color and delicate flavor. I like it best cool, but if it's still chilly outside, go ahead and serve it warm. If you have chive blossoms in your garden, garnish the soup with those.

2	bunches asparagus (about 2 pounds)
4	tablespoons ($^1/_2$ stick) unsalted butter
2	large shallots, chopped
2	cups heavy cream
	Kosher salt and freshly ground white pepper
$^1/_2$	teaspoon fresh lemon juice, plus more to taste
2	teaspoons finely chopped fresh chives
	Saffron Croutons (page 32)

Trim just the tough bottoms off the asparagus and cut the rest of the spears into 1-inch pieces.

Melt the butter in a 3- to 4-quart saucepan over medium-low heat. Add the shallots and cook, stirring occasionally, until the shallots are soft but not colored, about 5 minutes. Add the cream, 2 cups water, 2 teaspoons salt, and $^1/_2$ teaspoon white pepper. Increase the heat and bring the liquid to a boil. Add the asparagus, lower to a simmer, and cook until the asparagus is tender (taste a piece to see) but still quite green, about 5 minutes.

Puree the soup in batches in a blender. Pass it through a fine-mesh strainer, pressing on the solids with a ladle, into a bowl (if you plan to serve it cold) or a clean saucepan. (Discard the solids.)

Gently reheat the soup if serving it warm. Stir in the lemon juice; season to taste with additional salt and pepper and more lemon juice, if you like. Divide the soup among six cups or small bowls. Top with the chives and croutons and serve.

MAKE AHEAD: *The soup will keep, covered and refrigerated, for up to 2 days.*

A Fine-Mesh Strainer

In many of my recipes, I direct you to pass a mixture through a fine-mesh strainer, most often a vegetable puree or a cheese sauce that I want super-smooth. Your regular strainer or colander—the larger-holed one you use for draining pasta—won't cut it. What you need is a sieve. When you're after a smooth texture, the sieve, which is made of woven wire mesh, is the right tool, because it prevents all the bits of stems, seeds, and skins from passing through. You'll also need a ladle to press the mixture through the mesh.

In a restaurant, the sieve of choice is a chinois, named for the pointed Chinese hat it's shaped like. Good ones come with a pestle to help force the contents through and have brackets so that the chinois can fit across a bowl or pan. It may come with a stand as well to allow for easy hands-off draining of things like yogurt or homemade ricotta (see page 34). A chinois can be pricey ($100 or more), but it will last a lifetime. Look for them at kitchen specialty stores like Williams-Sonoma, restaurant supply stores, and online.

Chilled Tomato Consommé

MAKES 2 QUARTS;
SERVES 8 AS
A FIRST COURSE

If you could drink a fresh-picked tomato, it would taste like this. Serve this bright broth in clear glasses to appreciate its beauty, and top it with a smidgen each of fresh tomato, avocado, jalapeño, and cilantro. It's the perfect thing to serve at a summertime cocktail party.

FOR THE SOUP

5	pounds tomatoes (12–15, depending on size), coarsely chopped
1	small red onion, chopped
2	garlic cloves, chopped
2	tablespoons kosher salt, plus more to taste
1	jalapeño pepper, chopped
6–8	fresh basil leaves
12–15	fresh parsley leaves
	About 10 grinds of black pepper
1/2	teaspoon crushed red pepper flakes
1/2	teaspoon sherry vinegar, plus more to taste

FOR THE GARNISH

Avocado, peeled, pitted, and cut into tiny dice
Tomato, seeded and cut into tiny dice
Jalapeño pepper, stemmed, seeded, and very finely chopped
Whole fresh cilantro leaves

Put all the soup ingredients except the sherry vinegar in a blender or food processor and puree. Transfer the mixture to a medium saucepan and simmer over medium-low heat for about 10 minutes. As the mixture heats up, it will separate, or "break"; this is fine.

Line a fine-mesh strainer with a double layer of wet cheesecloth. Set the strainer over a bowl and strain the soup through it. Do not press on the solids, but do let them drain for 1 to 2 hours to extract as much clear liquid as possible.

Season with ¹/₂ teaspoon sherry vinegar to start. Chill well. Before serving, taste and add up to another teaspoon of the vinegar and a little salt to taste. Garnish each serving with some avocado, tomato, jalapeño, and cilantro.

MAKE AHEAD: *You can make the consommé a day ahead of serving, but its fresh flavor is best savored on the day it's made.*

Slicing Avocado

To slice an avocado neatly, cut the fruit lengthwise up to the large pit in the middle and gently twist apart the two halves. Remove the pit by whacking it with the sharp side of the knife so that the knife blade sticks into the pit, then use the knife to pull the pit out. (Remove the pit from the knife by pushing it off with your fingers from the dull side.) Scoop out the flesh in one piece by wedging a teaspoon between the skin and the flesh and removing the flesh in one go.

Cool Corn Soup with Mushrooms, Scallion, and Lemon

On a muggy summer day, my agent, Doe Coover, stopped in to see how the recipe-testing for the book was going. After taking a spoonful of this cool, sweet soup, she shut her eyes and breathed in deeply. "This is so delicious," she said. "Tell me it's very hard to make." My co-author and I looked at each other and smirked. This soup is simple: just four ingredients, if you don't count water, salt, and pepper.

The soup tastes best made with fresh-picked sweet (not starchy) summer corn. A simple garnish of mushrooms, scallion, and a squeeze of lemon adds brightness and texture (see the photo on page 82), but you should feel free to experiment with other accompaniments. One possibility is diced chorizo sautéed in a little olive oil with a bit of minced onion; top the soup with the sausage and a drizzle of the oil from the pan.

The soup is also great served warm—something to consider on a cool September night.

FOR THE SOUP

- 10 medium ears corn, shucked, silk removed
- 4 tablespoons (½ stick) unsalted butter
- ⅓ cup sliced shallot (about 1 large)
  Kosher salt and freshly ground black pepper
- 2 cups whole milk

FOR THE GARNISH

- 1 tablespoon extra-virgin olive oil
- 6 ounces mushrooms, preferably chanterelles, chopped (if small, leave whole or slice)
- 1 small shallot, finely chopped
  Kosher salt and freshly ground black pepper
- 2 tablespoons thinly sliced scallion
  About ½ teaspoon fresh lemon juice

TO MAKE THE SOUP: Remove the kernels from the cobs by slicing straight down each cob with a sharp chef's knife, turning the cob and repeating until most of the kernels are off. This is easier and neater if you cut the cob in half crosswise first and do the slicing on a baking sheet to make collecting the kernels easier. Using the dull side of the knife, scrape the now nude cob hard to extract the corn "milk," which you can combine with the kernels. Reserve a few of the corncobs.

In a medium saucepan, melt the butter over medium heat. Add the shallot and cook, stirring occasionally, until the shallot is tender but not colored, about 5 minutes. Reserve 1/2 cup of the corn kernels for the garnish and put the rest, including any liquid, in the saucepan. Season the corn with 2 teaspoons salt and about 10 grinds of pepper. Cook, stirring, for just a minute and then add the milk and 1 cup water. Bring the soup to a gentle simmer. (At this point, you may add 2 or 3 corncobs to simmer with the mixture and help add a bit more corn flavor. Just be sure to remove the cobs before you puree the soup.) Cook, stirring occasionally, until the corn is just tender, 8 to 12 minutes.

Puree the soup well in a blender or food processor, in batches if necessary. If you like a chunky soup, you can chill the soup as is. I prefer to strain the soup, which makes it much more refined. Pass it through a fine-mesh strainer, pressing hard on the solids with a ladle to extract as much flavor and liquid as possible, and chill.

TO MAKE THE GARNISH: Heat the oil in a small skillet over medium heat. Add the mushrooms and shallot, season with a pinch of salt and a couple grinds of pepper, and cook for 2 to 3 minutes, stirring occasionally, until both are tender. Add the reserved corn kernels and continue cooking for another 3 to 4 minutes, until tender. You're not looking for much color here. Transfer to a small bowl and add the scallion and a squeeze of fresh lemon juice. Taste and season with additional salt, pepper, or lemon juice, if needed.

Meanwhile, remove the soup from the refrigerator to take some of the chill off. (You want it cool, but the flavors will be muted if it's too cold.) Taste the soup and season with additional salt and pepper, if you like; soups made with milk or cream often need more salt than you think they do.

Divide the soup among four to six bowls and center a spoonful of the mushroom garnish in each bowl. Serve immediately.

MAKE AHEAD: *You can make both the soup and the mushroom garnish a day ahead of serving; keep both covered and refrigerated.*

Spicy Tomato Soup with Crispy Grilled Cheese

SERVES 6 Spicy and really easy to make, this is a great soup. But it's what the soup is paired with that makes it exceptional—crisp, full-flavored, croutonlike sandwiches that feel more like cheese that's been grilled than a traditional grilled cheese. (By the way, I know at least two people who swear they hate caraway yet love these sandwiches.) I make the grilled cheese on a well-buttered baking sheet, weighing the sandwiches down with another baking sheet on top. This ingenious method makes them super-thin, amazingly crispy, and beautifully browned. It also means you can make a lot at one time. Though delicious as a comforting main course, the grilled cheese can also be cut into tiny pieces and served as part of an hors d'oeuvres spread, with the soup in shot glasses; people go wild for it.

FOR THE SOUP

2	tablespoons extra-virgin olive oil
1	small onion, sliced
1	teaspoon crushed red pepper flakes (up to $1/2$ teaspoon more if you want it spicy, as I do)
2	28-ounce cans plum tomatoes
$1/4$	cup fresh basil leaves
	Kosher salt and freshly ground black pepper
6	tablespoons crème fraîche (optional)

FOR THE GRILLED CHEESE

	Good country, French, or Italian bread
$1^1/2$	tablespoons caraway seeds
8	tablespoons (1 stick) unsalted butter, at room temperature
$1/2$	pound Morbier or other good melting cheese, such as Italian fontina, Gruyère, or Mimolette (see page 165)

TO MAKE THE SOUP: Heat the olive oil in a large heavy saucepan over medium heat. Add the onion and red pepper flakes and cook, stirring occasionally, until the onion is tender, about 7 minutes. Add the tomatoes and $1^1/2$ cups water and cook, stirring occasionally, for 30 minutes. Add the basil, season lightly with salt and pepper, and let cool briefly before pureeing the soup in a food processor or a blender, in batches if necessary. Pass the soup through a fine-mesh strainer, pressing on the solids with a ladle. (Save the pulp, if you like; though it has no place in this soup, it's great on crostini or baked eggplant.) Keep the soup on medium-low heat if you plan to serve it right away.

TO MAKE THE GRILLED CHEESE: For easier slicing, stick the bread in the freezer briefly; it will be easier to slice when cold and firm. With a serrated knife, cut the bread into 12 exceedingly thin slices—as thin as you can without the bread falling apart. (I use a meat slicer and slice it about ¼ inch thick, and I cut it long enough so I can balance the sandwich across a soup bowl, though you can certainly serve the sandwiches alongside the bowls.)

Heat a small, dry skillet over medium heat. Add the caraway seeds and toast them, stirring occasionally, until fragrant, about 3 minutes. (It's easy to burn spices, so stick around during this part.) Transfer the seeds to a bowl. Go ahead and melt the butter in the same skillet. Let it cool a bit and then add 1 tablespoon of the toasted caraway seeds to it.

Heat the oven to 400°F. Have ready two heavy baking sheets of the same size so that one can nestle into the other. Line one with a sheet of parchment paper.

Slice the cheese thinly, too. (How thin is not as crucial here, as the cheese melts so thoroughly that it practically disappears into the bread.) Brush 6 of the bread slices with the melted butter and lay them on the parchment-lined baking sheet. Top each with a single layer of cheese and then top with another slice of buttered bread to make sandwiches. Put the sandwiches on the prepared baking sheet, leaving some space between them. Cover the sandwiches with a piece of parchment and stack the second baking sheet on top of the first; this will cook the sandwiches on both sides without the need to flip them and will also flatten them a bit. Bake until the sandwiches are golden brown and crisp, 15 to 20 minutes. Carefully peel away the top layer of parchment, transfer the sandwiches to a cooling rack, and serve warm or at room temperature. If there are any ragged bits of baked cheese hanging off the sandwiches, just trim them away by hand; you'll want to eat these, so go ahead.

To serve, divide the hot soup among six bowls. Float a tablespoon of crème fraîche on top of the soup, if you like, and garnish with some of the reserved toasted caraway seeds. Position a grilled cheese sandwich across the top of the bowl, if it fits without falling in, or beside the bowl, and serve.

MAKE AHEAD:

▌ *You can make the soup a few days ahead; refrigerate it, covered with plastic wrap, and then reheat it when ready to serve.*

▌ *I think it's easier to make the grilled cheese sandwiches earlier in the day or even a day ahead. Store them, once cooled, in a sealed container at room temperature.*

Creamy Leek and Potato Soup with Bay Scallops

SERVES 6 This elegant soup is easy: put leeks and potatoes in a pot and add cream, and the result is reminiscent of the best chowder. The sweet scallops—I can't resist Nantucket Bay scallops when they're in season in winter—are quickly browned and added just before serving to keep them from getting overcooked. To balance out the creamy sweetness, I add a couple of black olives cut into dainty slivers. A little unusual, perhaps, but their briny flavor works really well here, and their contrasting color is striking. Since the soup is so simple and quick, do consider serving it with the Black Olive Potato Chips, which are made by spreading olive paste between thin slices of potato and frying them till crispy in a little oil. They're certainly optional but are so freakin' good, you just have to try them.

1	tablespoon unsalted butter
2	large leeks (white parts only), well washed and dried, sliced lengthwise, then thinly sliced crosswise into half moons (about 1½ cups)
1	large Idaho potato (russet), peeled and cut into ¼-inch cubes
4	cups heavy cream
	Kosher salt and freshly ground black pepper
	Black Olive Potato Chips (optional; recipe follows)
12	ounces fresh bay scallops, preferably Nantucket Bay, or sea scallops
1	tablespoon vegetable oil
¼	cup finely chopped fresh chives
4–6	Niçoise olives, pitted and cut into slivers (see page 95)
	Fleur de sel

In a medium saucepan over medium-high heat, melt the butter. Add the leeks and cook, stirring, until translucent, about 2 minutes. Add the cubed potato, cover with the heavy cream, and simmer until the potato is tender and just cooked through, 10 to 12 minutes. Season with 1½ teaspoons salt and a few grinds of black pepper and keep the soup warm.

If serving the soup with the potato chips, make them now.

Season the scallops with salt and pepper. Heat the vegetable oil in a medium skillet over medium-high heat. When the oil is quite hot, add the scallops and sear without moving them until well browned on one side, about 30 seconds to 1 minute. Turn the scallops over and sear the other side. Be careful not to overcook, as they cook quickly. Take the skillet off the heat as soon as both sides are nicely browned.

Reheat the soup if necessary. Divide it among six bowls. Spoon the scallops on top. Sprinkle the chives and olive slivers around the scallops and crown the soup with the black olive potato chips, if using, and a sprinkle of fleur de sel.

Black Olive Potato Chips

Crisp, golden brown potato chips with the tangy flavor of black olives—these are truly addictive. And though they are fun to eat and look impressive, too, they're not hard to make, even for people who have a fear of frying. Since you're making only a handful of these small crisps, you just need to fill a small saucepan about halfway full of oil to fry them in batches.

1   large Idaho potato (russet)
    About 1 cup grapeseed, peanut, or canola oil
2   heaping tablespoons Black Olive Paste (page 6) or good
        purchased tapenade
    Fleur de sel

Peel the potato and trim it to a rectangular shape about 3 inches long and $1^{1}/_{2}$ inches across. With a mandoline or a very sharp knife, cut the rectangle into 24 paper-thin slices.

Heat enough oil to come halfway up the sides of a small saucepan over medium-high heat until a potato edge sizzles immediately when dipped into it (300° to 325°F).

Put between $^{1}/_{4}$ and $^{1}/_{2}$ teaspoon of the olive paste down the middle of half the slices. Top each slice with one of the remaining potato slices and press to seal. Fry a couple at a time in the hot oil, adjusting the heat as needed and turning the chips with a couple of spoons so they cook evenly, until golden brown and crisp, 1 to 2 minutes. They may open a little at the edges, but that's okay. Carefully remove them from the oil, drain on paper towels, and sprinkle with fleur de sel.

MAKE AHEAD: *The chips are best served soon after frying, but if serving is delayed, they're still irresistible at room temperature, if not quite as crispy.*

Olive "Fillets"

When I pit and chop olives for a garnish, I take the time to "fillet" them to get beautiful slivers. Using a very sharp knife, I slice the "meat" off by cutting alongside the pit; I slice one side off, turn the olive so its flat side is down, and cut off another, turning and slicing until there is little left on the pit. If the olives are very small, such as Niçoise, I leave the pieces whole; if large, I slice the fillets lengthwise into thin slivers. This method pits the olives without crushing them. The slices have a better texture and, when used as a garnish, won't bleed their juices.

Creamy Chestnut Bisque

When fresh chestnuts appear at the market, you know the holiday season is fast approaching. With their dark, hard shells, they literally look like a tough nut to crack. But you only have to roast them to get at the sweet mild meat inside. This is a wonderful soup to serve at the start of your Thanksgiving meal. Half the diced vegetables go into the soup, and half are reserved for the garnish; only the latter need to look pretty.

3 cups fresh chestnuts

2 slices bacon, diced

½ cup diced peeled celery; reserve any tender celery leaves for garnish

½ cup diced peeled carrot

½ cup diced onion

½ cup diced peeled parsnip

1 cup port, preferably ruby port

1 cup heavy cream

4 cups chicken broth, preferably Roasted Chicken Stock (page 108), or water
Kosher salt and freshly ground black pepper

1 tablespoon unsalted butter

¼ cup peeled, finely diced Granny Smith apple

1 tablespoon chopped fresh parsley
Fleur de sel

Heat the oven to 350°F. With a paring knife, score the chestnuts with an X on their flatter side and roast them on a baking sheet until the spot where they've been scored opens up, about 15 minutes. Let cool just until you can handle them and peel away the shell as well as the skin, which can be bitter. Reserve 6 of the chestnuts and chop the rest.

In a medium saucepan over medium heat, cook the bacon until crisp. Add about ¼ cup each of the celery, carrot, onion, and parsnip (reserve the rest for serving) and cook, stirring often, until tender and just slightly colored, 6 to 8 minutes. Add the chopped chestnuts and the port, increase the heat to medium-high, and cook until the wine is reduced by half. Add the cream and the broth and simmer until the vegetables are very tender and the flavors combined, about 40 minutes. Transfer the soup to a blender and puree until smooth. Pass through a fine-mesh strainer into a clean saucepan, pressing on the solids with a ladle. Season to taste with salt and pepper. If the bisque is too thick, thin it with a little water and taste it again for seasoning. Keep the soup warm if serving right away.

Just before serving, finely slice the reserved chestnuts. Melt the butter in a small skillet over medium heat. Add the remaining vegetables, apple, and chestnuts and cook, stirring, until just tender, 1 to 2 minutes. Season to taste with salt and pepper. Divide the soup among four to six bowls. Divide the sautéed vegetables among the bowls as well. Finish with a sprinkling of parsley, the reserved celery leaves, if you have them, and fleur de sel.

MAKE AHEAD:

▮ *You can roast and peel the chestnuts a day or two ahead of making the bisque and refrigerate them, covered.*

▮ *The bisque can be made 2 days ahead of serving it. Keep it covered with plastic wrap and refrigerated and reheat it gently.*

White Bean Soup with Sage and Hazelnuts

I am a fanatic about this soup. On first glance it looks humble and rustic, but I take a lot of care when I make it so the results are beautifully refined, with a balanced flavor and a gorgeous presentation. Carefully sautéing the ingredients so they cook through but don't color, simmering the beans to perfect tenderness, and taking the time to pass the soup through a fine-mesh strainer for a velvety texture are all part of the ritual of making it. And while it's quite tasty on its own, the accompaniments set it apart. Toasted hazelnuts add a buttery richness as well as a little crunch. Tiny mascarpone ravioli mimic the silken richness of the soup. I made this at an event attended by some big names in the cooking world, and my heart swelled as I listened to their praise for this soup.

Navy beans work well here, but if you can get your hands on Tarbais beans, use them instead. Buttery with a delicate and tender skin, these imported (and pricey) beans, harvested at the foothills of the Pyrenees, give the soup an irresistible texture.

¼	cup extra-virgin olive oil
2	celery stalks, peeled and chopped, 6 tender leaves reserved and chopped
1	medium white onion, chopped
1	pound dried white beans, such as navy beans (see headnote), soaked overnight in cold water
2	fresh sage sprigs
2	tablespoons kosher salt, plus more to taste
1½	teaspoons freshly ground white pepper
30–36	Mascarpone Raviolini (optional; recipe follows)
1	tablespoon hazelnut oil (for optional raviolini), plus more for drizzling
6	tablespoons chopped toasted hazelnuts
1	teaspoon fresh lemon juice
	Fleur de sel

In a soup pot, heat the olive oil over medium heat. Add the chopped celery and onion and cook, stirring occasionally and lowering the heat, if need be, until translucent but not browned, about 10 minutes. Drain the beans and add them, with 8 cups water, to the soup pot. Add the sage, bring to a boil, lower to a simmer, and cook, partially covered, adjusting the heat as necessary, until the beans are soft, about 2 hours. Remove the sage and puree the soup, in batches if necessary, in a blender. Pass the soup through a fine-mesh strainer into a saucepan, pressing on the solids with a ladle, and season with the salt and pepper. Add a little more water to the soup if it's too thick, and keep the soup warm if serving right away.

If serving the soup with the raviolini, bring a pot of well-salted water to a boil. Cook the raviolini until just tender. Gently drain and toss with 1 tablespoon hazelnut oil.

To serve, divide the soup among six bowls. Float 5 or 6 raviolini on top, if using. Finish each bowl with a sprinkling of hazelnuts, a drizzle of hazelnut oil, a few drops of lemon, and a pinch of fleur de sel before garnishing with the reserved celery leaves.

MAKE AHEAD: *You can make the soup 2 days ahead of serving it and refrigerate, covered with plastic wrap.*

Mascarpone Raviolini

MAKES AT LEAST 100 RAVIOLINI

These tiny melt-in-your-mouth ravioli are also delicious tossed in browned butter with chopped fresh sage (see the sauce recipe on page 170). Since this recipe makes a lot and freezes beautifully, you can do both.

1½ cups mascarpone
½ cup finely grated Parmigiano-Reggiano
Kosher salt and freshly ground black pepper
Unbleached all-purpose flour for dusting
½ batch Fresh Pasta Dough (page 115)
Extra-virgin olive oil

In a mixing bowl, whisk together the mascarpone, Parmesan, about ³/₄ teaspoon salt, and about ¹/₄ teaspoon pepper. Adjust the seasoning to taste and put the mixture in a piping bag fitted with a ¹/₄-inch tip.

Lightly flour a baking sheet and your work surface. Roll out the pasta dough using the thinnest setting on your pasta machine, as directed on page 116. Using a 1¹/₂-inch round cutter, cut out rounds of pasta. Working in batches, place about 20 rounds down on your work surface (cover the rest with plastic wrap or a towel). Pipe about ¹/₂ teaspoon of the cheese filling onto the center of 10 of the rounds. Using a small pastry brush, lightly moisten one side of one of the other 10 rounds with water. Place that round, moistened side down, over a round with filling. Gently press the two rounds together, first very gently near the center by the filling to force out any air bubbles and then more forcefully to seal the edges together to form the raviolini. For a better seal and a more uniform look, use a slightly smaller round cutter, dull side down, to press and seal the edges together.

Place the raviolini on the baking sheet and refrigerate until ready to cook.

To cook, drop the raviolini into a pot of boiling salted water. Stir gently and let cook until they float, 3 to 4 minutes. Remove the raviolini from the water with a slotted spoon, coat them with a little extra-virgin olive oil to keep them from sticking, and use to garnish the bean soup on page 98.

MAKE AHEAD: *The raviolini will hold for a few hours in the refrigerator and can be frozen as well; freeze them on the baking sheet until rock-hard and then transfer to an airtight container.*

Chicken Consommé

Consommé is one of those things that every enthusiastic home cook should try at least once, just to witness the transformation from a murky, cloudy stock to a stunningly translucent liquid with a superbly intense flavor.

This consommé makes an excellent first course. Serve it on its own or garnish it with a few celery leaves or, if you're lucky enough to have it, some shaved fresh white truffle. For something a little racier, float paper-thin rings of fresh red-hot red pepper (pepperoncini) on top. You could add some of the chicken meatballs (page 149) to the consommé for a heartier soup, or serve it with tortellini, for *tortellini en brodo*; mascarpone raviolini (facing page) are also delicious (cook the pasta separately and then add it to the broth). I've also been known to add cooked alphabet pasta. It's about the most soothing food you could eat.

Don't panic if your first attempts yield a soup that's not perfectly clear. Though the steps are pretty straightforward, the method, which includes adding egg whites to the consommé as it cooks, may take a little getting used to. A slightly cloudy soup will still taste delicious, but you may just want to use it as a stock and save showing off your consommé in a clear glass bowl for your next attempt.

1	3–3½-pound chicken, giblets removed
2	celery stalks, chopped
1	medium onion, chopped
1	medium carrot, peeled and chopped
1	plum tomato, chopped
2	tablespoons vegetable oil
2	garlic cloves, crushed
4	fresh thyme sprigs
2	bay leaves
2	teaspoons coriander seeds
1	teaspoon black peppercorns
1	small bunch fresh parsley
4	large egg whites
	Kosher salt and freshly ground black pepper

Heat the oven to 400°F. Remove the chicken breast (leaving the breastbone behind) and reserve for another use. Remove as much skin and fat as possible from the rest of the bird and discard it. Cut the chicken into pieces.

Remove the meat from the thighs and add it as well as one third each of the celery, onion, carrot, and tomato to a food processor and pulse until finely chopped and well combined. (This mixture adds flavor to the consommé.)

Put the rest of the chicken as well as the legs in a heavy baking pan and roast until golden brown, 45 minutes to an hour.

Meanwhile, heat the oil in a large soup pot over medium heat. Add the remaining celery, onion, carrot, and tomato, and the garlic and cook, stirring occasionally, until golden brown, 10 to 15 minutes. Add the browned chicken to the pot. Pour off and discard any accumulated fat from the baking sheet, then scrape the brown bits left behind on the sheet into the pot. Add 4 quarts cold water and the thyme, bay leaves, coriander seeds, and peppercorns. Finely chop about 2 tablespoons of the parsley and reserve it; add the rest of the bunch to the soup pot. Bring to a simmer over medium heat—don't let it boil—reduce the heat to low, and cook, skimming the top occasionally, until the broth is reduced by half and is very flavorful, about 4 hours. (You don't have to watch the pot too closely during this time.)

Line a fine-mesh strainer with a double layer of wet cheesecloth. Set the strainer over a saucepan, preferably one that's taller than it is wide. Remove the bones from the pot and discard. Strain the broth into the saucepan. (At this point, this is an excellent chicken broth.) Cool the broth to room temperature. (If it's too hot, it will cook the egg whites that get added later too quickly.) You can set the saucepan in an ice-water bath in the sink or in a large bowl.

In a large bowl, whisk the egg whites until frothy. Add the chicken and vegetable mixture from the food processor and the reserved chopped parsley to the egg whites (the mixture will be quite liquid). Return the broth to the stove over medium-low heat. Using a heatproof rubber spatula, stir in the egg-white mixture. Adjust the heat as needed to bring the broth barely to a simmer; do not let the mixture boil. Periodically scrape the bottom of the saucepan—the goal is to prevent the solids from sinking to the bottom, where they might burn. As the egg whites heat up, they will coagulate and rise to the top, along with the other solids, to form what's called a raft—essentially a filter that catches the suspended particles in the liquid. Once you see the egg whites begin to coagulate, turn the heat down and stop scraping the bottom of the pan to allow the raft to form, which should take 20 to 30 minutes. Do not let the mixture boil.

During this time the liquid beneath the raft will become beautifully clear. To take a peek, use a ladle to gently draw off some of the liquid. If the raft covers the entire surface area, gently press down on it to force some liquid up. But be careful; messing with the raft too much can cause the soup to become cloudy.

To finish, set the strainer up again with another piece of wet, doubled cheesecloth and position it over a large bowl. Do not try to remove the raft. Instead, carefully ladle the consommé through the cheesecloth-lined strainer, pressing down on the raft as needed to draw off the liquid. This time do not press on the solids left behind in the strainer, or they will cloud the consommé. Let the consommé cool completely in the refrigerator and remove any solidified fat that may float to the top before reheating and serving it. Season with salt and pepper before serving.

MAKE AHEAD: *The consommé will keep for 2 to 3 days covered in the refrigerator and for a few weeks in the freezer.*

Chicken and Vegetable Soup with Caraway Gnocchi

Wanting something warm and comforting to eat on a cold late-fall day, I immediately thought of chicken soup. But what to add to it? My inspiration came from Lombardy, the northernmost region of Italy, which borders on Switzerland. In this Alpine area, both cabbage and caraway are commonly used in the kitchen. I decided to add cabbage (and its cousins, cauliflower and broccoli) to the soup and caraway to the gnocchi. Serve this stewlike soup for dinner on a chilly Sunday afternoon and all will feel right in the world.

By searing the chicken in the pot it's to cook in, you get all the flavor from those tasty browned bits left behind in the pot. I usually throw a whole bird in the pot, which yields more meat than I need for the soup (the tender chicken is great for chicken salad and in tacos and quesadillas). But you can substitute skin-on, bone-in chicken thighs; they will be easier to maneuver in the pot and will yield just enough meat for the soup. If you go with the whole bird, truss it with some kitchen twine so the legs and wings don't flop around. While this step is not vital, tying the bird up will make turning it in the pot much easier, allowing for a better sear and less swearing.

1	tablespoon olive oil
1	3–3$^{1}/_2$-pound chicken, giblets removed, or 4 large skin-on, bone-in chicken thighs
2	large celery stalks, coarsely chopped
1	large carrot, peeled and coarsely chopped
1	large onion, coarsely chopped
2	garlic cloves, crushed
4	fresh thyme sprigs
4	fresh parsley sprigs
2	bay leaves
	Kosher salt
	A few grinds of black pepper
1$^{1}/_2$	cups finely shredded green cabbage (about $^{1}/_4$ head)
1	cup tiny-cut ($^{1}/_2$-inch) broccoli florets
1	cup tiny-cut ($^{1}/_2$-inch) cauliflower florets
	Caraway Gnocchi (recipe follows), freshly made or frozen
	Celery leaves for garnish (optional)
	Fleur de sel

In a large, heavy pot, one that's big enough to hold the chicken with some room around it, heat the olive oil over medium heat until quite hot. Add the chicken and sear on one

side, adjusting the heat so you hear a sizzle, until it's quite brown. Turn the chicken and continue to brown it all over. This will take at least 10 minutes.

Take the chicken out of the pot and put it on a baking sheet to catch any juices. To the pot, add the celery, carrot, onion, garlic, thyme, parsley, bay leaves, 1 tablespoon salt, and pepper and cook, stirring occasionally, just to sweat the vegetables. Return the chicken to the pot and add 8 cups (2 quarts) cold water. Cook the chicken over medium-low heat until the meat easily pulls off the bone, about 1 hour and 15 minutes. (The chicken can hang out in the liquid for longer than that off the heat if you can't get to it right away.)

Transfer the chicken to a clean baking sheet. Pass the soup through a fine-mesh strainer into a large saucepan, using a ladle to press on the solids. When the chicken is cool enough to handle, remove and discard the skin. With your fingers, remove all the meat and shred it into bite-sized pieces. If you are using a whole chicken, set aside half for the soup. (Reserve the rest of the chicken for another use.)

When ready to serve, skim the soup of any fat on its surface if necessary. Heat the soup over medium heat. Add the cabbage, broccoli, and cauliflower and cook until just tender, about 8 minutes. Add the chicken.

Meanwhile, bring a pot of well-salted water to a gentle boil. Add the gnocchi and cook until they float to the top and are tender, 3 to 4 minutes. Using a slotted spoon, remove the gnocchi and divide them among six large soup bowls. Use a ladle to divide the soup among the bowls. Serve garnished with celery leaves, if you like, and a pinch of fleur de sel.

MAKE AHEAD:
▌ *Though I find this soup soothing to make and eat in a single day, you can divide the work over a couple of days by cooking and shredding the chicken a day or two ahead. Refrigerate it and the broth separately, covered.*
▌ *The gnocchi can be made ahead and frozen as directed on page 107.*

Caraway Gnocchi
MAKES ABOUT 100 GNOCCHI

Because these gnocchi were created for the soup on page 104 and don't have to hold on to a sauce, they don't need grooves, which means shaping them is simply a matter of rolling the dough and cutting it into pieces. You can make the gnocchi from start to finish while the chicken for the soup simmers or make it ahead and freeze it. The recipe is also easily doubled.

1–1¼	pounds medium- to high-starch potatoes, such as Idaho (russet), whole and unpeeled
1	tablespoon caraway seeds
¾	cup unbleached all-purpose flour, plus more as needed
1	large egg
1½	teaspoons kosher salt

Bring the potatoes to a boil in well-salted cold water and cook until very tender (a metal cake tester inserted will pull out easily), about 30 minutes.

Meanwhile, toast the caraway seeds over medium heat in a small dry skillet until fragrant, about 3 minutes. Let cool and lightly crush the seeds with a mortar and pestle or with the bottom of a heavy saucepan.

Drain the cooked potatoes and allow to cool just until you're able to handle them. Peel the potatoes while still quite hot (the skin will come off more easily) and put them through a ricer into a large bowl. Let cool to room temperature.

Have ready a parchment-lined, lightly floured baking sheet that will fit in your freezer (or use multiple plates or platters).

Dump the potatoes onto a lightly floured work surface. Sprinkle the $^{3}/_{4}$ cup flour over the potatoes and fluff it into them, using your fingers and a light touch. Gently gather the potatoes into a mound. Create a well in the center of the mound. Whisk together the egg and salt in a small bowl and pour it into the well. Mix by kneading the dough, sprinkling on more flour as needed (you may need as much as $^{1}/_{4}$ cup more), until it just forms a ball and feels delicate and a little bit sticky. Sprinkle the caraway seeds over the dough and knead them in, adding a little more flour if the dough is very sticky. You want it to feel soft and pliable. Set the dough aside and clean the work surface of any hard bits of dough.

Sprinkle the work surface lightly with flour. Roll the dough out with a rolling pin until about $^{1}/_{2}$ inch thick. Use a bench scraper (or a knife) to cut the dough into strips between $^{1}/_{2}$ and $^{3}/_{4}$ inch wide. Roll each strip under your hands to round the edges and form a log and then cut the logs into $^{3}/_{4}$-inch pieces. Put the gnocchi on the baking sheet or plate, making sure they don't touch. If not using right away, freeze the gnocchi on the baking sheet until rock-hard and then store in 2 batches in airtight containers in the freezer.

MAKE AHEAD: *The gnocchi will keep for weeks in the freezer and can go right from the freezer to the pot to cook.*

Roasted Chicken Stock

While my recipes that call for chicken broth can be prepared with good store-bought chicken broth, they will taste a lot better when made with this deeply flavored homemade version. An addition of fresh herbs toward the end of cooking gives the broth a bright flavor.

1	3–3½-pound chicken, giblets removed
¼	cup vegetable oil
1	carrot, peeled and chopped
1	white onion, chopped
1	celery stalk, peeled and chopped
1	garlic clove, chopped
2	cups dry white wine
1	tablespoon coriander seeds
1	tablespoon black peppercorns
2	bay leaves
2	sprigs fresh parsley
2	sprigs fresh thyme

Cut the breast meat off the chicken (leaving the breastbone behind) and reserve it for another use. Cut off the legs and thighs, too, and reserve them for another use. (You can leave the wings.) Remove any excess fat—a little meat on the bones is welcome—and cut the carcass into 3- to 4-inch pieces.

In a large soup pot, heat the oil over medium-high heat. Add the bones and let them brown well (stir them only every few minutes), about 15 minutes. Add the carrot, onion, celery, and garlic and cook, stirring occasionally, until they, too, are well browned, about 10 minutes. Pour off any excess fat, add the wine, and cook until the wine has reduced by a little more than half. Add 4 quarts water, the coriander, peppercorns, and bay leaves, and bring to a gentle boil. Reduce to a lively simmer and cook until reduced to about 1 quart, occasionally skimming the surface with a ladle; this reducing step can take as long as 2 hours, but you can be doing other things during this time. Add the parsley and thyme and let steep for 5 minutes.

Strain the stock through a fine-mesh strainer before using or storing.

MAKE AHEAD: *The beauty of stock is that you can make it one day and then use it long after. Freeze it in varying amounts in airtight containers so you can pull out just what you need for a particular recipe.*

Notes

a passion for pasta

FRESH PASTA DOUGH   115

ODD FELLOW MARINARA   120

BUTCHER SHOP BOLOGNESE   121

ORECCHIETTE WITH CAULIFLOWER, ANCHOVIES,
AND PISTACHIOS   123

PASTA WITH POTATOES AND PESTO   126

LINGUINE WITH SPICY CLAM SAUCE   128

SPICY LOBSTER BOLOGNESE   130

TORN PASTA FAGIOLI WITH SHRIMP POLPETTINI   133

RIGATONI WITH SPICY SAUSAGE AND CANNELLINI BEANS   135

PAPPARDELLE WITH TANGY VEAL RAGU   138

CHEESE AGNOLOTTI WITH BUTTER SAUCE, CELERY, APPLE,
AND PROSCIUTTO   140

ROASTED CORN AND TOMATO LASAGNETTES   143

CHICKEN MEATBALL LASAGNETTES   147

RICOTTA GNUDI   153

GNOCCHI   154

TRUFFLED GNOCCHI WITH PEAS AND MUSHROOMS   157

PRUNE-STUFFED GNOCCHI WITH FOIE GRAS SAUCE   159

CHEESE RISOTTO   164

TOMATO AND ARUGULA RISOTTO WITH PROSCIUTTO   166

MAINE CRAB, LEMON, AND ZUCCHINI BLOSSOM RISOTTO   168

MUSHROOM- AND FONTINA-STUFFED CRESPELLES WITH
BROWN BUTTER–SAGE SAUCE   170

I did not grow up in a household where Nonna hand-rolled her pasta dough on the kitchen table and hung strands of fettuccine over the backs of chairs to dry. All of the noodles (we didn't call it pasta then) that my Irish family ate came out of a light blue Prince box, and I half believed the old commercial that made it look like spaghetti grew on trees. So it makes me especially proud that it's my fresh pastas and gnocchi that have gotten me the most attention.

I learned to make fresh pasta when I worked for Todd English at Figs. Like so much of Italian cooking at the time, it felt completely foreign to me. (Back then I hardly knew there was such a thing as fresh herbs, so forget about fresh pasta.) It took a little time before I got the difference. Fresh pasta absorbs a sauce completely differently from dried; you almost don't perceive that there was once a pasta and a sauce distinct from each other, because the two entities meld into one glorious dish. And while boxed pasta is convenient, with a chewy texture just right for some recipes, it can never be as sublime as fresh pasta.

At Figs, I mastered the mechanics of making fresh pasta by studying cookbooks and cranking out lots of dough. But it took an extended trip to Italy, where I cooked every day with the wife of the farmer at whose home I was staying, for me to see the process as something much more soulful. Making pasta and gnocchi with Mita in her rustic Tuscan kitchen, I learned to trust my instincts more than any recipe, to really feel the dough, and to understand that every time I make a batch of dough, the amount of flour added will be different (and that is how it should be). Most important, Mita taught me not to be afraid. Before my visit, I handled pasta dough gingerly, as if it might somehow dissolve right before my eyes. I practically held my breath when I sent it through the rollers, and I was scared that I was going to make the pasta tough if I dared to flour it during rolling. (The fear was similar to how I felt about babies before I had one of my own.) Mita exuded a nonchalant confidence as she handled her pasta dough. From her I learned that after the dough has been kneaded, you can flour it all you want to keep it from sticking to the rollers. If a sheet of pasta tears after going through the rollers, who cares? You just fold it up and send it through again. I also learned that even a less-than-stellar batch of fresh pasta tastes better than boxed pasta.

I returned to the United States with a renewed passion for pasta, often turning out five different fresh pasta dishes a night at the restaurant. I make pasta all the time at home as well. At almost every gathering I host,

fresh pasta is on the menu, such as the ravioli I serve along with lamb every Easter. I make batches of fresh pasta on weekends with my daughter, Marchesa, who loves to help roll it. And if someone has a birthday party, I'm more likely to show up with a pan full of gnocchi than with a bottle of wine or flowers.

If you love good food, I suggest you get into the habit of making fresh pasta, too. The first time you make your own, it may feel arduous, but the more you do it, the more familiar you get with handling the dough and rolling it, the easier it becomes. The same can be said for gnocchi, and in fact my method for shaping them is easier than most; quicker, too.

Though I am not a fan of rice, risotto is another matter altogether. As the rice cooks and swells, it loses its grainy feel and becomes voluptuous and creamy. Risotto is not only much more delicious but much easier to make than plain old steamed rice. It's a great canvas for showcasing other flavors, which is why I generally serve it as its own course and not on the side.

Fresh Pasta Dough

**MAKES ABOUT
1 POUND PASTA;
SERVES 4 TO 6**

I came to my love of fresh homemade pasta relatively late in life, and like any good convert, I zealously try to spread the good word. If you already make fresh pasta, you know what I'm talking about. Nothing can come near it for delicacy and tenderness. And while I have included recipes that taste great with dried pasta, they taste so much better if you use fresh.

I love the rich flavor and tenderness of pasta dough made with all egg yolks. But for home cooks who are just learning to make fresh pasta, an all-egg-yolk dough can be tricky to work with. I strike a balance between tenderness and ease of handling with a recipe that uses twice as many egg yolks as whole eggs.

Unless you're a whiz with a rolling pin, you'll want to thin the dough in a pasta machine (the kind that rolls dough, not the pasta extruder you see on infomercials). A hand-cranked one works fine, while a motorized one gets the job done faster.

Finally, if you need a half batch of pasta, as for the raviolini on page 100, you can cut this recipe in half. But a better idea is to go ahead and make the whole batch. The benefits are myriad: you have extra dough made if you need it, and any left over can be cut to whatever shape you like and frozen.

2   cups unbleached all-purpose flour, plus more as needed
1   teaspoon kosher salt, plus more for pasta water
2   large eggs
4   large egg yolks

Combine the flour and salt on a clean work surface. If it's not already in a small mound, gather it into one. Use your fist and a circular motion to transform the mound into a wide well. Crack the whole eggs into the center of the well and add the yolks. Beat the eggs with a fork just as you would to make scrambled eggs. Very gradually incorporate some of the flour into the eggs by bringing in a little at a time from the perimeter of the

well. Be careful not to break through the wall of the well or the egg will race out all over the counter—a total bummer. When the dough becomes too stiff to mix with a fork, use your fingers to work the eggs and flour together, adding only enough of the flour to make a cohesive ball of dough. You may not need to use all the flour; the amount you use will vary every time you make fresh pasta, depending on your eggs, your flour, and even the weather. To see if you have added enough flour, press a clean, dry finger deep into the dough. If nothing sticks to your finger, your dough is in good shape. If not, work in a little more flour now or, if it feels close, as you knead the dough.

Move the dough over to one side and scrape your work area clean of any excess flour, especially any hardened bits, and then clean your hands as well. Lightly reflour the surface and knead the dough by pushing it away from you with the heel of your hand, folding it over, giving it a quarter turn, and pushing it away again. Continue kneading, adding a sprinkling of flour if the dough feels sticky, until it feels as soft and supple as your earlobe; this can take 5 to 8 minutes. Sprinkle the dough with a little flour, wrap it in plastic or a cloth, and let it rest for half an hour before rolling it.

Set your pasta machine to its widest setting. Cut the dough in half and keep the half you're not using wrapped while you work (some of the recipes calling for fresh pasta need only a half batch of dough). Roll the dough lightly in flour and flatten it into a rectangle that is roughly the width of your pasta machine. Run the dough through the machine at this setting twice to give the dough a final kneading.

Set the machine to its next thinnest setting and run the dough through. Continue running the dough through the machine's settings so it gets progressively thinner each time; you don't *have* to hit every setting on the dial, as is so often insisted, but do thin the dough gradually. If you run the dough through the machine and it shreds or tears or is too thin, simply fold it over and run it through a wider setting to smooth it out. If your dough sticks, you can flour it well without worry; the dough will not incorporate too much flour at this point.

As the length of the dough increases, you may find it a little unwieldy. With an electric (as opposed to hand-cranked) pasta machine, you can stand pretty far away and gather the dough as it comes out of the machine, gently folding it over onto itself, so it looks like ribbon candy. Or you can cut shorter lengths with a sharp knife and run each piece through each setting. Do whatever works best for you.

For most pastas, you want to roll the dough until it's very thin, like a silk scarf; if you hold it up to the light, you should see your hand through it. On some pasta machines, this will mean the thinnest setting; on others it may be the second thinnest.

At this point, you can use the pasta sheets as directed in the various recipes for fresh pasta that follow. Or you can cut the pasta sheets into fettuccine, tagliatelle, or similar shapes. Start by cutting the sheets into rectangles roughly a foot long. Attach a pasta cutter to your pasta machine and run the pasta through. Or cut the pasta by hand with a sharp knife or ravioli cutter. Let the pasta sheets air-dry for an hour or so before cutting into shapes. You can then stack the sheets to make cutting more efficient.

Here's how I cut the following:

FETTUCCINE: Most pasta rollers come with an attachment for cutting this pasta.

PAPPARDELLE: Make wide noodles with rippled edges by cutting the pasta sheet into 1-inch-wide strips with a fluted ravioli cutter.

TAGLIATELLE: Make thin noodles by cutting the pasta sheets into $1/4$-inch-wide strips with a sharp chef's knife.

TRENETTE: Make slightly wider noodles by running the pasta through to the second-to-last setting and cutting the sheet into about $1/3$-inch-thick strips, on one side with a knife for a straight edge, and on the other side with a ravioli cutter for a rippled edge.

MAKE AHEAD:

▌ *I prefer to keep moving when I am making fresh pasta, but if you are interrupted, you can refrigerate the pasta dough for a few hours before rolling it. Let it come to room temperature before rolling. Too long before drying, cooking, or freezing and it will discolor.*

▌ *Cut pasta, such as fettuccine, may be neatly frozen by wrapping strands around your hand to create nests. Put the nests on a floured baking sheet, freeze them until rock-hard, and transfer to an airtight container or freezer bag. Cook them straight from the freezer.*

▌ *I almost never dry pasta. But if you want to make it ahead, you can dry it the traditional way by hanging it over a dowel and letting it air-dry or by laying it out on a baking sheet in a single, uncrowded layer with an extra sprinkling of flour and leaving it overnight.*

Odd Fellow Marinara

MAKES ABOUT
4 CUPS,
ENOUGH FOR 1
POUND OF PASTA
TO SERVE 6

I sell this spicy, chunky tomato sauce by the jar, and I'm a little worried that sales will go down when people see how easy it is to make at home. Its name, a play on the mafioso "good fellow," pays homage to the historic name of the building across the street from my restaurant, the Odd Fellows building, which now houses the Boston Center for the Arts. When I have lots of local, ripe tomatoes, which is only for about one month in the summer, I start with fresh tomatoes for this sauce; otherwise I use good canned tomatoes or, in the case of Pomì brand tomatoes, which I like, boxed ones. I love this sauce over Ricotta Gnudi (page 153).

1	tablespoon extra-virgin olive oil
1	small onion, thinly sliced
2	garlic cloves, finely chopped
1/2	teaspoon crushed red pepper flakes, plus more to taste
1/4	cup dry white wine
1	28-ounce can crushed tomatoes, preferably imported San Marzano tomatoes, or 1 similar-sized box of Pomì brand chopped tomatoes
	Kosher salt
2–3	fresh basil leaves
	Freshly ground black pepper

Heat the olive oil in a medium saucepan over medium heat. Add the onion, garlic, and crushed red pepper flakes. Cook, stirring occasionally, until the onion is just tender but not colored, about 8 minutes. Add the wine, increase the heat to medium-high, and cook for a few minutes until it's reduced by about half. Add the tomatoes with their juices and 1/2 teaspoon salt. Simmer for about 10 minutes, stir in the basil, and season with a few grinds of pepper and additional salt and red pepper flakes if needed.

MAKE AHEAD: *This sauce is so quick that I don't usually bother making it ahead, but it will keep for 3 or 4 days, covered and refrigerated. It's a great sauce to have around, especially if you have kids in the house. If they're like mine, they eat a lot of pasta.*

Butcher Shop Bolognese

MAKES ABOUT
6 CUPS,
ENOUGH FOR 1½
POUNDS OF PASTA
TO SERVE 8

The "secret" ingredient in this rich, meaty, creamy, traditional-style Bolognese sauce is chicken livers. Finely chopped and combined with the ground meat, they contribute an amazing depth of flavor without making the sauce livery (which means their addition can be our little secret). Though the sauce is delicious using one or two of the ground meats listed, it tastes best with all three; the lamb especially gives it character. This super-easy recipe can be doubled and freezes well. I serve it over homemade tagliatelle or gnocchi, but it's great with dried pasta, too, especially a wider noodle.

1	tablespoon extra-virgin olive oil
1	medium onion, finely chopped
1	large celery stalk, finely chopped
1	large carrot, finely chopped
5	ounces chicken livers, trimmed and finely chopped
¼	cup chopped fresh sage
	Kosher salt and freshly ground black pepper
1½	pounds ground meat, preferably ½ pound each of veal, pork, and lamb
1½	cups dry red wine
1½	cups chicken broth, preferably Roasted Chicken Stock (page 108), or beef broth
1	14½-ounce can (1½ cups) chopped canned tomatoes
½	cup chopped fresh basil
½	cup heavy cream, or more to taste (optional)
	Freshly grated Parmigiano-Reggiano

Heat the olive oil in a large deep skillet or Dutch oven over medium heat. Add the onion, celery, and carrot and cook, stirring occasionally, until tender, 8 to 10 minutes. Add the chicken livers and sage, season with a little salt and pepper, and cook, stirring, until the livers lose their red color, 2 to 3 minutes.

Add the ground meat in batches, letting it brown a little before adding more. Season with a pinch of salt and a few grinds of pepper and cook, stirring, until no red or pink color remains. Pour off most of the fat. Add the wine, increase the heat to high, and boil, stirring occasionally to break up any clumps of meat, until the wine is almost gone, 10 to 15 minutes. Add the broth, tomatoes, and basil. Bring to a boil and then lower

the heat to a gentle simmer; you should see an occasional bubble but not a boil. Cook, uncovered, until the sauce is thick, dark, and rich, for at least 1 hour. (You can keep cooking it longer over low heat, and it will only get better; I cook mine for hours at home and dip a piece of bread into the sauce every time I walk by the pot.) Stir in the cream, if using, and simmer for at least another 10 minutes to heat it through; longer is fine.

Serve the sauce over pasta, topped with freshly ground black pepper and grated Parmesan.

MAKE AHEAD: *The sauce will keep for a couple of days in the refrigerator covered with plastic wrap and freezes beautifully, too. If going right from the hot pot to the freezer, cool the sauce first by putting it in a bowl set over an ice bath in the sink (stir it occasionally) before storing in an airtight container.*

Orecchiette with Cauliflower, Anchovies, and Pistachios

SERVES 6

This recipe is an adaptation of a dish I first had in Sicily, where anchovies are used with abandon. It's a good habit, as they add a salty, earthy flavor without fishiness and really perk up the cauliflower. In Italy, pine nuts, not pistachios, are typically added to a pasta sauce like this one, but I think pistachios are better. Since I don't like to waste the leaves at the base of the cauliflower head, I chop and cook them with the cauliflower. (See the photo on page 124.)

½	cup shelled unsalted pistachios
8	tablespoons (1 stick) unsalted butter, cut into pieces
1	medium head cauliflower, cut into small florets
5	oil-packed anchovies, drained, rinsed, and finely chopped
1	garlic clove, finely chopped
2	cups chicken broth, preferably Roasted Chicken Stock (page 108)
1	pound orecchiette
½	cup chopped fresh parsley
¾	cup finely grated Parmigiano-Reggiano, plus more for sprinkling
½	teaspoon crushed red pepper flakes, plus more to taste
	Kosher salt and freshly ground black pepper
6	tablespoons extra-virgin olive oil
	Fleur de sel

Heat the oven to 350°F. Spread the pistachios out on a small baking sheet and bake until lightly toasted, about 5 minutes. Once cool, coarsely chop them.

In a large, deep skillet, melt the butter over medium heat until it smells nutty and is golden brown. Add the cauliflower and cook, stirring, for a minute or two. Add the anchovies and garlic and cook, stirring, for another couple of minutes; the anchovies will dissolve into the butter. Add the chicken broth and cook until the cauliflower is tender, about 5 minutes.

Meanwhile, bring a large pot of well-salted water to a boil. Cook the orecchiette until al dente. Reserve ½ cup of the pasta water before draining the pasta. Add the orecchiette, parsley, Parmesan, and crushed red pepper flakes to the cauliflower and stir to combine. Season to taste with salt and pepper. If the pasta seems dry, add a little of the reserved water. Divide among six serving bowls and sprinkle with the toasted pistachios and more red pepper flakes, if desired. Finish with a drizzle of olive oil and pinch of fleur de sel.

ORECCHIETTE WITH CAULIFLOWER, ANCHOVIES, AND PISTACHIOS (PAGE 123)

PRUNE-STUFFED GNOCCHI WITH FOIE GRAS SAUCE (PAGE 159)

Pasta with Potatoes and Pesto

This is my take on a traditional Ligurian pasta that's both summery and satisfying. In many recipes, the potatoes are cooked with the pasta. But when they are cooked together, there's a good chance one will be tender before the other. Instead, I boil the potatoes, green beans, and pasta in succession, using the same water. Salt the water a little less than usual because it will boil for longer and the saltiness may become too pronounced. You may want to double the pesto, so you have leftovers.

FOR THE PESTO

½ cup pine nuts, toasted in a dry skillet or the oven until golden brown

½ cup fresh basil leaves, well washed and dried, plus 4 small leaves for garnish

2 garlic cloves, coarsely chopped

¾ cup extra-virgin olive oil

Kosher salt and freshly ground black pepper

FOR THE PASTA

1 Idaho (russet) potato, peeled and cut into ½-inch cubes (about 1½ cups)

3 ounces green beans, cut into ½-inch lengths on the diagonal (about ½ cup)

½ pound trenette, tagliatelle, or fettuccine, preferably homemade (see page 115)

Kosher salt and freshly ground black pepper

1 cup lightly packed Parmigiano-Reggiano shavings (from about a 2-ounce chunk)

Fleur de sel

TO MAKE THE PESTO: Reserve 1 heaping tablespoon of the pine nuts and put the rest in a blender. Add the ½ cup basil, garlic, olive oil, ½ teaspoon salt, and a few good grinds of pepper. Puree well.

TO MAKE THE PASTA: Bring a pot of salted water to a boil (see headnote). Have ready a bowl of ice water. Cook the potato at a gentle boil until just tender, about 8 minutes. With a slotted spoon or skimmer, transfer it to the ice water to halt the cooking. Add the green beans to the pot, cook till just tender, 3 to 5 minutes, and shock them in ice water to cool. Finally, add the pasta to the boiling water and cook until al dente. Reserve about ½ cup of the pasta water and drain the pasta. Return the pasta to the pot. Drain the potatoes and green beans well and add them to the pot with the pasta. Add the pesto and toss gently over low heat, adding a little of the reserved pasta water to loosen the sauce. Season to taste with salt and pepper.

Divide the pasta among four bowls. Garnish each with some of the shaved Parmesan, the reserved pine nuts, and a basil leaf. Finish with a tiny sprinkle of fleur de sel and serve.

MAKE AHEAD: *You can make the pesto up to a couple of days ahead. Cover it well with plastic wrap to prevent the top from darkening. (It will still taste good if it does blacken a little on top but won't look as pretty.) The pesto also freezes well for up to a month.*

Linguine with Spicy Clam Sauce

SERVES 4   Pasta with clam sauce is one of those dishes I crave from time to time. Though this is a pretty classic rendition, some traditionalists may take issue with the fact that I finish the pasta with a little cheese. I like the way it brings all the flavors together. Fresh linguine or, even better, fresh pasta torn into pieces (see page 133) is my preference for this dish—the fresh pasta absorbs the sauce beautifully, so every bite tastes of the sea—but dried pasta works fine.

36	littleneck clams, well scrubbed
¼	cup dry white wine
2	tablespoons olive oil, plus more to finish
1½	tablespoons finely chopped garlic
¼	teaspoon crushed red pepper flakes, plus more to taste
	Kosher salt
1	pound linguine, preferably homemade (see page 115)
2	tablespoons chopped fresh parsley
	About 1 teaspoon fresh lemon juice
1–2	tablespoons finely grated Parmigiano-Reggiano

Heat a large saucepan or Dutch oven over high heat. Add the clams and wine, cover, and cook, stirring once about halfway through, until the clams open, 5 to 10 minutes. Remove the clams from the pan with a slotted spoon. Discard any clams that do not open. Carefully pour the juices through a fine-mesh strainer into a small bowl, leaving any sediment behind in the pan. When the clams are cool enough to handle, remove them from their shells and chop them coarsely.

Heat the olive oil in a clean skillet over medium-high heat. Add the clams and garlic and let the clams sizzle undisturbed for 2 to 3 minutes, lowering the heat if the garlic starts to color. Add the red pepper flakes and a couple of tablespoons of the reserved clam juices and stir. Remove the sauce from the heat. Taste it and add more red pepper flakes and a little salt, if needed, keeping in mind that the clam liquid will be salty as well.

Bring a large pot of well-salted water to a boil and cook the pasta until just tender. Reserve ½ cup of the pasta water. Using a slotted spoon, transfer the pasta to the skillet with the clams, add the parsley, and gently toss everything together over medium heat, adding a little of the reserved pasta water to loosen the sauce, if need be. Drizzle a couple of teaspoons of olive oil and the lemon juice over the pasta.

Divide the pasta and clams among four bowls. Divide the sauce that remains in the pan among the bowls and sprinkle the pasta with Parmesan.

MAKE AHEAD: *You can cook, shuck, and chop the clams up to a day ahead of finishing the sauce. Store the clams in the reserved juice, covered, in the refrigerator. Use a slotted spoon to remove them from the juice for cooking, but do reserve the juice, as you'll be adding most, if not all, of it to the sauce as well.*

Spicy Lobster Bolognese

If you love lobster (is there anyone who doesn't?), you will love this pasta. Not only does it feature big bites of fresh lobster, but it includes a lobster broth that infuses the pasta itself with lobster flavor. Most of the ingredients come from the pantry spice drawer. (For an extra-spiffy result, you may want to take the time to dice the vegetables.)

2	1¼-pound lobsters
¼	cup vegetable oil
2	celery stalks, peeled and finely chopped
1	large white onion, finely chopped
1	large carrot, peeled and finely chopped
1	cup dry white wine
2	tablespoons tomato paste
1	bay leaf
1	teaspoon coriander seeds
½	teaspoon crushed red pepper flakes, plus more to taste
4	garlic cloves, finely chopped
6	ripe tomatoes, cored, seeded, and chopped
½	pound dried spaghetti
2	tablespoons extra-virgin olive oil
8–10	fresh basil leaves, stacked, rolled up tightly, and sliced thinly crosswise into a chiffonade
	Fleur de sel

To parcook the lobsters to remove their meat, bring a large pot of water to a boil. Have ready a large bowl of ice water. Boil the lobsters for 5 minutes (they will not be fully cooked), then plunge them into the ice water. Once the lobsters have cooled, twist the tails off the bodies, remove the meat from the tails (save the shells), and cut each tail lengthwise into 2 pieces, removing the intestinal tracts. Remove the claw meat by snapping off the little pincers first. Using the back of a heavy chef's knife or good kitchen scissors, crack open the claws and remove the meat in a single piece, again reserving the shells. Remove the knuckle meat, too. Refrigerate the lobster meat until ready to use. Chop the lobster shells into 2-inch pieces for the broth.

To make the lobster broth, heat 2 tablespoons of the oil in a large saucepan over medium-high heat. Add the lobster shells and cook, stirring, until lightly browned, 3 to 5 minutes. Add about $1/2$ cup each of the celery, onion, and carrot (reserve the rest) and cook, stirring, until lightly browned, 3 to 5 minutes. Add the wine, tomato paste, bay leaf, coriander seeds, and crushed red pepper flakes. Bring to a boil, add 1 quart water, and simmer for about 45 minutes. Remove the large pieces of shell and then strain the liquid into a bowl through a fine-mesh strainer. You should have about 2 cups of broth.

To make the pasta sauce, heat the remaining 2 tablespoons oil in a large skillet or saucepan over medium heat. Add the reserved celery, onion, and carrot and cook, stirring, for a few minutes. Add the garlic and continue to cook until the vegetables are tender and lightly browned, about 5 minutes. Add the lobster broth, bring it to a simmer, then add the chopped tomatoes. Simmer the sauce for 15 to 20 minutes to cook the tomatoes and thicken it.

Meanwhile, bring a large pot of well-salted water to a boil. Cut the reserved lobster meat into large bite-sized pieces. Cook the spaghetti until just shy of al dente. Reserve some of the pasta water and drain the spaghetti. Add the spaghetti and the lobster meat to the sauce, along with some of the pasta water if the sauce seems dry. Toss, taste, and add more crushed red pepper flakes, if you like; I add up to another $1/2$ teaspoon, but I like this very spicy. Cook for a few more minutes to heat the lobster through and to finish cooking the pasta.

Divide the pasta among four bowls. Drizzle each serving with a little olive oil, garnish with the basil, and finish with a pinch of fleur de sel.

MAKE AHEAD: *You can parcook the lobster and make the broth up to a day ahead; store both in the refrigerator, covered.*

Torn Pasta Fagioli with Shrimp Polpettini

SERVES 6 Pasta and beans is one of the most comforting dishes around, and I am always playing with the notion of it. In this pasta, I add tiny shrimp *polpettini,* or "meatballs" (easily made in a food processor) and loads of fresh sage and rosemary. I like to use fresh pasta cut into squares, rectangles, or irregular shapes of about 2 inches (triangles, trapezoids). In Italy they call these shapes *maltagliati,* which translates as "badly cut," because they are generally what is left over after the pasta has been cut into other shapes. Or you can use dried pasta, breaking up wide flat noodles and cooking them a little longer.

FOR THE POLPETTINI

³⁄₄	pound shrimp, peeled, deveined, and coarsely chopped
¹⁄₄	cup plus 2 tablespoons panko (Japanese bread crumbs; see page 209)
1	large egg
2	tablespoons heavy cream
	Finely grated zest of 1 lemon
	Kosher salt and freshly ground black pepper

FOR THE SAUCE AND PASTA

¹⁄₂	cup extra-virgin olive oil, plus more for serving
¹⁄₂	medium white onion, diced
3	garlic cloves, very finely chopped
1	tablespoon chopped fresh sage
1	tablespoon finely chopped fresh rosemary
2	15-ounce cans white beans, drained and rinsed
	Kosher salt and freshly ground black pepper
¹⁄₂	batch Fresh Pasta Dough (page 115), rolled as directed and cut with a knife into irregular shapes of about 2 inches, or ¹⁄₂ pound dried wide flat noodles, such as pappardelle, broken into 2-inch lengths
	Fleur de sel
	Thinly sliced fresh sage leaves for garnish (optional)

TO MAKE THE POLPETTINI: Combine the shrimp, panko, egg, cream, lemon zest, 1 teaspoon salt, and a few grinds of pepper in a food processor and puree until smooth. (To test for seasoning, roll a small amount into a ball and poach in barely simmering water. Let cool, taste, and add more salt and pepper if necessary.)

To roll the meatballs, wet your hands slightly and roll the mixture into balls about the size of a large marble. Set the meatballs down on a baking sheet (you will have 30 to 40), cover with plastic wrap, and refrigerate until ready to use.

TO MAKE THE SAUCE: Heat $\frac{1}{4}$ cup of the olive oil in a large saucepan over medium heat. Add the onion, garlic, sage, and rosemary and cook, stirring, until the onion is tender, about 5 minutes. Add the beans, 2 cups water, and a little salt and pepper. Bring to a simmer. Cook for about 5 minutes and then transfer about half the beans to a food processor or blender and puree until smooth, adding a little bit of water if very thick. Return the pureed beans to the pot with the whole beans.

TO ASSEMBLE THE DISH: Bring a large pot of well-salted water to a boil. Add the shrimp *polpettini* to the pot of beans and simmer gently over medium heat until the meatballs are cooked through, about 4 minutes. Meanwhile, cook the pasta until al dente. Reserve a cup of the pasta water and drain the pasta. Add the pasta to the beans, along with the remaining $\frac{1}{4}$ cup olive oil, and toss gently. If the sauce looks dry, add a little of the reserved pasta water to it. Season to taste with salt and pepper.

Divide among six bowls. Top with a drizzle of extra-virgin olive oil, a pinch of fleur de sel, and a sprinkling of sage for color, if you like.

MAKE AHEAD: *The meatballs can be made a day ahead and refrigerated, covered in plastic wrap. You can also freeze them in an airtight container for up to a month. The beans can be made 2 days ahead and refrigerated, covered; reheat them gently, and add water to them if they look very dry.*

Rigatoni with Spicy Sausage and Cannellini Beans

SERVES 6 This sauce pairs well with denser dried pasta like rigatoni. Hearty, comforting, and perfect for a chilly night, this is an easy weeknight meal, since it relies primarily on pantry staples: canned beans, canned tomatoes, and dry pasta. If you want a mellower dish, use sweet Italian sausage in place of the spicy and less crushed red pepper.

2	tablespoons extra-virgin olive oil
4	garlic cloves, finely chopped
1	large Spanish onion, coarsely chopped
1	pound hot Italian sausage (see headnote), casings removed
1	cup dry red wine
1	28-ounce can diced Italian tomatoes or 1 similar-sized box of Pomì brand chopped tomatoes
1/2	teaspoon crushed red pepper flakes, plus more to taste
	Kosher salt and freshly ground black pepper
1	pound dried rigatoni
1	19-ounce can cannellini beans, drained and rinsed
1/2	cup freshly grated Parmigiano-Reggiano, plus more for serving
2	tablespoons coarsely chopped fresh basil, plus more for serving
2	tablespoons unsalted butter, cut into pieces

Heat the olive oil in a large skillet over medium heat. Add the garlic and cook, stirring, until it is fragrant and light golden, about 2 minutes. Add the onion and sausage and cook, breaking up the sausage with a wooden spoon, until the sausage is no longer pink, about 5 minutes. Add the wine, increase the heat to high, and cook until the wine is reduced by half, about 10 minutes. Stir in the tomatoes, their juices, and the crushed red pepper flakes. Season with a pinch of salt and a few grinds of pepper. Reduce the heat to medium and cook until the sauce thickens slightly and develops flavor, about 25 minutes.

Meanwhile, bring a large pot of well-salted water to a boil. Add the rigatoni and cook until al dente. Reserve ½ cup of the pasta water before draining the pasta. Add the rigatoni to the pan with the sauce and stir to coat it. Add the beans, Parmesan, basil, and butter and stir gently. Cook until the beans are heated through, about 3 minutes. Taste and add more crushed red pepper flakes, if you like. If the pasta looks dry, add some of the reserved pasta cooking water.

Divide the pasta among six large bowls and top with additional cheese and basil. Serve immediately.

MAKE AHEAD: *You can make the sauce an hour or so ahead and keep it warm on the stove, or make it a day or two ahead, refrigerate it, covered, and reheat it gently before adding the pasta and beans.*

Pappardelle with Tangy Veal Ragu

A long braise makes the meat amazingly tender, while the marrow in the bones gives the tomatoey sauce a luscious, full-bodied feel and a rich meaty flavor. Veal shanks, the ones used in the famous Italian dish osso buco—that is, cut into thick bone-in pieces—can be pricey but are widely available. If you can find a whole shank, you can substitute that; it may be cheaper and will taste just as good. Boneless veal stew meat will work in a pinch but won't give you nearly as big a flavor as a bone-in braise.

4	pounds thick veal shanks (4–6 shanks, depending on thickness) or whole veal shank
	Kosher salt and freshly ground black pepper
1/2	cup all-purpose flour for dredging
1/4	cup extra-virgin olive oil
4	garlic cloves, very finely chopped
3	medium carrots, peeled and finely chopped
2	celery stalks, finely chopped
1	medium onion, finely chopped
2	cups dry red wine
3/4	cup balsamic vinegar
1	35-ounce can peeled Italian tomatoes, drained and coarsely chopped, juices reserved
2	cups beef broth
1	fresh rosemary sprig (about 4 inches long)
1/4	cup finely chopped fresh basil
1	pound pappardelle, preferably homemade (see page 115)
	Freshly grated Parmigiano-Reggiano

Tie the shanks around the middle with kitchen twine if not already tied by the butcher and season them well with salt and pepper. (The tying is not crucial, but it does make handling them easier.)

Put the flour in a dish. Dredge the veal in the flour and shake off the excess. In a large heavy pot or Dutch oven, heat the olive oil over medium-high heat. Add the veal, in batches if necessary, and cook undisturbed for a few minutes to brown well on one side. Turn and continue to cook until well browned all over. Transfer the veal to a plate.

Add the garlic, carrots, celery, and onion to the pot and cook over medium heat, stirring frequently, until lightly browned, about 5 minutes. Add the wine and balsamic vinegar and cook over high heat, stirring occasionally, until the liquid has reduced to a thick syrup, about 25 minutes. Add the tomatoes and their juices, beef broth, rosemary sprig, 2 tablespoons of the basil, and 2 cups water. Return the veal to the pot, season with salt and pepper, and bring to a simmer. Cover partially and cook over low heat, stirring occasionally, until the veal is very tender, about 2½ hours.

Transfer the veal to a plate and let cool slightly before cutting the meat into 1-inch pieces.

Strain the sauce into a large saucepan through a fine-mesh strainer, pressing on the solids to extract as much liquid and flavor as possible; discard the solids. If there is any visible fat on top of the sauce, spoon it off. Simmer the sauce over medium-high heat until reduced to 2½ cups, 10 to 15 minutes. Stir in the veal and the remaining 2 tablespoons basil and season with salt and pepper. Keep the veal ragu warm over low heat.

To serve, bring a large pot of well-salted water to a boil and cook the pappardelle until al dente. Drain thoroughly and return to the pot. Add the veal ragu and toss gently. Divide the pasta among six large bowls and sprinkle with the Parmesan.

MAKE AHEAD: *If you plan to make the ragu ahead, consider refrigerating the sauce before it's been reduced, since it's easy to remove the fat once the sauce has cooled and the fat has hardened. Refrigerate the meat and the unreduced sauce separately, covered, for up to 3 days. Or reduce the sauce and combine the meat and the sauce, refrigerate it, and reheat it all together over low heat. The ragu can also be frozen in an airtight container for a month or two.*

Cheese Agnolotti with Butter Sauce, Celery, Apple, and Prosciutto

SERVES 6; MAKES 50
TO 60 AGNOLOTTI

Agnolotti (ah-nyoh-LOH-tee) are little semicircles or squares of stuffed pasta. In this case, I fill the pasta with a single creamy, pungent cheese. I serve the agnolotti in a butter sauce with crisp celery, sweet apple, and salty prosciutto for a dish that's a study in contrasts.

FOR THE AGNOLOTTI

Fresh Pasta Dough (page 115)

1   container Epoisses cheese (about 9 ounces; see page 142)
     or the same amount of Brie or Taleggio

FOR THE SAUCE

½   cup chicken broth, preferably Roasted Chicken Stock (page 108)

8   tablespoons (1 stick) butter, cut into pieces

1   cup finely grated Parmigiano-Reggiano (about 2 ounces),
     preferably grated with a rasp-style (Microplane) grater

2   slices prosciutto, diced (about 6 tablespoons)

1   small, crisp apple, such as Honeycrisp or Granny Smith,
     peeled and cut into small dice

1   celery stalk, peeled and cut into small dice
     Kosher salt and freshly ground black pepper
     Squeeze of fresh lemon juice

8   celery leaves for garnish (optional)

TO MAKE THE AGNOLOTTI: Roll the pasta dough out to its thinnest setting, as described on page 116. Cut the pasta sheets into 4-x-12-inch strips. Working with one strip at a time (keep the others covered in plastic wrap so they don't dry out), place the strip with the long edge facing you. Put blobs of the cheese (each about a teaspoon's worth) along the middle of the pasta strip at 1½-inch intervals. Fold the top edge of the pasta down over the cheese. Brush the bottom edge lightly with water and fold the cheese-filled portion over again onto the wet edge. Gently press between each piece of cheese to help seal the pasta and then cut between them with a knife to form separate agnolotti; they will be shaped like little pillows. Dust them with flour to keep them from sticking and put them on a baking sheet dusted lightly with flour. Refrigerate or freeze the pasta if not using right away.

TO MAKE THE SAUCE: Put the broth in a large skillet and bring it to a boil. Add the butter a little at a time, whisking it to combine; it should thicken slightly. Whisk in the Parmesan and reduce to a gentle simmer. Add the prosciutto, apple, and celery to the sauce when you are ready to cook the pasta; you want these to cook a little, but the apple and celery should still have some crunch. Taste the sauce and season with a little salt, if needed, and pepper. Keep it warm over very low heat while you cook the pasta.

When ready to serve, bring a large pot of well-salted water to a boil. Add the agnolotti to the boiling water and cook until they float, 1 to 2 minutes. With a Chinese skimmer or other slotted spoon, transfer the agnolotti to the sauce, then squeeze a little lemon juice over all and toss gently to combine. Divide the pasta and sauce among six large bowls and garnish with the celery leaves, if you like.

MAKE AHEAD: *The agnolotti can be made and refrigerated, covered with plastic wrap on the baking sheet, for a day or frozen for up to 2 weeks. Freeze them on the baking sheet in a single layer. When rock-hard, they can be transferred to an airtight container.*

Epoisses

Epoisses, a cow's-milk cheese from Burgundy, France, comes in a small wooden box that does little to contain its strong aroma. As my friends in the cheese business say, Epoisses (ay-PWOSS) is a "stinky" cheese. They mean that as a compliment. Epoisses has an earthy aroma that puts you on the farm right along with the cows. Its flavor, however, is milder than its fragrance suggests: rich, somewhat salty, and a little tangy, because its rind has been washed with a brandylike eau-de-vie. Perfect with a hearty red wine after dinner, Epoisses has a smooth, puddinglike texture that makes the most luscious agnolotti. As you break into one with your fork, the cheese oozes out. Look for Epoisses at a good cheese market.

A fine substitute is Taleggio, which is usually easier to find. A cow's-milk cheese from Italy, it also has a washed rind and an aroma stronger than its flavor, and its texture is quite similar to that of Epoisses. Brie is another option, but its flavor is nowhere near as intriguing as that of either Epoisses or Taleggio, though it has a similar texture.

Roasted Corn and Tomato Lasagnettes

SERVES 6

Lasagna and summertime are two words that don't usually go together, but these individual, freestanding lasagnas celebrate two of the season's best offerings: fresh sweet corn and tomatoes. This recipe is perfect for entertaining for lots of reasons. For one, it's a knockout. Imagine stacked rounds of pasta layered with a creamy corn béchamel, roasted corn kernels, and roasted tomatoes. For another, all of the recipe's components can be made in advance (and in any order), which means you can spread out the work. Building the little stacks is easy, and the completed (but uncooked) lasagnettes will hold for up to a day in the fridge. All you have to do is heat them up in the oven (which takes just minutes) and make a simple butter sauce. This gorgeous pasta will be the star of the night. Precede or follow it with some simply grilled lamb chops to round out the meal.

> Fresh Pasta Dough (page 115)
> Olive oil
>
> 5 large ears corn, shucked, silk removed
> 3 teaspoons sugar
> 6 medium tomatoes
> 1 teaspoon fresh thyme leaves
>   Kosher salt and freshly ground black pepper
> 14 tablespoons (1¾ sticks) unsalted butter
> 1 cup whole milk
> ¼ cup unbleached all-purpose flour
> ¼ cup fine dry bread crumbs, preferably panko (Japanese bread crumbs)
> ¼ cup finely grated Parmigiano-Reggiano, preferably grated with a
>   rasp-style (Microplane) grater
> 6 small fresh basil leaves (optional)

To make the pasta rounds, roll out half of the pasta dough to the thinnest setting, as directed on page 116. (Reserve the rest and use it as you like.) Cut the pasta sheets into 8- to 10-inch lengths to make them more manageable for boiling. Bring a large pot of well-salted water to a boil and have ready a large bowl filled with ice water. Add a good drizzle of olive oil to the water (the olive oil will keep the sheets from sticking together). Cook the pasta sheets until al dente, about 3 minutes. Gently transfer the sheets to the bowl of ice water to halt the cooking. Once cool, drain the sheets well.

Line a baking sheet with parchment paper and lightly oil it. With a 3-inch round cutter, cut out 28 to 30 circles of dough (you're making a few extra just in case) and place them in a single layer on the prepared baking sheet. (I save the pasta scraps and use them in soups, in pasta fagioli, like the one on page 133, or in place of the linguine with clam sauce on page 128.) If the rounds don't fit in one layer, oil a piece of parchment paper, put it on top, and start a second layer. If not using the pasta rounds within an hour or so, cover them with plastic wrap and refrigerate them for up to 2 days.

To roast the corn, heat the oven to 400°F. Remove the kernels from the corncobs by slicing straight down each cob with a sharp chef's knife, turning the cob and repeating until most of the kernels are off. (This can be easier and neater to do if you cut the cob in half crosswise first.) Do the slicing on a baking sheet, so you can roast the kernels on it. Using the dull side of the knife, scrape hard along the now nude cob to extract the corn "milk," which you can combine with the kernels. Set aside 2 cups of the corn kernels and spread the remaining kernels out on the baking sheet so that they are mostly in one layer. Sprinkle $1\frac{1}{2}$ teaspoons of the sugar over the corn and roast until most of the kernels are deeply browned in spots, 15 to 20 minutes. Let cool until ready to use. Leave the oven on.

Meanwhile, stem the tomatoes and cut them into quarters. With the tomato quarters skin side down and using a paring knife held parallel to the work surface, cut away the seeds so that you're left with a fleshy tomato "petal." (Put the tomato innards into a small saucepan with some olive oil and garlic and simmer for a quick sauce for another time, if you like.) Line a baking sheet with a reusable nonstick liner, such as a Silpat (see page 64), or with parchment paper, and lay the tomatoes on it skin side down. Sprinkle with the remaining $1\frac{1}{2}$ teaspoons sugar, the thyme leaves, a few pinches of salt, and a few grinds of pepper. Drizzle a tablespoon or so of olive oil over the tomatoes and roast until the tomatoes blister and color around the edges, about 10 minutes. Let cool until ready to use.

To make the corn puree for the corn béchamel, melt 2 tablespoons of the butter over medium heat in a medium saucepan. Add the reserved 2 cups raw corn kernels and $\frac{1}{2}$ teaspoon salt and cook, stirring occasionally, for 2 to 3 minutes. Add the milk, bring to a boil, and cook until the corn is completely tender, about 6 minutes. Let the corn and milk cool a bit, then puree it in a blender, pass it through a fine-mesh strainer into a clean saucepan, and reserve off the heat.

To make the béchamel, melt 4 tablespoons of the butter in a small saucepan over medium to medium-high heat. Add the flour and cook, whisking constantly, until the mixture (called a roux) no longer tastes floury, about 5 minutes; season with $\frac{1}{4}$ teaspoon salt. Put the corn puree back on medium heat. Whisk the roux a little at a time into the warm corn puree. Continue to cook, whisking constantly, until the mixture thickens somewhat, about 4 minutes; it will thicken more as it cools. Pour the béchamel out onto a large plate to cool it quickly.

Toss the bread crumbs with the cheese in a small skillet and cook over medium heat, stirring occasionally, for just a few minutes, until the crumbs are golden brown. (You can also toast the bread crumbs and cheese in your oven if it's still hot.) Reserve off the heat.

To assemble the lasagnettes, lay 6 rounds of pasta down on a baking sheet with a little room between them. Top each with about 1½ teaspoons of the béchamel, about the same amount of roasted corn, and 1 tomato petal. Cover with another pasta round and top this with just the béchamel and roasted corn. Add another pasta round and top this one with the béchamel, roasted corn, about 1½ teaspoons of the bread crumbs, and 1 tomato petal. Top with a final pasta round, and finish with a layer of béchamel (you may not need to use all of it), roasted corn, bread crumbs, and remaining tomato petals.

To serve, heat the oven to 300°F. Add 2 to 3 tablespoons of water to the pan with the lasagnettes and lay a sheet of oiled parchment over them. Bake until hot throughout, 10 to 15 minutes.

Meanwhile, make a quick butter sauce by heating ¼ cup water in a small saucepan and whisking in the remaining stick of butter, a little at a time, until emulsified and slightly thickened. Season with a little salt.

Divide the butter sauce among six wide, shallow bowls or rimmed plates. Use a spatula to transfer the lasagnettes carefully to the bowls. Serve each topped with a fresh basil leaf, if you like.

MAKE AHEAD:

▌ *You can refrigerate the cooked pasta rounds, covered with oiled parchment paper and plastic wrap, for up to 2 days.*

▌ *Both the corn and the tomatoes can be roasted up to a day ahead and refrigerated covered with plastic wrap. The corn puree can be made a day or two ahead, or you can make the entire corn béchamel a day ahead and refrigerate, covered with plastic.*

▌ *The fully assembled lasagnettes can be held in the refrigerator, lightly covered in plastic wrap, for a full day ahead of cooking.*

Chicken Meatball Lasagnettes

SERVES 6 I once made these tiny individual servings of lasagna for Julia Child. (That time I used pheasant instead of chicken, but otherwise this is the same recipe.) Julia loved it. It's one of my favorites, too, in part because it's so cute: little rounds of pasta stacked and separated by marble-sized meatballs. Unlike traditional meat lasagna, this one is not chock-full of cheese and there's no tomato sauce; instead, a creamy béchamel binds the layers together, and the sauce is a deeply flavored roast chicken jus. There's no getting around the fact that the components in this dish take some time to make, but they can all be made well ahead of serving the dish, and the final assembly is easy.

Fresh Pasta Dough (page 115)
Olive oil
4 tablespoons (½ stick) unsalted butter
¼ cup unbleached all-purpose flour
¾ cup whole milk
⅓ cup heavy cream
Kosher salt
⅓ cup crème fraîche
Freshly ground white pepper
Chicken Meatballs (recipe follows)
Chicken Jus (page 150)
Shaved Parmigiano-Reggiano

To make the pasta rounds, roll out half of the pasta dough to the thinnest setting, as directed on page 116. (Reserve the remaining dough and use it as you like.) Cut the pasta sheets into 8- to 10-inch lengths to make them more manageable for boiling. Bring a large pot of well-salted water to a boil and have ready a large bowl filled with ice water. Add a good drizzle of olive oil to the water (the olive oil will keep the sheets from sticking together). Cook the pasta sheets until al dente, about 3 minutes. Gently transfer the sheets to the bowl of ice water to halt the cooking. Once cool, drain the sheets well.

Line a baking sheet with parchment paper and lightly oil it. With a 3-inch round cutter, cut out 30 circles of dough (plus a few extra just in case) and place them in a single layer on the prepared baking sheet. (I save the pasta scraps and use them in soups, in pasta fagioli, like the one on page 133, or in place of the linguine with the clam sauce on page 128.) If the rounds don't fit in one layer, oil a piece of parchment paper, put it on top, and start a second layer. If not using the pasta rounds within an hour or so, wrap them in plastic, and refrigerate them for up to 2 days.

To make the béchamel, melt the butter in a small saucepan over medium heat. Add the flour and cook, whisking constantly, until the mixture no longer tastes floury and smells a little nutty but has not darkened, 5 to 8 minutes. Add the milk, heavy cream, and 1 teaspoon salt and cook, whisking, until thickened, 5 to 7 minutes. Take the pan off the heat and whisk in the crème fraîche. Season the béchamel to taste with white pepper and additional salt and pour it out onto a large plate to cool it quickly.

To assemble the lasagnettes, lay 6 rounds of the pasta down on a baking sheet with a little room between them. Top each with about 1½ teaspoons of the béchamel and then place 3 meatballs over the béchamel. The layers won't be perfectly even; you can also halve the meatballs if whole ones prove too unwieldy. Continue this layering until you have 4 layers of the meatballs (you may not need all the meatballs) and 5 layers of the rounds.

To serve, heat the oven to 300°F. Add 2 to 3 tablespoons of water to the baking sheet with the lasagnettes and lay a sheet of oiled parchment over them. Bake until heated through, 10 to 15 minutes.

Use a spatula to transfer the lasagnettes carefully to six wide bowls or rimmed plates. Spoon a few tablespoons of jus around each lasagnette and top with some shaved Parmesan.

MAKE AHEAD:

❚ *Both the meatballs and the chicken jus can be made well ahead of assembling; see those recipes for details.*

❚ *You can refrigerate the cooked pasta rounds, covered with plastic wrap, for up to 2 days.*

❚ *You can make the béchamel a day or two ahead of using it and refrigerate, covered with plastic wrap.*

❚ *You can take a well-earned rest after assembling the lasagnettes, because once assembled, they can hold in the refrigerator, lightly covered with plastic wrap, for a day or two.*

Chicken Meatballs

MAKES 100 MEATBALLS

I created these delicately flavored little meatballs to make individual-sized servings of lasagna, but they're also good added to pasta with marinara and to soup, such as Chicken Consommé (page 101). When I was a kid, my mother added saltines soaked in milk to her meatballs. I use the Japanese bread crumbs called panko, available now at almost all supermarkets. I have a pet peeve with meatballs: I hate it when I bite into one and all I taste is raw onion. That's why I use shallots instead and cook them thoroughly.

1	3-pound chicken, giblets removed
1	tablespoon vegetable oil
2	shallots, very finely chopped
2	garlic cloves, very finely chopped
½	cup heavy cream
1	cup panko (Japanese bread crumbs; see page 209) or fine dry homemade bread crumbs
6	tablespoons finely grated Parmigiano-Reggiano
1	large egg, lightly beaten
1	teaspoon chopped fresh thyme
	Kosher salt and freshly ground black pepper

Heat the oven to 350°F and line two baking sheets with parchment paper.

Cut the chicken into pieces. Remove the meat from the legs, thighs, and breast, discarding all skin and sinew. Save the bones to make the Chicken Jus (page 150). Finely chop 1½ pounds of the meat or coarsely grind it in a food processor.

In a small skillet, heat the oil over medium heat. Add the shallots and garlic and cook, stirring, until very tender but not colored, about 8 minutes. Let cool. In a small bowl, pour the cream over the panko and stir. In a larger bowl, combine the chicken meat with the cooled shallots and garlic, cheese, egg, thyme, 1 tablespoon salt, and about ¾ teaspoon pepper. Add the soaked panko and use your hands to combine everything—the panko will be thick and pastelike—gently but thoroughly.

At this point, it's a good idea to test for seasoning. Take a little of the mixture, flatten it into a patty, and sauté it until cooked through. Taste and add more salt and pepper as needed.

Mimolette

Mimolette is a hard cow's-milk cheese. Because of its size and its thick, rough, dimpled rind, it bears a striking resemblance to a cantaloupe, and the interior is bright orange. (As in some cheddars, the color comes from annatto, a flavorless derivative of achiote seeds.) Though Mimolette is a French cheese, its flavor calls to mind such Dutch favorites as Edam and Gouda. Like Gouda, Mimolette is quite mild when young but becomes more deeply nuanced as it ages. Take a bite and you'll experience smoky, caramel, Scotch whisky flavors. Mimolette is delicious served as part of a cheese course, and it also melts beautifully, which is why I like to use it in risotto and in cheese sauce (page 244). Cheddar melts similarly, but aged cheddars are sharper and don't offer the same complexity of flavor. If you can't find Mimolette, an aged Gouda is a better choice.

Roll the chicken mixture into meatballs about ³⁄₄ inch in diameter (the size of a grape); to keep the meatball mixture from sticking to your hands, keep your hands wet as you roll. Line the meatballs up on the prepared baking sheets without letting them touch and bake until cooked through, about 8 minutes. Cool. If not using within an hour or so, cover with plastic wrap and refrigerate.

MAKE AHEAD: *You can refrigerate the cooked meatballs, covered with plastic wrap, for a couple of days, or freeze them for longer storage. To keep them from clumping together, let them cool and then freeze them on the cooled baking sheet until hard before transferring them to a freezer bag.*

Chicken Jus
MAKES 2 CUPS

If you have extra jus, use it to enrich a risotto, stew, sauce, or braise.

¹⁄₄ cup vegetable oil
Bones from 1 chicken (see Chicken Meatballs, page 149), chopped into 3-inch pieces
1 carrot, peeled and chopped
1 white onion, chopped
1 celery stalk, peeled and chopped
1 garlic clove, chopped
2 cups dry white wine
4 quarts chicken broth or water or a mix of both
1 tablespoon coriander seeds
1 tablespoon black peppercorns
2 bay leaves
2 fresh thyme sprigs
Kosher salt and freshly ground black pepper

In a large soup pot, heat the oil over medium-high heat. Add the bones and let them brown well, stirring occasionally, about 15 minutes. Add the carrot, onion, celery, and garlic and cook, stirring occasionally, until they are well browned, about 10 minutes. Pour off any excess fat, add the wine, and cook until the wine has reduced by a little more than half. Add the chicken broth, coriander, peppercorns, and bay leaves and bring to a gentle boil. Reduce to a lively simmer and cook, occasionally skimming the surface with a ladle, until reduced to about 4 cups; this can take up to 2 hours, but you can be doing other things during this time. Strain the liquid through a fine-mesh strainer into a smaller saucepan and continue to cook it until reduced to about 2 cups. Add the fresh thyme and allow it to steep for 2 minutes before removing it. Strain the jus again, if desired, and season to taste with salt and pepper.

MAKE AHEAD: *You can hold the jus for a few days in the refrigerator, covered, or freeze it for up to a month in an airtight container.*

Ricotta Gnudi

If you took the pasta off traditional ravioli, the cheese filling would be naked, right? Ricotta gnudi (NOO-dee) is little more than ricotta cheese formed into tiny dumplings that simmer to an ethereal lightness. Since this "pasta" is all about the ricotta, use the best quality you can find (or make it yourself following the recipe on page 35). I like to serve these delicate dumplings with Odd Fellow Marinara (page 120), a butter-sage sauce (see page 170), or my Butcher Shop Bolognese (page 121). You can give them grooves as directed or leave them plain.

1	pound fresh ricotta (see page 34), drained in a cheesecloth-lined strainer if very wet
3/4–1	cup unbleached all-purpose flour, plus more as needed
1	large egg, lightly beaten
1/3	cup finely grated Parmigiano-Reggiano (optional), preferably grated with a rasp-style (Microplane) grater
1	tablespoon kosher salt
1/2	teaspoon freshly ground white pepper

In a large mixing bowl, combine the ricotta, 3/4 cup of the flour, the egg, Parmesan (if using), salt, and pepper. Use a wooden spoon to mix the ingredients together well. Lightly flour your work surface and a baking sheet for holding the shaped gnudi. With floured hands, knead the ricotta mixture briefly; it will be quite wet and sticky at this point. Dump the mixture out onto your work surface.

Cut off a piece of the gnudi dough and try rolling it into a 3/4-inch-thick log. If you can't get it to roll, add a little more flour to the dough and try again. You want as little flour as possible to bind this together so the result will be light. Cut the log into 1-inch pieces and then roll them into little balls. Hold a fork with the tines facing down, and roll each ball down the length of the tines or use a gnocchi board (see page 158). Place on the floured baking sheet. Repeat until all of the dough is rolled and cut. Freeze the gnudi, about 1 hour. (Because they are so soft, they are much easier to handle if frozen, so do this even if you plan to use them soon.)

To serve, bring a large pot of well-salted water to a gentle boil. In batches, drop the frozen gnudi into the water and cook until they float, 1 to 2 minutes. As each batch cooks, remove the gnudi with a slotted spoon and keep them warm or transfer them directly to the sauce with which they are being served.

MAKE AHEAD: *You can freeze some or all of the gnudi for a couple of weeks. Freeze them in a single layer on a baking sheet until rock-hard and then transfer to a freezer bag.*

Gnocchi

SERVES 8

Like homemade pasta, homemade potato gnocchi (NYOH-kee) is revelatory. If you've only eaten packaged, you may think of these potato dumplings as solid, heavy little lumps. But gnocchi made with care by hand are incomparably light. There are, however, a few tricks to making them that way. One is to start with high-starch potatoes, which cook up dry and fluffy. That texture makes incorporating the flour easier, which means the potatoes won't get overworked and leaden. To mash the potatoes, use a ricer (see page 156); nothing else will do. Then add just enough flour to strike a balance between not enough (which makes the gnocchi fall apart when boiled) and too much (which makes them heavy). A good gnocchi dough will feel pliable, soft, and a little sticky.

You can serve gnocchi with just about any sauce you would serve with pasta. A brown butter sauce flavored with sage, like the one on page 170, is delicious, as is Tangy Veal Ragu (page 138) or Butcher Shop Bolognese (page 121). You can also flavor the gnocchi with chopped fresh herbs and freshly grated cheese, if you like.

2–2¼	pounds medium- to high-starch potatoes, such as Idaho (russet), whole and unpeeled (2–3 potatoes)
	Kosher salt
1½–2	cups unbleached all-purpose flour
2	large eggs

Put the potatoes in a medium pot of salted water. Bring to a boil and cook until very tender (a cake tester or toothpick inserted will pull out easily), about 30 minutes. Drain the potatoes well and allow them to cool just until you're able to handle them. Peel the potatoes while still quite hot (the skin will come off easily) and rice them onto a baking sheet to cool.

Have ready a parchment-lined, lightly floured baking sheet or platter in a size that will fit in your freezer. Dump the cooled potatoes onto a lightly floured work surface. Sprinkle 1½ cups of the flour over the potatoes and fluff the flour into the potatoes, using your fingers and a light touch. Gently gather the potatoes into a mound. Create a well in the center of the mound and add 1½ teaspoons salt. Crack the eggs into the well and, using your fingers, combine all the ingredients. Knead the dough by pushing it away from you with the heel of your hand, folding it over, giving it a quarter turn, and pushing it away again. Continue kneading, sprinkling on a little more flour as needed, until the dough just forms a ball and feels delicate and a little bit sticky. Set the dough aside and clean the work surface of any hard bits of dough.

Sprinkle the work surface lightly with flour. Roll the dough out with a rolling pin to about ½ inch thick. Use a bench scraper or knife to cut the dough into strips about ½ inch wide. Roll each strip under your hands to form a log and cut the logs into 1-inch pieces. If you like, you can give your gnocchi grooves. Using a gnocchi board, shape the pieces into balls and roll them down the board as directed on page 158.

If you are not cooking the gnocchi right away, freeze them on the baking sheet or platter in a single layer until frozen solid. Once frozen, you can transfer them to a freezer bag or other airtight container.

Cook the gnocchi in boiling salted water until they float to the top, about 5 minutes. Drain well and serve with your favorite sauce.

MAKE AHEAD: *The gnocchi will keep well for about 3 months in the freezer and can go right from the freezer to the pot to cook.*

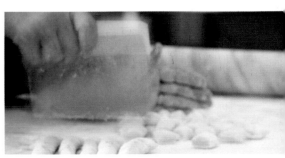

VARIATIONS

TRUFFLED GNOCCHI: *Add 2 tablespoons white truffle oil to the well along with the eggs.*

TOMATO GNOCCHI: *Puree 1 cup sun-dried tomatoes (plumped in warm water if very dry, then drained) and add them and ½ cup tomato paste to the well along with the eggs.*

For the Lightest Gnocchi, Use a Ricer

There are a few tools I insist on, and a potato ricer for gnocchi is one of them. Using a ricer, which looks like a rounded garlic press on hormones, is about the only way to guarantee the potatoes will have the right light, lump-free consistency. If you don't have one, you'll be glad I forced you into buying it, because a ricer also makes wonderful, supremely smooth, fluffy mashed potatoes. You can find ricers at most home-goods stores—Oxo makes a good one—for about $20.

Truffled Gnocchi with Peas and Mushrooms

SERVES 4   Mushrooms paired with gnocchi make so much sense to me, since both have earthy flavors. To further emphasize the combination, I add a little good-quality truffle oil to the gnocchi dough itself and drizzle a bit on just before serving. Peas, especially sweet fresh ones, brighten up this creamy dish. Delicious as this is, it's even better with some (about 1 cup) freshly cooked lobster meat added right before serving.

2	tablespoons unsalted butter
8	ounces mushrooms, preferably chanterelles, halved if large, cleaned and trimmed (about 2 cups)
2	cups heavy cream
1/2	cup peas (fresh or thawed frozen)
1	tablespoon finely chopped fresh thyme
1/2	recipe Truffled Gnocchi (see the Variation, page 156)
	Kosher salt
	Freshly ground black pepper
1	tablespoon finely chopped fresh chives
	Truffle oil

Melt the butter over medium-high heat in a large skillet. Add the mushrooms and cook, stirring occasionally, until tender, about 5 minutes.

In a medium saucepan, bring the cream to a boil and cook over medium heat until reduced by half. Add the cream, peas, and thyme to the mushrooms and cook over low heat, stirring occasionally, while you cook the gnocchi.

Cook the gnocchi in boiling salted water until they float to the top, about 5 minutes. Drain well and toss the gnocchi with the cream sauce. Season the gnocchi well with salt and pepper before dividing it among four bowls. Garnish each serving with the chopped chives and a drizzle of truffle oil.

MAKE AHEAD: *You can make the mushroom sauce earlier in the day. Refrigerate it, covered with plastic wrap, if it will sit out for more than half an hour and reheat it gently before adding the rest of the ingredients.*

How Gnocchi Get Their Grooves

If you make gnocchi often, creating the distinctive grooves is easy to do with a gnocchi board, which looks like a small, ridged wooden paddle. If you don't have one, you can use a fork, though it isn't as wide and convenient. You'll need to press harder on the fork, which can smash the gnocchi. To roll them on the board, I use my flattened hand, not my thumb, since I prefer the gnocchi to be evenly rounded rather than having the deeply indented shell shape that rolling with the thumb creates. Finding your groove when making gnocchi can take a while if you're new to it. Don't worry if the gnocchi are not all exactly the same size and shape; consistency will come with practice. And though the ridges will help a sauce cling better to the gnocchi as well as make them more texturally interesting, you can leave the dumplings ridge-free and call it a day.

Prune-Stuffed Gnocchi with Foie Gras Sauce

SERVES 6   These gnocchi—my most requested recipe—were inspired by an idea from a cook from Bergamo, in northern Italy, who worked at No. 9 Park. Alberto mentioned the dessert gnocchi filled with prune puree for which his hometown was famous. I transformed that idea into a savory dish and made it ultra-luxurious by adding a rich foie gras–butter sauce. The gnocchi sound as though they might be heavy, but they actually feel quite light; more than that, they are velvety, smooth, and creamy. Save this dish for a very special occasion, when you are pulling out all the stops, since the recipe takes some time and, frankly, a good amount of cash. That said, even a beginning cook can execute it well. The oversized, stuffed gnocchi—they look like little boats—are actually fun to make, and they freeze beautifully.

I like to use Vin Santo to flavor the prunes. Made with dry grapes full of concentrated flavor that go through a special fermentation, the wine has a deep golden color and tastes of roasted nuts and caramel. A good Madeira, such as a dark and sweet Malmsey, would work as well. Finally, Marcona almonds are fat nuts from Spain commonly sold fried and salted (you can find them at Whole Foods, Trader Joe's, and even Costco). Coarsely chopped and sprinkled on top of the gnocchi, they add a welcome crunch and a saltiness that counters the sweet and rich flavors already on the plate. (See the photo on page 125.)

FOR THE GNOCCHI

22	pitted prunes
1	cup Vin Santo or Madeira, plus more if needed
2–2¼	pounds medium- to high-starch potatoes, such as Idaho (russet), whole and unpeeled
1½–2	cups unbleached all-purpose flour, plus more as needed
2	large eggs
	Kosher salt and freshly ground black pepper
⅛	teaspoon freshly grated nutmeg

FOR THE SAUCE

8	ounces foie gras (see page 163), half at room temperature (reserve the other half, refrigerated, for serving)
8	tablespoons (1 stick) unsalted butter, cut into pieces, at room temperature
½	cup finely chopped shallots (about 2 large)
15	small fresh thyme sprigs
15	black peppercorns
15	coriander seeds
2	cups Vin Santo or Madeira

2   tablespoons chopped salted Marcona almonds or regular almonds,
     lightly toasted and salted

3   fresh chervil sprigs, whole leaves and small clusters of leaves picked off,
     or small parsley leaves

     Fleur de sel

TO MAKE THE GNOCCHI FILLING: Put all but 2 of the prunes in a small saucepan with the
Vin Santo, adding a little more, if need be, to cover the prunes completely. Cook the
prunes over medium heat, reducing the amount of liquid until the pan is almost dry,
about 30 minutes. Set aside and let cool. Once cool, chop the prunes very finely or puree
them in a food processor if you want to pipe the filling. Chop the 2 reserved (unsoaked)
prunes as well but keep them separate; you will use them to garnish the gnocchi.

TO MAKE THE GNOCCHI DOUGH: Put the potatoes in a medium pot of salted water. Bring
to a boil and cook until very tender (a cake tester or toothpick inserted will pull out
easily), about 30 minutes. Drain the potatoes well and allow them to cool just until you're
able to handle them. Peel the potatoes while still quite hot (the skin will come off easily)
and rice them onto a baking sheet to cool.

　　　Dump the cooled potatoes onto a lightly floured work surface. Sprinkle 1½ cups
of the flour over the potatoes and fluff the flour into the potatoes, using your fingers and
a light touch. Gently gather the potatoes into a mound. Create a well in the center of the
mound. Whisk together the eggs and 1 teaspoon salt in a small bowl and pour them into
the well. Add a couple of grinds of pepper and the nutmeg. Using your fingers, combine
all the ingredients. Knead the dough by pushing it away from you with the heel of your
hand, folding it over, giving it a quarter turn, and pushing it away again. Continue
kneading, sprinkling on a little more flour as needed, until it forms a ball and the dough
feels delicate and just a little bit sticky. Set the dough aside and clean the work surface of
any hard bits of dough.

　　　Sprinkle the work surface lightly with flour. Roll out half of the dough to about
¼ inch thick. Using a 3-inch round cookie cutter, punch out rounds of dough. Reroll the
scraps and cut out as many circles as you can. Line up the circles in rows for easy, efficient,
assembly-line stuffing. If you have room, roll out the second half of the dough; if not, do

it after this batch of gnocchi has been stuffed and shaped. But work without interruption, as the potato dough will become less easy to work with as it sits.

TO STUFF THE GNOCCHI: Have ready a parchment-lined, lightly floured baking sheet or platter that will fit in your freezer.

Put about a teaspoon of the cooked chopped prunes in the center of each dough circle, leaving a ¹/₂-inch margin all around. (If you pureed the prunes, you can pipe the filling with a pastry bag.) Fold the dough in half to make a half-moon shape. You can seal the dough by pressing the edges together with your fingers, but for a better seal and a more uniform look, use a slightly smaller round cookie cutter to trim ¹/₄ inch off the rounded side of the gnocchi. Next, flip up the half-moon so that it's standing on its rounded edge. Use a finger to put a little (¹/₄-inch-deep) indentation in the middle of the side that's facing up. (This dent helps hold the sauce on the gnocchi.) As the gnocchi are stuffed and shaped, transfer them to the parchment-lined baking sheet (don't let them touch each other or they will stick). Freeze the gnocchi on the sheet for at least 30 minutes. (They're easier to handle when frozen and will keep their shape better this way, too.) Once they are rock-hard, you can put them into the airtight container of your choice or cook them right away. Repeat the entire process with the second half of the dough, if you have not already rolled it out.

TO MAKE THE SAUCE: Pass the room-temperature foie gras through a fine-mesh strainer into a medium bowl. (This is easier than it sounds, and the strainer removes all small veins for a smooth sauce.) Use a wooden spoon to combine the foie gras and butter. Shape the mixture into a log on a piece of plastic wrap, parchment, or waxed paper. Wrap it well and refrigerate until firm.

Meanwhile, put the shallots, thyme, peppercorns, and coriander in a medium saucepan. Pour the Vin Santo into the pan and cook on high heat until the liquid has reduced practically to a glaze. Lower the heat to medium-low and whisk in about one sixth of the foie gras butter. As it melts, add a little more. When all of the foie gras butter has been whisked in, pass the sauce through a clean fine-mesh strainer. Keep the sauce warm (but not hot) as you finish the dish. (If the sauce gets too hot, the foie gras–butter emulsion can "break," or separate; if that happens, whisk in a little warm water just before serving.)

To serve, bring a large pot of salted water to a gentle boil.

Slice the remaining 4 ounces foie gras into 1-inch-thick slices; use the tip of a small knife or a skewer to remove any large, obvious veins. Season well with salt and pepper. Heat a nonstick pan over medium heat. Add the foie gras and cook until well browned on all sides, up to 1 minute per side. (Don't overcook it, or you will end up with a puddle of pricey fat.) Remove from the heat and keep warm.

Reheat the sauce if necessary over medium-low heat.

Cook the gnocchi in batches, gently lowering 5 or 6 of them at a time into the water with a large-holed slotted spoon or Chinese strainer. The gnocchi are done when they rise to the top, 2 to 3 minutes. Fish the gnocchi out with the strainer and keep warm until all the gnocchi are cooked.

To serve, cut the scared foie gras into smaller pieces to go on top of the gnocchi. Divide the gnocchi among six plates, lining them up so their dented sides face up to catch and hold the sauce. Spoon the sauce over the gnocchi, top the gnocchi with the foie gras, and sprinkle a little of the chopped almonds, reserved chopped prunes, and chervil over all. Finish with a pinch of fleur de sel.

MAKE AHEAD:

I *The stuffed gnocchi will keep for weeks in the freezer and can go right from the freezer to the pot to cook.*

I *The foie gras butter can be made 2 days ahead, wrapped in plastic wrap, and refrigerated. It can also be frozen for up to 6 months; thaw before using.*

I *The foie gras sauce can be made ahead and either chilled or frozen for up to 1 month. If frozen, let it thaw for a day in the refrigerator before reheating over low heat. Add ¼ cup cream to the pan to help the sauce stay emulsified.*

Foie Gras

Foie gras (fwah grah) is the liver from a duck or goose that was specially fattened to make the organ oversized and consequently rich and delicious. (Foie gras in the United States is from duck, whereas in Europe it is almost always from goose.)

Even people who think they don't like liver fall in love fast when they experience their first bite of seared foie gras melting in their mouth. It's one of those foods that literally make people moan with pleasure. I often make terrines and pâtés featuring its silky texture and rich flavor, but my most famous dish with it is the prune-stuffed gnocchi on page 159.

Some specialty markets carry foie gras, but unless you live near one, you will have to mail-order a whole liver, which is made up of two lobes and weighs between 1 and 1½ pounds and costs $70 to $80. Hudson Valley Foie Gras sells foie: visit the website www.hudsonvalleyfoiegras.com or call 845-292-2500. D'Artagnan (www.dartagnan.com; 800-327-8246) is another good source.

The livers come in a few grades. Grade A is the best and therefore the most expensive, but go ahead and buy grade B if it's cheaper. Grade B foie gras is slightly less perfect; it's often a little smaller and has minute traces of blood. You can freeze what you don't use.

A whole foie gras needs a little prep work. Gently pull the two lobes apart. Sometimes a clump of white fat is nestled between the lobes; peel this off with your fingers and throw it away. As you open up the liver, you will see a vein connecting the lobes. Remove it. I find it easier to do this when the foie gras is at room temperature and feels as pliable as butter. Use a knife to cut the vein and pull on it to free it. I don't bother to get rid of smaller veins if I am browning foie gras, because the discoloration they have isn't noticeable. When using foie gras in a terrine, I gently probe the liver with the tip of a paring knife or skewer to remove the veiny network. Once I am finished trimming the foie gras, I gently mash the pliable liver back into its lobe shape, wrap it in plastic wrap, and refrigerate it to make slicing easier. Frozen is not quite as good as fresh, but it's still delicious.

Cheese Risotto

Loaded with tangy cheese, this dish may remind you more of the best-ever macaroni and cheese than a typical risotto. My favorite cheese for it is Mimolette, but it's also very tasty with aged Gouda. Serve this as a starter to a light meal or with a crisp salad for lunch. It's amazing with fresh truffle shaved over it, but I know most people don't have access to fresh truffles. A few drops of truffle oil add a welcome musky note, too.

2	tablespoons extra-virgin olive oil
½	small onion, diced (about ⅓ cup)
1	cup Arborio rice
¼	cup dry white wine
4	cups chicken broth, preferably Roasted Chicken Stock (page 108), heated
2	ounces Mimolette, aged Gouda, or Edam cheese, very finely grated with a rasp-style (Microplane) grater
2	tablespoons unsalted butter, at room temperature
⅓	cup heavy cream, whipped to medium peaks
	Kosher salt and freshly ground white pepper
	Shavings of fresh black truffle (optional)
	Truffle oil (optional)
	Fleur de sel

Heat the oil in a medium saucepan over medium heat. Add the onion and cook, stirring occasionally, until tender but not browned, about 8 minutes. Add the rice and cook, stirring, for about 1 minute to toast the grains slightly. Add the wine and cook until it is almost absorbed. Add about 1 cup of the broth and cook, stirring every minute or two, until almost all of the broth has been absorbed. Continue cooking, adding more broth, and stirring in this manner until the risotto is creamy and al dente, 20 to 25 minutes. (At this point the risotto may be held for up to 2 days, as described on page 169.)

Add the butter and the cheese. Stir briskly to incorporate and melt the cheese. Fold in the whipped cream, taste, and season with salt and a few good grinds of white pepper. Spoon the risotto into six bowls or onto rimmed plates. If using, garnish each with as much shaved fresh truffle as you can afford or with a few drops of truffle oil. Add a pinch of fleur de sel and serve.

Tomato and Arugula Risotto with Prosciutto

This summery risotto is sumptuous. Flecked with red and green from ripe tomato and peppery arugula, it is served folded in prosciutto so that the fat melts right into the rice. Make sure you use the real deal (prosciutto di Parma) for the most unctuous result. Because the risotto itself is so delicately flavored, I use water instead of broth.

4	thin slices prosciutto di Parma
4	medium tomatoes
5	tablespoons extra-virgin olive oil
1	large garlic clove, finely chopped
	Kosher salt and freshly ground black pepper
1/2	medium onion, finely chopped
1	cup Arborio rice
1/3	cup dry white wine
3	tablespoons unsalted butter, at room temperature
3	ounces (about 3 handfuls) baby arugula leaves, well washed and dried
1/2	cup heavy cream, whipped to medium peaks
	Squeeze of fresh lemon juice
1/2	cup finely grated Parmigiano-Reggiano

Before you start cooking, take the prosciutto out of the refrigerator if necessary so that it warms up a bit before serving.

Stem the tomatoes and cut them into quarters. With the tomato skin side down and using a paring knife held parallel to the work surface, cut away the seeds so you're left with a fleshy tomato "petal." (Throw the tomato innards into a small saucepan with some olive oil and garlic and simmer for a quick sauce for another time, if you like.) Slice the petals thinly. Heat 3 tablespoons of the olive oil in a medium skillet over medium heat. Add the garlic and cook until fragrant, about 1 minute. Add the tomatoes, season with salt and a little pepper, and cook, stirring occasionally, until the tomatoes have softened a bit, about 5 minutes. Remove from the heat but keep warm near the stove.

In a medium saucepan, heat the remaining 2 tablespoons olive oil over medium heat. Add the onion and cook, stirring occasionally, until tender but not browned, about 8 minutes. Add the rice and cook, stirring, for about 1 minute to toast the grains slightly. Add the wine and cook until almost all of it has been absorbed. Add about 1 cup hot water and cook, stirring every minute or two, until almost all of the water has been absorbed. Continue cooking, adding more water and stirring in this manner, until the risotto is creamy and al dente, 20 to 25 minutes. (At this point the risotto may be held for up to 2 days, as described on page 169.)

To serve, lay a piece of prosciutto on each large serving plate so that half is centered and the other half hangs off the plate (you will fold it over the risotto later). Stir the butter, the arugula, and about half of the tomatoes into the risotto. Gently fold in the whipped cream and season to taste with a little salt and pepper and a few drops of lemon juice. Divide the risotto among the four plates, spooning it over the prosciutto. Sprinkle the cheese over the risotto and top it with the remaining tomatoes. Fold the other half of the prosciutto over so that it covers some of the risotto.

Whipped Cream Lightens Risotto

It may seem odd to add whipped cream—not whipping cream, but heavy cream whipped to medium peaks—to risotto, but just a little bit of it folded in near the finish contributes richness and gives the risotto a wonderful texture. Beat the cream until you can pull out a stopped beater or whisk and leave a peak that holds its shape without sinking back into the bowl. The whipped cream then "melts" into the rice, coating it beautifully, and the air you've incorporated lightens the risotto's texture considerably.

Maine Crab, Lemon, and Zucchini Blossom Risotto

This is a wonderful warm-weather risotto. You can omit the zucchini blossoms, but they add a gorgeous color as well as a bit of flavor. More farmers' markets are carrying them these days, and if you grow your own zucchini, you can harvest some yourself.

3½	tablespoons extra-virgin olive oil
1	small or ½ medium onion, finely chopped (about 1 cup)
2	cups Arborio rice
1	cup dry white wine
4	cups chicken broth, preferably Roasted Chicken Stock (page 108), or water, heated, plus more if needed
	Kosher salt and freshly ground white pepper
2	medium zucchini, trimmed and diced (about 4 cups)
3	tablespoons heavy cream
1½	teaspoons freshly grated lemon zest (from ½ lemon)
	Juice of ½ lemon, plus more to taste
2	tablespoons unsalted butter, at room temperature
1	pound fresh lump crabmeat, picked over
6	zucchini blossoms
½	cup finely grated Parmigiano-Reggiano (optional)

In a medium saucepan or Dutch oven, heat 2 tablespoons of the olive oil over medium heat. Add the onion and cook, stirring occasionally, until tender but not browned, about 8 minutes. Add the rice and cook, stirring, for 1 to 2 minutes to toast the grains slightly. Add the wine and cook until most of it has been absorbed. Add about 1 cup of the broth and cook, stirring every minute or two, until almost all of the broth has been absorbed. Continue cooking, adding more broth and stirring in this manner, until the risotto is creamy and al dente, 20 to 25 minutes. Stir in 1 teaspoon salt and a few grinds of white pepper. (At this point the risotto may be held for up to 2 days, as described on the opposite page.)

Meanwhile, heat the remaining 1¹/₂ tablespoons olive oil in a large skillet over medium heat. Add the zucchini and cook, stirring occasionally, until browned and just tender, adjusting the heat as needed, 3 to 4 minutes. Season with a few good pinches of salt and a few grinds of white pepper and reserve in the pan off the heat.

In a small bowl, whip the cream to medium peaks. Add the lemon zest and juice and season with a little salt and white pepper.

To serve, add the butter and then the zucchini and crab to the risotto. Stir gently over medium-low heat, adding a little water or broth, if needed, to loosen the mixture a bit. Tear the zucchini blossoms into small pieces, fold them and the whipped cream into the risotto, and season to taste with salt, white pepper, and lemon juice. Sprinkle with Parmesan, if you like.

Making Risotto Ahead

You can use the same trick that many chefs use to parcook the risotto so the dish can be made ahead. Once the rice is al dente, take it off the heat and spread it out on a baking sheet so that it cools evenly. The rice can stay at room temperature for 1 to 2 hours or refrigerated, covered with plastic wrap after it reaches room temperature, for up to 2 days. When reheating cooled risotto, you may need to add a little more heated broth or water to loosen and soften it. Once it is quite warm, you can finish it as directed.

Mushroom- and Fontina-Stuffed Crespelles with Brown Butter–Sage Sauce

A crespelle is a thin Italian pancake similar to a crepe. Whole wheat flour gives it a more substantial, less sweet flavor than that of a traditional crepe. The pancakes are rolled around a savory filling of wild mushrooms, robust herbs, and gooey cheese and baked in the oven; the result is similar to cannelloni.

FOR THE CRESPELLES

- ¾ cup whole wheat flour
- ½ cup all-purpose flour
- ½ teaspoon kosher salt
- ¼ teaspoon sugar
- 1½ cups whole milk
- ¼ cup heavy cream
- 1 large egg
- 1 tablespoon melted unsalted butter, plus more butter for the pan

FOR THE FILLING

- 2 tablespoons grapeseed or canola oil
- 12 ounces mushrooms, preferably a mix of wild and domestic, cleaned, trimmed, and cut if very large (otherwise leave whole)
- Kosher salt and freshly ground black pepper
- 2 tablespoons unsalted butter
- 1 shallot, finely chopped
- 1 garlic clove, finely chopped
- ¼ cup dry white wine
- Chopped leaves from about 4 fresh thyme sprigs
- 6 ounces Italian fontina, thinly sliced
- 4 ounces arugula or other tender greens, well washed and dried, stemmed, and coarsely chopped if leaves are big

FOR THE SAUCE

- 8 tablespoons (1 stick) unsalted butter
- 6 sage leaves, stacked, rolled, and thinly sliced crosswise
- 1–2 teaspoons fresh lemon juice
- Kosher salt
- Fleur de sel

TO MAKE THE CRESPELLES: Whisk together the flours, salt, and sugar in a small bowl. In a larger bowl, whisk together the milk, cream, and egg. Whisk the dry ingredients into the wet ones and then whisk in the melted butter. Let the batter rest in the refrigerator for at least an hour to let the flour absorb the liquid (you'll get a more tender crespelle that way).

Heat a crepe pan if you have one (I don't) or an 8- or 9-inch nonstick or well-seasoned cast-iron pan over medium-high heat. Melt a smidge of butter in the pan and pour or ladle about $\frac{1}{4}$ cup of the batter into the pan (enough to coat the bottom). Lift the pan off the stove and tilt it to spread the batter around in an even layer. Cook, adjusting the heat as needed, until the batter has set and the bottom is nicely browned, about 2 minutes. Flip the crespelle over (you may need to dislodge it first with a spatula or a shake of the pan) and briefly cook the other side. Transfer to a plate and proceed with the remaining batter, adding more butter to the pan as needed. You should be able to make 8 to 10 pancakes.

If you're not using the crespelles right away, stack them between pieces of parchment paper, let cool completely, and then wrap the stack in plastic wrap to keep moist until ready to use.

TO MAKE THE FILLING: Heat the grapeseed oil in a large skillet over medium-high heat. Add the mushrooms, season them with salt and pepper, and cook, stirring occasionally, until lightly browned and tender, about 5 minutes. Push the mushrooms over to one side of the pan and, in the space created, add the butter. Once it's melted, add the shallot and garlic and cook until tender. Add the white wine and cook, stirring, until the wine is reduced by half. Add the thyme leaves, stir everything together, season to taste with salt and pepper, and cook for an additional minute before removing from the heat.

TO ASSEMBLE THE CRESPELLES: Lay the best-looking crespelles down on a work surface and divide the mushroom mixture evenly among them, leaving a little room around the edge. Likewise divide the fontina and arugula. Roll each crespelle around the filling as if you were rolling a cigar and put them seam side down on a baking sheet.

TO MAKE THE SAUCE AND SERVE: Heat the oven to 325°F. Heat the crespelles until the cheese is melted and they are warmed through. Meanwhile, melt the butter in a small saucepan over medium to medium-high heat until it smells nutty and the milk solids in the butter brown (be careful not to let it burn). Add the sage leaves and lemon juice and season with a little kosher salt. Divide the warm crespelles among plates and drizzle the brown butter sauce over them. Finish each plate with a pinch of fleur de sel.

MAKE AHEAD: *Like crepes, crespelles are a wonderful springboard for ad-lib cooks because they take to both sweet and savory fillings. (Roll them around jam and top them with whipped cream for an impromptu dessert.) The batter will keep well for a day, covered, in the refrigerator. Cooked crespelles, separated by parchment and wrapped tightly in plastic wrap, are fine in the fridge for a couple of days and can be frozen in various quantities for longer storage. If you freeze them, add a layer of aluminum foil over the plastic. Defrost frozen crespelles in the refrigerator until pliable.*

Notes

from the sea

SEARED SEA BASS WITH SPICY SOFFRITO   178

PAN-FRIED COD WITH CHORIZO AND CLAM RAGOUT   180

SALMON WITH ROASTED RATATOUILLE AND SAFFRON AÏOLI   182

SEARED SALMON WITH WHITE BEANS AND SPINACH   185

FRITTO MISTO WITH CARAMELLO SAUCE   188

SAFFRON-STEAMED MUSSELS WITH CRÈME FRAÎCHE   192

SPICY CLAM STEW   194

SCALLOP AND PUREED CELERY ROOT GRATINÉE   196

SEARED SEA SCALLOPS WITH SAUCE VERTE AND
TOASTED HAZELNUTS   198

LEMON AÏOLI LOBSTER ROLLS   200

LOBSTER WITH TOASTED SCALLION–MUSHROOM VINAIGRETTE   202

W
hen I was growing up, peas came from a can, herbs from a jar, and cheese out of a plastic sleeve. The exception was fish. Every Friday, following the dietary code of pre–Vatican II Catholicism, we had fish for dinner. And, with the exception of the occasional fish stick, that meant fresh fish picked up by my stepfather down by the waterfront on his way home from work. As often as we could afford, he brought home live lobsters, which we kids promptly set loose on the kitchen floor. On his few vacation days a year, we headed out to Nantasket's Paragon Park and ate lunch at his favorite fish shack, where we gorged ourselves on fried local clams and scallops.

If I learned one food lesson from my stepfather, it was that the best fish goes as quickly as possible from the sea to the plate. All of which makes the way I met my husband, Charlie, ironic. One day when I was working, he came to the back door of the restaurant and tried to talk me into buying frozen fish from his storage facilities. (Unknown to him, Gloucester fishermen were strolling in through the front door to show off what they had caught that morning.) I refused Charlie's fish but asked him to come in for a cup of coffee, which he in turn declined. (I later found out he doesn't like coffee.) Eventually he stopped trying to get me to buy his fish and I stopped trying to get him to drink coffee. Somehow we managed to get married.

Though the fish I cook comes mostly from nearby waters, my style of cooking fish is more reminiscent of Italy and the Mediterranean, where fish is treated simply to let its delicate flavor come through. That's why you won't find many marinades, spice rubs, or coatings in my fish recipes. I pair the seared or roasted fish with pristine seasonal ingredients that complement, not obscure, its flavor.

There are just a couple of tricks to keep in mind when preparing fish. Let it stay out at room temperature for about 20 minutes before cooking; it will cook more evenly if it's not cold to start. Don't salt the fish until after you have cooked it. Salt draws the moisture to the surface, and that can make it difficult to sear the fish well, so you won't get a delicious crust. In fact, if your fish looks wet, pat it dry with a paper towel just before it hits the pan. After giving the fish an initial burst of heat, I often cook it low and slow, finishing it in the oven, which reduces the chance it will overcook.

SEARED SEA BASS WITH SPICY SOFFRITO (PAGE 178)

Seared Sea Bass with Spicy Soffrito

The Italian *soffrito,* usually a mix of chopped garlic, onion, celery, and green pepper, is often used as an aromatic base for soups, stews, and sauces, similar to the French mirepoix. In this recipe, the soffrito is given a spicy turn with the addition of a little jalapeño and crushed red pepper flakes and taken to the forefront as the accompaniment for a beautifully seared piece of fish. For this reason, you may want to take the time to dice the vegetables finely for a pretty presentation. This recipe makes about 1½ cups of soffrito, which is more than you'll need, but having it on hand is like having a culinary secret weapon. (See the photo on page 176.)

1	small white onion, finely chopped
1	small carrot, peeled and finely chopped
1	celery stalk, peeled and cut into small dice
½	yellow bell pepper, seeds removed, finely chopped
½	red bell pepper, seeds removed, finely chopped
½	green bell pepper, seeds removed, finely chopped
½	jalapeño pepper, seeds removed, finely chopped
1	large garlic clove, finely chopped
3	tablespoons extra-virgin olive oil, plus more for cooking the fish and serving
1½	teaspoons sherry vinegar, plus more to taste
1½	teaspoons honey
¼	teaspoon crushed red pepper flakes, plus more to taste
	Kosher salt and freshly ground black pepper
4	sea bass fillets, each about 6 ounces
¼	cup finely chopped fresh parsley
	Fleur de sel (optional)

In a medium saucepan, combine the onion, carrot, celery, all the peppers, garlic, 3 tablespoons olive oil, vinegar, honey, and crushed red pepper flakes. Season with ½ teaspoon salt and a few grinds of pepper. Cook over medium heat, stirring occasionally, until the liquid in the pan has reduced and the vegetables are very tender, 45 minutes to 1 hour. Season to taste with additional salt, pepper, red pepper flakes, and vinegar.

To serve, heat 1 to 2 tablespoons olive oil in a large nonstick skillet over medium-high heat. Pat the fillets dry and add them to the pan skin side down. Cook, undisturbed, until lightly browned on one side, about 3 minutes. Gently turn the fish over and cook until just barely firm to the touch, another 3 to 4 minutes, depending on thickness. (If you can't fit them all in one pan with room around each fillet, cook them either in two pans or in batches, transferring them as they cook to a baking sheet and keeping them warm in a 300°F oven.) Season lightly with salt and pepper and serve each fillet skin side up, over a few tablespoons of the warm soffrito. Finish with a drizzle of extra-virgin olive oil, a sprinkling of parsley, and if you like, a pinch of fleur de sel.

MAKE AHEAD: *Covered and refrigerated, the leftover soffrito will keep for a week. Use it in salads, on sandwiches, as an accompaniment to antipasti, and in soups and stews.*

Buying the Best Seafood—and Keeping It Fresh

Use all of your senses when evaluating fish. Whole fish should look bright and shiny, with scales intact. The gills, if you can see them, should be red, which means the fish is so fresh there is still oxygen present. Judging fillets and steaks is a little trickier, but most species of lean or white fish should be white and almost translucent, with no discoloration. If you can't touch the fish yourself, ask the person behind the counter to give it a poke while you are looking; if it doesn't spring back, it means the fish is old and mushy. Finally, ask to smell the fish you plan to buy; it should *not* smell fishy but should smell fresh and mild. When you get your fish home, rinse it under cold water, pat it dry, wrap it airtight, and keep it in the coldest part of your fridge. Ideally you should cook it the same day you buy it; it will keep for a day or two max.

Do not seal live clams, oysters, mussels, crabs, lobsters, or crayfish in airtight containers (or put them in water), or you will kill them and they will spoil; refrigerate them covered with just a damp cloth or paper towel.

Pan-Fried Cod with Chorizo and Clam Ragout

SERVES 4 This is a great dinner to make when good friends are coming over. It is based on a dish that was brought to the Boston area by Portuguese immigrants, and its ingredients are unpretentious. This beautiful presentation, however—a golden, crisp cod fillet perched on top of slivers of sweet bell pepper, spicy nubbins of sausage, and briny whole clams—elevates the dish to something special. And it's really easy to make.

As for the clams, I love razor clams, especially baked or fried, but I use them mainly because they're so easy to find in and around Boston. If you can't get razor clams, use littlenecks or cockles.

	About 3 tablespoons extra-virgin olive oil
1	garlic clove, finely chopped
1/2	cup dry white wine
2	fresh thyme sprigs
1/4	cup fresh parsley leaves
1/2	teaspoon crushed red pepper flakes
2	pounds clams (littlenecks, cockles, or razors), well scrubbed
3/4	cup diced dried Spanish chorizo (about 1/4 pound)
2	large or 3 medium red bell peppers, stemmed, seeded, and cut into thin slices
2/3	cup Wondra flour or all-purpose flour
4	tablespoons (1/2 stick) unsalted butter
4	skinless cod fillets, each about 6 ounces
	Kosher salt and freshly ground white pepper
	Fleur de sel

In a deep, heavy skillet or Dutch oven, heat about 1 tablespoon of the olive oil over medium heat. Add the garlic and cook until fragrant but not colored, about 1 minute. Add the wine, thyme, half of the parsley, the red pepper flakes, and the clams. Stir to combine. Increase the heat to medium-high, cover the pan, and let the clams steam open, 5 to 7 minutes. With a large slotted spoon, transfer the open clams to a bowl. Discard any unopened clams. Pour the liquid from the pan through a fine-mesh strainer into a small bowl.

Wipe the pan clean and return it to medium heat. Add another tablespoon of olive oil and the chorizo and cook, stirring occasionally, until the sausage begins to render its fat. Add the peppers and cook, stirring occasionally, until the peppers become just

tender, about 10 minutes. Pour the reserved clam juice over the sausage and peppers, leaving any sediment behind. Cook until most of the juice has evaporated.

If using razor clams, remove the clams from their shells and trim away and discard all but the neck, a strip about the size of your finger that is the only edible part of the clam. Add all the clams, plus any accumulated juices, to the pan. Cook, stirring occasionally, until the clams are heated through, about 5 minutes. Keep the ragout warm while you prepare the cod.

Line a cooling rack with paper towels. Spread the flour out on a plate near the stove. Heat a large nonstick skillet over medium-high heat and add the butter and a tablespoon of olive oil. Season the cod fillets with salt and white pepper, lightly dredge them in the flour, and gently shake off any excess. Add the fillets to the pan and cook without moving the fish until deeply golden on one side, about 4 minutes. Flip the fish over and cook the other side until golden brown, another 4 minutes. Remove the fillets from the pan and let them drain on the paper towels for a few minutes.

Reheat the ragout if necessary and stir in the remaining parsley. Place a large spoonful of the ragout in the center of each plate or bowl and place a cod fillet on top. Sprinkle with a bit of fleur de sel and serve immediately.

MAKE AHEAD: *The ragout can be made up to a day ahead of serving. Once cooled, store in the refrigerator, covered. Reheat before serving.*

Salmon with Roasted Ratatouille and Saffron Aïoli

SERVES 4

Ratatouille is a wonderful thing, especially at the height of summer, when squash and eggplants are abundant. But all too often, it's mushy and flavorless. That's because the traditional method can wind up steaming the vegetables instead of browning them. In my version, the vegetables are roasted, which guarantees they get nicely caramelized. They become a tasty bed for the seared salmon. If you happen to have caper berries (the berry of the caper plant, as opposed to the bud, which is what a caper is), they make a jaunty garnish, one per plate, split lengthwise.

1	small zucchini
1	small yellow summer squash
1	small Italian eggplant
	Extra-virgin olive oil
	Kosher salt and freshly ground black pepper
4	medium tomatoes (I like Tasty Toms)
1	garlic clove, cut into slivers
2	tablespoons grapeseed or canola oil
4	pieces salmon fillet, 5–6 ounces each, preferably skin on
	Saffron Aïoli (recipe follows)
12	small fresh basil leaves
	Fleur de sel

Heat the oven to 375°F and line a baking sheet with parchment paper. Cut the zucchini, squash, and eggplant into batons that resemble French fries, about 5 inches long. (An easy way to do this is to start by trimming away the rounded edges to square them off. Then slice them ½ inch thick, stack a few slices, and cut the slices into ½-inch-wide sticks.) You'll want 4 batons for each vegetable, but if you have extra, cook them as well; they're great in salads.

Brush the vegetable batons all over with olive oil, lay them in a single layer on the baking sheet, and season them generously with salt and a little pepper.

Slice off the tops and bottoms of the tomatoes. Top each tomato with a sliver or two of garlic and a drizzle of olive oil and season with salt and pepper. Put the tomatoes on the same baking sheet as the vegetable batons if there is room (or line another sheet with parchment paper). Roast the vegetables until tender but still holding their shape, about 10 minutes. Remove the tomatoes from the baking sheet and let the other vegetables continue roasting until tender and slightly caramelized, another 5 minutes or so. Set aside at room temperature.

Heat the grapeseed oil over medium-high heat in a large skillet. When the pan is hot, add the fillets, skin side down. Cook without moving them until the skin is browned and crispy, 3 to 5 minutes. (Be patient. If you try to lift the salmon too soon, the skin will stick to the pan.) With a spatula, carefully flip the fish over and cook for another 3 to 5 minutes, depending on how you like your salmon cooked. Lightly season the salmon with salt and pepper.

To serve, divide the vegetable batons among four plates. Place the salmon on top. Place a roasted tomato on the plate and top the fish with a dollop of aïoli. Garnish with the basil leaves (3 per plate) and sprinkle with a little fleur de sel.

MAKE AHEAD: *You can cut the vegetables earlier in the day. Refrigerate them in a bowl with a damp paper towel over them. You can also cook them 1 day ahead and reheat them gently when ready to serve.*

Tongs: Just Say No!

My kitchen at home and my restaurant kitchens are tong-free. That may sound surprising, since so many chefs use this tool. But tongs make it too easy to manhandle food. By their design they keep you too far from the pan; I prefer to get as close as safely possible to better judge browning and doneness. More important, tongs don't allow for finesse, which is especially vital when cooking delicate foods like fish fillets. Instead of tongs, use a spatula or two spoons to turn and flip foods. That way you get closer to the food and can cradle and turn it with care.

Saffron Aïoli

MAKES ABOUT 1½ CUPS

The saffron turns this aïoli a gorgeous color. Any leftover sauce is delicious dolloped on grilled fish or served with asparagus.

1	tablespoon saffron threads
1	large egg yolk
1	tablespoon fresh lemon juice
	Kosher salt and freshly ground black pepper
1¼	cups grapeseed or canola oil

In a small pan, heat the saffron in 1 teaspoon water over medium-low heat for a minute to bring out its flavor and color. Let cool.

In a medium bowl, whisk the yolk, saffron mixture, 1 teaspoon of the lemon juice, 1 teaspoon salt, and ½ teaspoon pepper until combined. Slowly drizzle in the oil, whisking nonstop until the mixture begins to emulsify. As the mixture thickens, whisk in the remaining 2 teaspoons lemon juice and continue to whisk in the oil until the aïoli has achieved a thick, mayonnaise-like consistency. (Alternatively, make the aïoli in a small food processor, combining all the ingredients except the oil and 2 teaspoons of the lemon juice. With the motor running, slowly add the oil and reserved lemon juice, processing until thickened.) Taste and adjust the seasonings.

MAKE AHEAD: *You can make the aïoli a day ahead; just keep it covered and refrigerated.*

NOTE: If consuming raw eggs is a health issue for you, look for pasteurized eggs, which are becoming more common at the supermarket and are sold by the dozen just like regular eggs.

STIR   MIXING IT UP IN THE ITALIAN TRADITION

Seared Salmon with White Beans and Spinach

Salmon, white beans, and spinach make a soothing dinner. Colorful, too. But what makes this recipe extraordinary is the olive-lemon relish, which adds an exclamation mark to each bite. (See the photo on page 186.)

¼ cup olive oil
1 pound fresh spinach, tough stems removed, leaves well washed and dried
  Cooked White Beans (page 195) or a 15-ounce can of white beans,
    rinsed and drained
  Kosher salt and freshly ground black pepper
2 tablespoons grapeseed or canola oil
4 salmon fillets, 5–6 ounces each, preferably skin on
  Olive-Lemon Relish (optional; recipe follows)
  Fleur de sel

Heat 2 tablespoons of the olive oil in a large nonstick skillet over medium-high heat. Add a large handful of the spinach and toss gently. As it wilts and makes room in the pan, add more spinach. When all the spinach is wilted, pour off any liquid in the pan, then press on the spinach with the back of a large spoon to release any more liquid and discard that liquid as well. If it is still wet, drain on paper towel and return to the pan. Add the cooked beans and the remaining 2 tablespoons olive oil and gently heat all together. Season to taste with salt and pepper.

To cook the salmon, heat the grapeseed oil over medium-high heat in a large skillet. When the pan is hot, add the fillets, skin side down. Cook without moving them until the skin is browned and crisp, 3 to 5 minutes. (Be patient. If you try to lift the salmon too soon, the skin will stick to the pan.) With a spatula, carefully flip the fish over and cook for another 3 to 5 minutes, depending on how you like your salmon cooked. Season with salt and pepper.

To serve, divide the beans and spinach among four plates. Place the salmon on top, skin side up. Top the salmon with a little of the relish, if using, and dot some around the plate, if you like. Finish with a pinch of fleur de sel.

MAKE AHEAD:
❙ *If using dried beans, you can cook them a day or two ahead, cover, and refrigerate.*
❙ *The bean and spinach mixture can hold, off the heat, for an hour or so before you sear the fish. You can also refrigerate it for up to a day, covered, and gently reheat it before serving.*

Olive-Lemon Relish

MAKES ABOUT 1 CUP

It's amazing what a little of this relish can do for a simple dish like seared salmon (page 185), transforming it into something spectacular, thanks to its intriguing blend of textures and flavors. Also try the relish—based on a recipe from chef Suzanne Goin—on bruschetta or with roasted chicken, grilled eggplant, or lamb.

½	cup pitted, chopped Picholine olives or other green, brine-cured olives
1	lemon, preferably Meyer, peeled and segmented and chopped, juice squeezed and reserved
2	tablespoons extra-virgin olive oil
2	tablespoons chopped fresh parsley
1	small shallot, finely chopped
½	teaspoon honey, plus more to taste if using a regular lemon
½	teaspoon white wine vinegar, preferably Chardonnay
¼	teaspoon kosher salt, plus more to taste
	Freshly ground black pepper to taste

In a medium bowl, gently toss all the ingredients, including the reserved juice, together. Taste and add more honey, salt, and pepper, if needed.

MAKE AHEAD: *The relish will keep for a few days in the refrigerator, covered.*

Segmenting Citrus

When you want pretty sections of citrus without pith and peel, prepare them this way: Cut a little off the top and bottom of the fruit so it can stand upright. Using a sharp knife, remove the peel and pith by slicing close to the flesh with a gentle sawing motion from top to bottom, following the curve of the fruit. Holding the fruit over a bowl to catch the juice, cut away each segment by running the knife down along an interior membrane toward the center. When the knife hits the center of the fruit, turn the blade and slice up the other side of the membrane in the same manner, releasing the individual segment. Continue until all the segments are freed. Squeeze the remaining juice from the membrane and reserve it together with the whole segments.

Fritto Misto with Caramello Sauce

SERVES 6

Fritto misto means "mixed fry" in Italian. This version is based on one I had at a restaurant about an hour's drive north of Milan. The chef, Gualtiero Marchesi, cooked with an Asian influence, and his *fritto misto* was exceedingly light and fresh, like a tempura. Along with the fried vegetables and fish, he served a clear sweet-and-sour sauce, which I have reproduced by adding a little vinegar to a light caramel. Feel free to substitute any vegetables cut to a similar size or just about any thin white fish fillet. I also like to throw in a small handful of fresh tender herbs, such as chervil, parsley, or tarragon.

1¹/₂	cups all-purpose flour
	Kosher salt and freshly ground black pepper
	Sparkling water or club soda (optional)
2	cups sugar
6	tablespoons rice wine vinegar or white wine vinegar
	About 4 cups peanut or canola oil for frying
1–1¹/₂	pounds fillet of sole or other thin white fish fillets
2	large carrots, peeled and thinly sliced (¹/₈ inch thick) on the diagonal
1	large red onion, sliced ¹/₄ inch thick
1	bunch broccoli, trimmed and cut into bite-sized florets
¹/₄	pound green beans, trimmed
¹/₄	cup tender fresh herb leaves, such as chervil, parsley, or tarragon (optional)

In a large bowl, combine the flour, ¹/₂ teaspoon salt, and ¹/₄ teaspoon pepper. Gradually whisk in 2 cups ice-cold water (sparkling water or club soda will give you an even lighter batter), mixing only until blended; it's okay if there are some lumps.

Meanwhile, put the sugar and ¹/₂ cup water in a medium saucepan over medium-low heat and cook, occasionally swirling the pan, until the sugar has dissolved. Increase the heat to medium-high and continue to cook until the sugar has just begun to turn the slightest bit amber, about 10 minutes. The sugar may look cloudy and bubbles will cover the surface, but it will smooth out once the vinegar is added. Take the sugar off the heat and stir in the vinegar, being careful, as it may sputter a bit. Add a pinch of salt, stir again, and return to the heat for 2 minutes more to concentrate the flavors of the sauce. Transfer the sauce to a bowl and let it cool to room temperature. Don't be tempted to taste it until it has cooled considerably; it is very hot.

Fill a large saucepan about halfway with the oil and heat it over medium-high heat until it registers 375°F on a candy/fry thermometer. Cut the fish into strips about 1 inch wide and 2 to 3 inches long and have it, the vegetables, and the herbs, if using, close to the stove. Cover a baking sheet or large plate with paper towels and have that nearby, too.

Because the oil will pick up the flavor of the fish, fry the vegetables first. Using your fingers, submerge a couple of vegetables in the batter, then hold them up over the batter bowl to let any excess batter drip back in. Carefully lower the vegetables into the hot oil. Add more batter-dipped vegetables to the hot oil, being careful not to overcrowd the pan; you will need to fry in batches. Using a slotted spoon or Chinese skimmer, turn the pieces as they cook until all sides are lightly golden, adjusting the heat as needed. Remove the vegetables from the oil with the slotted spoon or skimmer and drain on the paper towels. Continue frying the remaining vegetables. If you're using herbs, occasionally toss some into the oil (without a dip into the batter) along with the vegetables. Next, move on to the fish, battering and frying and draining it similarly. Place the fish, vegetables, and herbs, if using, on a platter or on individual plates, season the *fritto misto* with additional salt, if needed, and serve it with the sauce for dipping.

MAKE AHEAD:

▌ *All of the vegetables as well as the fish can be trimmed and sliced ahead of time, wrapped well in plastic, and refrigerated.*

▌ *The sauce is best made ahead, since it needs time to cool. It can sit at room temperature for a day. You can also refrigerate it, covered, for up to a week, but you will need to warm it gently to thin it.*

▌ *Feel free to make the batter up to a day ahead; cover and refrigerate it.*

FRITTO MISTO WITH CARAMELLO SAUCE (PAGE 188)

SAFFRON-STEAMED MUSSELS
WITH CRÈME FRAÎCHE (PAGE 192)

Saffron-Steamed Mussels with Crème Fraîche

When I use saffron, I use a lot. I'm not going to be half-assed about it and call for the usual "pinch" or "a few threads." So, yes, this recipe contains 2 teaspoons saffron threads. Because the sauce for the mussels is also chock-full of aromatics—garlic, fennel, leeks, and celery—and mellowed with a smidge of crème fraîche, that amount works perfectly, adding saffron's unmistakable fragrance and flavor without overwhelming the dish. (See the photo on page 191.) I love mussels with French fries (see page 280). If you don't go that route, do have some crusty bread around to sop up the sumptuous sauce.

2	large leeks, trimmed (white parts only)
1	celery stalk
½	fennel bulb
2	large or 3 medium tomatoes
6	tablespoons (¾ stick) unsalted butter
3	tablespoons extra-virgin olive oil
2	garlic cloves, finely chopped
2	teaspoons saffron threads
½	teaspoon crushed red pepper flakes
2	cups dry white wine
	Kosher salt
3–4	pounds mussels, scrubbed, beards removed if necessary
½	cup crème fraîche (or ½ cup heavy cream mixed with the juice of ½ lemon)
	Freshly ground black pepper
1	teaspoon fresh lemon juice

Cut the leeks in half lengthwise and then into matchsticks. Rinse well in cold water and dry. Remove and reserve any celery leaves from the stalk, then trim, peel, and thinly slice the stalk. Slice the fennel bulb as thin as possible, preferably on a mandoline, and then cut those slices into matchsticks (keep the fennel separate from the leeks and celery; it and the tomatoes are added at the end). Quarter the tomatoes, scoop out the seeds and pulp, and chop the flesh into tiny dice.

Heat a large pot over medium heat. Melt the butter with 2 tablespoons of the olive oil. Add the leeks, celery, and garlic and cook until softened but not browned, about 7 minutes. Crumble the saffron threads into the pot. Add the red pepper flakes, wine,

$^1\!/_2$ teaspoon salt, and the mussels. Increase the heat to medium-high, stir to distribute the flavorings, cover the pot, and cook, stirring again after a couple of minutes, until a peek inside the pot shows that the mussels have all opened, 7 to 10 minutes. Remove the pot from the heat and, using a slotted spoon, transfer the mussels and vegetables to a large bowl, leaving any liquid behind in the pot. Discard any unopened mussels. Cover the mussels to keep them warm while finishing the sauce.

Pour the cooking liquid into a bowl or measuring cup, leaving any sediment behind. Wipe the pot clean and then return the cooking liquid to it, again leaving any sediment behind. Boil the liquid over high heat until reduced by half. Reduce the heat to medium-high and whisk in the crème fraîche. Reduce to a simmer and cook the sauce until hot, about 2 minutes. Remove from the heat and season to taste with salt and pepper.

Just before serving, combine the fennel, tomatoes, and any reserved celery leaves in a bowl with the remaining 1 tablespoon olive oil and the lemon juice. Season to taste with salt and pepper.

Put the mussels back into the pot and reheat them briefly, if necessary.

Divide the mussels among four to six pasta bowls (or put them in one large bowl and have people serve themselves). Pour the crème fraîche sauce over the mussels and top them with the tomato-fennel mixture. Or, if you're feeling fancy, arrange the mussels around the tomato-fennel mixture and drizzle with the sauce.

MAKE AHEAD: *You can prepare the leeks, celery, fennel, and tomatoes ahead of time; keep them refrigerated separately. Take them out of the refrigerator as you start the leeks to let them warm up a bit, and combine them just before serving.*

Spicy Clam Stew

SERVES 4

Though this stew is mostly about the clams, the addition of tender white beans balances the briny clams and spicy red pepper flakes to create a soothing and hearty dish. For a really quick dinner, you can substitute a drained 15-ounce can of good beans and skip the bean-cooking step. Serve some nice crusty bread with this. Even better, slather thickly sliced bread with olive oil and grill it.

2	tablespoons extra-virgin olive oil, plus more to finish
2	garlic cloves, chopped
3	dozen littleneck or mahogany clams, well scrubbed and rinsed in cold water
1½	cups dry white wine
	Cooked White Beans (recipe follows) or a 15-ounce can white beans, rinsed and drained
2	cups chopped tomatoes (canned or fresh)
1	teaspoon crushed red pepper flakes
2	scallions, thinly sliced

Heat the olive oil in a soup pot or a large, high-sided skillet over medium heat. Add the garlic and cook, stirring, until fragrant and lightly colored, 2 to 3 minutes. Add the clams and wine, increase the heat to medium-high, and cook until the wine reduces by about half. Stir in the cooked beans, tomatoes, and red pepper flakes. Cover the pot and cook until the clams open, about 15 minutes. Take the clams out of the pot with a slotted spoon, discarding any that have not opened, and let the sauce cook for another 5 minutes or so to reduce and intensify in flavor. Return the clams to the pot to reheat them. Divide the stew among four serving bowls, sprinkle with scallions, and drizzle with a little olive oil.

MAKE AHEAD: *You can cook the beans a day or two ahead of making the stew and refrigerate, covered.*

Cooked White Beans

MAKES ABOUT 1½ CUPS

While canned beans will do in many recipes, cooking the beans yourself almost always results in tastier beans, because you can add some additional flavorings. The texture can be better, too: silken and tender, not mushy.

½	carrot, peeled and chopped
½	celery stalk, peeled and chopped
½	small white onion, chopped
1	garlic clove, smashed
1	teaspoon black peppercorns
1	teaspoon coriander seeds
1	bay leaf
¼	teaspoon crushed red pepper flakes
¼	pound (about ¾ cup) dried white beans, such as cannellini, soaked overnight in cold water

Tie up everything but the dried beans in a cheesecloth sachet (see page 224). Drain the beans from their overnight soak and put them in a clean pot. Add water to cover by an inch, add the sachet, and cook over medium-low heat until very tender (bite into some to tell), 1½ to 2 hours. Drain the beans and discard the sachet. Spread the beans out on a baking sheet to cool evenly so they won't get mushy.

NOTE: If you have a pressure cooker, try cooking the beans in it; not only do they cook faster, but their texture is unbelievably silky.

Scallop and Pureed Celery Root Gratinée

SERVES 4 This dish is super-simple yet tastes luxurious. Sweet, rich scallops are nestled in an earthy, creamy celery root puree and topped with crisp bread crumbs, diced Granny Smith apple, and fresh chives.

1	celery root (about $1/2$ pound), peeled and chopped
1	cup whole milk
$3^{1}/_{2}$	tablespoons unsalted butter, at room temperature
	Kosher salt and freshly ground white pepper
1	cup dry bread crumbs, preferably panko (Japanese bread crumbs; see page 209)
$1^{1}/_{2}$–2	tablespoons vegetable oil, preferably grapeseed oil, plus more if needed
1	pound sea or bay scallops, side muscle removed, patted dry
$1/2$	Granny Smith apple, peeled and finely diced
1	tablespoon finely chopped fresh chives
	Celery Emulsion, page 25 (optional)

For the celery root puree, combine the celery root and milk in a small saucepan, bring to a simmer over medium heat, cover, and cook until the celery root is tender when pierced with a metal skewer or toothpick, about 20 minutes. Transfer the celery root and the liquid to a blender and add $1^{1}/_{2}$ tablespoons of the butter, 1 teaspoon salt, and a few good grinds of white pepper. Puree and pass through a fine-mesh strainer into a saucepan. Keep the puree warm on the stove.

Melt the remaining 2 tablespoons butter in a small saucepan, add the bread crumbs, and toss. Keep the bread crumbs warm on the stove.

To sear the scallops, heat $1^{1}/_{2}$ tablespoons of the oil in a large nonstick skillet over medium-high heat. When the oil is good and hot, add the scallops in batches, leaving plenty of space between them so they sear rather than steam. Let them cook, undisturbed, until very well browned, 1 to 2 minutes. Use a couple of spoons to turn each one over gently and cook, adding more oil, if needed, until barely cooked through, another 1 to 3 minutes, depending on thickness.

Divide the celery root puree among four plates. Season the scallops with salt and white pepper and divide them among the dishes, putting the scallops on top of the puree. Divide the buttery bread crumbs among the plates, sprinkling them over the scallops. Garnish with the diced apple, the chopped chives, and a spoonful of celery emulsion, if you like.

STIR MIXING IT UP IN THE ITALIAN TRADITION

MAKE AHEAD: *You can make the celery root puree and the celery emulsion a day or two ahead of assembling the dish, cover with plastic wrap, and refrigerate. Buzz the emulsion with a hand blender just before serving.*

NOTE: To serve this as a traditional baked gratin, don't sear the scallops. Leave bay scallops whole; quarter the sea scallops. Divide the celery root puree among four individual gratin dishes. Season the scallops with salt and pepper and place them on top of the puree, dividing them among the dishes. Sprinkle them with the buttery bread crumbs, dividing the crumbs evenly. Broil the gratins briefly to brown the crumbs lightly, then finish cooking in a 350°F oven until the puree is hot and the scallops are cooked through, 6 to 8 minutes. Remove the gratins from the oven and garnish with the diced apple, chopped chives, and a spoonful of celery emulsion, if you like.

Seared Sea Scallops with Sauce Verte
and Toasted Hazelnuts

Serving sea scallops with a boldly flavored fresh herb sauce is a great way to balance their inherent richness. Toasted hazelnuts contribute crunch but also a little fat, which means you don't have to add the butter that too often makes scallops too rich. Serve the scallops with Olive Oil–Glazed Baby Vegetables (page 272); green beans, steamed or boiled, also go well with the sauce.

If your hazelnuts have skins, rub them against each other in a paper towel or a clean dish towel to remove much of their papery skins (don't worry if some remains), then chop and toast as directed.

Kosher salt

Small bunch fresh chives

6 fresh chervil sprigs

4 fresh parsley sprigs, stems removed

4 fresh tarragon sprigs, stems removed

2 garlic cloves, peeled

2 anchovy fillets, rinsed well and chopped

1 tablespoon capers, rinsed well

1 small shallot, chopped

Freshly ground black pepper

6 tablespoons extra-virgin olive oil, plus more if needed

1 cup chopped skinned hazelnuts

1 pound (about 12 if very large) sea scallops, side muscles removed

To make the sauce verte, bring a small saucepan of salted water to a boil. Fill a medium bowl with ice water. Add the chives, chervil, parsley, and tarragon to the boiling water and blanch for 8 to 10 seconds. Immediately remove with a slotted spoon and place in the ice water to stop the cooking process and retain the herbs' bright green color. Remove the herbs from the water and squeeze out the excess. Chop the herbs coarsely and put them in a blender. Add the garlic cloves, anchovies, capers, shallot, 1 teaspoon salt, a few grinds of pepper, and 4 tablespoons of the oil and puree until smooth. If too thick, add a little more oil.

To toast the hazelnuts, heat the oven to 350°F. Spread the nuts out on a small baking sheet and toast in the oven until fragrant and lightly browned, 8 to 10 minutes.

To sear the scallops, heat the remaining 2 tablespoons oil in a large nonstick skillet over medium-high heat. When the oil is good and hot, add the scallops in batches, leaving space between them so they sear rather than steam. Let them cook, undisturbed, until very well browned and crisp, 1 to 2 minutes. Use a couple of spoons to turn each one over gently and cook, adding more oil, if needed, until barely cooked through, another 1 to 3 minutes, depending on size.

Divide the scallops among four plates and drizzle about 2 tablespoons of the sauce verte over each serving. Divide the hazelnuts among the plates, sprinkling them on and around the scallops.

MAKE AHEAD: *You can make the sauce verte up to 1 day ahead and keep it covered and refrigerated.*

Make Sure Your Scallops Are "Dry"

When buying scallops, ask the fishmonger if the scallops are dry, which means they haven't been soaked in a sodium solution. The solution whitens and plumps the scallops, but when you cook them, all the liquid leaches out, making it impossible to give them that flavorful brown crust you want. In the display case, dry scallops will look darker, more tan than white, and will not be sitting in liquid.

Lemon Aïoli Lobster Rolls

If there is a secret to this classic lobster roll, it's that I use a *lot* of lobster, freshly cooked and cut into substantial yet easy-to-eat pieces. If I use mayonnaise, it has to be Hellmann's, and I brighten it with a touch of fresh lemon juice. More often, though, I combine the lobster with a little lemon aïoli, which has a fresher flavor than any jarred mayonnaise. I also add a little celery, chopping it very finely so there's not too much crunch. The lobster salad then is stuffed (overstuffed, actually) into a top-split hot dog roll that's been lavishly buttered and browned on the griddle.

To round out the plate, try the fries on page 280, the slaw on page 264, and the easy homemade pickles on page 267.

I use the same lobster salad to make my signature lobster BLT, serving the lobster on toasted ciabatta rolls and topping it with a couple of slices of crisp bacon (preferably Niman Ranch applewood-smoked bacon) and a few pieces of the tomato confit on page 28. (See the photo on the opposite page.) Instead of fries, I serve the BLT with homemade potato chips (page 267).

4	lobsters, each about 1¼ pounds
1	cup Lemon Aïoli (page 47) or 1 cup Hellmann's mayonnaise mixed with 1 teaspoon fresh lemon juice
½	cup peeled, very finely chopped celery
	Kosher salt and freshly ground black pepper
4	top-split hot dog rolls (I like Pepperidge Farm)
4	tablespoons (½ stick) unsalted butter, at room temperature
1	tablespoon finely chopped fresh chives

Bring a large pot of water to a boil and fill a clean sink or very large bowl with ice water. Cook the lobsters, covered, for about 10 minutes. Plunge them into the ice water to halt the cooking. Twist the tails off the bodies. Cut each tail lengthwise into 2 pieces, removing the intestinal tracts. Remove the claw meat by snapping off the little pincers first. Using the back of a heavy chef's knife or good kitchen scissors, crack open the claws and remove the meat. Remove the knuckle meat too. Cut the meat into generous bite-sized pieces. Gently toss the lobster meat with the aïoli and celery. Season to taste with salt and pepper and refrigerate until ready to serve.

To serve, open up the rolls as wide as you can to accommodate all the lobster meat. Butter the hot dog rolls on the outside and toast them on a griddle or in a skillet until nicely golden brown. Taste the lobster salad again to see if it needs more seasoning (cold foods often do) and divide it among the 4 rolls, overstuffing them. Garnish the lobster with the chives.

MAKE AHEAD: *As fresh as possible is best for lobster salad, but you can make it a few hours ahead and keep it refrigerated, covered.*

Lobster with Toasted Scallion–Mushroom Vinaigrette

SERVES 2 AS A

MAIN COURSE OR 4

AS AN APPETIZER

Plump, buttery pieces of lobster topped with a toasty, tangy vinaigrette—this is perfect late-summer, dinner-on-the-deck eating. Serve the lobster on top of a light-as-air blini studded with fresh corn kernels (page 271) or some crusty bread.

FOR THE VINAIGRETTE

1   bunch scallions

3/4   cup plus 2 tablespoons grapeseed oil or mild olive oil, plus more for
        cooking the mushrooms

4   ounces wild mushrooms, preferably chanterelles, coarsely chopped
        (about 1/2 cup)

1   shallot, finely chopped

2   teaspoons sherry vinegar
        Kosher salt and freshly ground black pepper

FOR THE LOBSTER

2   lobsters, each about 2 pounds

8   tablespoons (1 stick) butter, cut into pieces

1   small fresh thyme sprig
        Kosher salt

TO MAKE THE VINAIGRETTE: Trim the roots and tops off the scallions and chop them into 5-inch lengths. (Finely slice some of the remaining greens and reserve as a garnish.) Heat the 2 tablespoons oil in a skillet over medium-high heat. Add the 5-inch scallion pieces and cook, stirring occasionally, until they are toasty brown all over, about 5 minutes. Remove from the pan and drain on a couple of layers of paper towels. Add a little more oil to the pan, if needed, and when it is nice and hot, add the mushrooms. Cook, stirring occasionally, until they, too, are a nice golden brown, and drain on paper towel. In a bowl, combine the shallot and the vinegar and let sit for 5 minutes while the mushrooms cool a bit. Add the 3/4 cup oil and whisk to combine. Add the toasted scallions and mushrooms, season with a little salt and pepper, and whisk gently to combine.

TO PARCOOK THE LOBSTER: Bring a large pot of water to a boil. Fill a clean sink or a very large bowl with ice water. Boil the lobsters for 5 minutes (they will not be cooked through) and then plunge them into the ice water. Twist the tails off the bodies, remove the meat from the tails, and cut each tail lengthwise into 2 pieces, removing the intestinal tracts. Remove the claw meat by snapping off the little pincers first. Using the back of a heavy chef's knife or good kitchen scissors, crack open the claws and remove the meat in a single piece. Remove the knuckle meat too. If not finishing the dish right away, refrigerate the lobster meat until ready to use.

TO SERVE: Heat 1 tablespoon water in a medium saucepan over medium heat. Whisk in the butter a little at a time to create a smooth, emulsified sauce. Add the thyme sprig, a pinch of salt, and the lobster meat. Finish cooking the lobster in the butter, occasionally spooning the butter over the pieces, for about 5 minutes.

Divide the lobster among two or four plates. Drizzle the vinaigrette on and around it, dividing the mushrooms and scallions in the vinaigrette among the plates. Garnish with the reserved sliced scallions and dot the plate with some of the leftover lobster cooking butter.

MAKE AHEAD:

▐ *You can make the vinaigrette up to 2 days ahead and refrigerate, covered. Let it come to room temperature or warm it gently before serving.*

▐ *The parcooked lobster will hold for at least a day if well wrapped and refrigerated.*

LEMONY BREADED CHICKEN CUTLETS   208

TALEGGIO-STUFFED PROSCIUTTO-WRAPPED CHICKEN WITH TOMATO
AND OLIVE SALAD   210

BRAISED CHICKEN THIGHS WITH ROSEMARY AND GARLIC   213

POULET AU PAIN   215

CORNISH GAME HEN CACCIATORE WITH CREAMY
MASCARPONE POLENTA   218

SEARED DUCK BREASTS WITH SPICED CHERRIES   222

DUCK CONFIT   225

CRISPED DUCK CONFIT WITH KUMQUAT MARMALADE   228

SPICE-RUBBED ROAST GOOSE   229

chicken, duck, and a goose

A friend of mine told me that every time the magazine where she works publishes another article on the best way to roast, braise, or sauté a chicken, the editors get complaints from readers who say they are tired of it. Yet when the magazine does surveys to find out which recipes score the best, guess what always comes out on top? Chicken.

Like those readers, I have a love-hate attitude toward chicken. Ask me what my favorite foods are, and chicken will never make the list. But ask me what I had for lunch yesterday, and I'll probably mention salad topped with slices of seared chicken breast. I guess that old saying about familiarity breeding contempt is true of chicken, too.

Like a pair of sweatpants, chicken can feel a bit utilitarian. Can't think of what to make for dinner tonight? How about chicken? And while you would never list old sweats among your favorite outfits, they sure feel great when you slip them on. The dishes I've included in this chapter fall mainly into that comfort-food category: a rosemary-infused braise, a grown-up version of breaded chicken cutlets, and roasted chicken encased in bread— how much more comforting can you get than *that*?

There is, however, an entire world of poultry beyond chicken that is even more flavorful, and elegant besides. I'm talking about duck and goose and those little game birds we chefs love so much. If you can cook a chicken, you can cook these birds, too. Indeed, my recipe for roast goose is as straightforward as roasting a chicken, and the duck with spiced cherries is actually quite quick to make.

Whichever kind of bird you're cooking, try to buy the best. If you can afford it, buy only organic and preferably free-range or free-roaming. These birds taste better (and are better for you) than their poor factory-farmed, hormone- and antibiotic-injected relations. I like the birds from Bell & Evans, available in supermarkets. D'Artagnan birds, which are carried in butcher shops and some supermarkets, are also a good choice; you can mail-order them as well (www.dartagnan.com).

POULET AU PAIN (PAGE 215)

Lemony Breaded Chicken Cutlets

SERVES 6

I often pretend I'm making this chicken just for my daughter, Marchesa, but actually I love it myself. Crisp, browned, and boneless, it has fresh herbs in the panko topping and is served with a buttery sauce. Cutlets like these are usually pan-fried, but with that method you risk burning the coating before the chicken cooks through. I partially cook the cutlets before patting the coating on; then I crisp them up in the oven. Serve with Roasted Eggplant with Golden Raisin–Pine Nut Vinaigrette and Feta (page 75) or Braised Tuscan Kale (page 276).

12	tablespoons (1¹⁄₂ sticks) unsalted butter, at room temperature
¹⁄₄	cup chopped fresh herbs (I like a mix of parsley, tarragon, and chives, but any tender herbs will work)
	Kosher salt and freshly ground black pepper
6	boneless, skinless chicken breasts, tenderloins removed and reserved for another use
¹⁄₂	cup all-purpose flour
4–6	tablespoons olive oil
2	cups chicken broth, preferably Roasted Chicken Stock (page 108)
1¹⁄₂	cups panko (Japanese bread crumbs)
1–2	lemons

In a small bowl, combine 8 tablespoons (1 stick) of the butter with the fresh herbs, using a fork or wooden spoon to distribute the herbs well. Season generously with salt and pepper.

Flatten each chicken breast to an even thickness by covering it with plastic wrap (or putting it in a food storage bag) and whacking the thickest end with a meat mallet or a heavy pan until the breast has a uniform thickness of about ¹⁄₃ inch.

Lightly salt and pepper the chicken breasts on all sides. Pour the flour onto a plate and dredge the breasts in the flour, coating well on both sides and shaking off the excess. Heat 2 tablespoons of the olive oil in a large skillet over medium-high heat (the chicken should sizzle when it hits the pan). Add 2 or 3 of the chicken breasts, being sure there is room around each. Cook until golden brown, about 2 minutes, then flip and brown the other side similarly. Transfer the chicken to a baking sheet and repeat the browning with the remaining breasts, adding more oil as necessary. (The chicken will not be fully cooked at this point.)

Heat the chicken broth in a saucepan over high heat until reduced by two thirds (there will be about $^2/_3$ cup left in the pan). Remove the pan from the heat.

Heat the oven to 375°F. Put the panko in a wide, shallow bowl. Melt the herb butter in a small saucepan over low heat and pour the melted butter over the panko. Season with a little salt and pepper and toss to mix well. Spread the panko evenly over the top of the chicken breasts. Pat the crumbs down with your fingers so they completely cover each piece. Place the breasts on a baking sheet and bake until the chicken is fully cooked and the crumbs are lightly browned, about 10 minutes (12 minutes if the chicken was refrigerated); an instant-read thermometer inserted into the thickest part of the chicken will read 165°F.

Bring the chicken broth back to a boil. Reduce to a simmer and whisk in the remaining 4 tablespoons butter, about $^1/_2$ tablespoon at a time. Add the juice from $^1/_2$ lemon and season with salt and pepper. Drizzle the sauce over the chicken and serve with lemon wedges, if you like.

MAKE AHEAD: *You can keep the browned (but not breaded) chicken at room temperature for up to half an hour before continuing with the recipe; otherwise, refrigerate it, covered with plastic wrap, for up to 24 hours. Let it warm up at room temperature if you refrigerated it before putting on the panko.*

Panko Perfection

When I want a crisp cutlet or a crunchy topping for a gratin, I reach for panko. These Japanese bread crumbs are coarse, irregularly shaped, and look more like flakes than crumbs. Because of their large surface area, they don't compress as much as regular bread crumbs when you pat them on; they feel lighter and almost lacy—more delicate and tender—and they stay crisp longer. Panko also absorbs less oil when fried. You will find panko at Asian markets and in many supermarkets in the Asian or international section or with the other bread crumbs.

Taleggio-Stuffed Prosciutto-Wrapped Chicken with Tomato and Olive Salad

SERVES 6   This recipe starts with boneless, skinless chicken breasts and utterly transforms them. The prosciutto wrap adds flavor, color, and texture and keeps the chicken extremely moist. Inside, creamy, full-flavored Taleggio cheese slowly melts so that when you cut into the breast, you encounter the cheese's earthy aroma before enjoying the way its ooziness plays off the bright salad. Because you can make most of the recipe ahead, and because it looks just awesome on the plate, this is a good one for company. For weeknight cooking, you can forgo the salad, but do serve the chicken with something crisp and bright to counter the cheesy, salty goodness.

FOR THE CHICKEN

6	boneless, skinless chicken breasts
6	ounces Taleggio (or another full-flavored creamy cheese), sliced into 6 pieces
	Kosher salt and freshly ground black pepper
2	tablespoons fresh tarragon leaves
12	thin slices prosciutto
2	tablespoons extra-virgin olive oil, plus more as needed

FOR THE SALAD (OPTIONAL)

3	large ripe tomatoes, cored, halved, seeded, and each half cut into 6 pieces
1/2	cup pitted Kalamata olives
4	small celery stalks, peeled and sliced very thinly on an exaggerated diagonal
1	bunch fresh parsley, tough stems trimmed away, well washed and dried
1/2	medium red onion, very thinly sliced
3	tablespoons extra-virgin olive oil
1	tablespoon fresh lemon juice
1/4	teaspoon kosher salt
	Freshly ground black pepper

TO MAKE THE CHICKEN: Using a sharp knife, cut a 2-inch pocket lengthwise along the thickest side of each breast, being careful not to cut through completely to the other side. Put a piece of cheese in each pocket and press the breast closed. Season the breasts with a little salt and pepper and then top them with the tarragon. Wrap the prosciutto around the breasts; you'll need 2 pieces per breast to completely cover the chicken; the prosciutto can overlap a bit.

Heat the oven to 375°F. Heat the oil in a large skillet over medium to medium-high heat (the chicken should sizzle when it hits the pan). Sear the breasts, in batches, 4 to 5 minutes per side, adding more oil as necessary to keep the bottom of the pan coated. (Don't worry if the breasts are not fully cooked at this point, as they will be finished in the oven.)

Put the seared chicken breasts on a baking sheet and bake until cooked through, 8 to 12 minutes (an instant-read thermometer inserted into the thickest part of the chicken will read 165°F). Remove the chicken from the oven and let it rest while you toss the salad.

TO MAKE THE OPTIONAL SALAD: Combine the tomatoes, olives, celery, parsley, and onion in a medium bowl. In a small bowl, whisk together the olive oil and lemon juice. Season with the salt and a few grinds of pepper.

TO SERVE: Divide the salad among six plates and place the chicken on top of or alongside the salad. For an even prettier presentation, you can slice each breast diagonally into 4 pieces before plating it. Serve immediately, while the cheese is still oozing.

MAKE AHEAD:

▌ *The seared breasts can sit at room temperature for up to an hour and can be refrigerated for up to 24 hours, covered with plastic wrap, before serving. The cold chicken will require a few more minutes in the oven.*

▌ *The salad components can be assembled, but not dressed, up to a day ahead; refrigerate the salad, covered with plastic wrap, until ready to serve.*

Braised Chicken Thighs with Rosemary and Garlic

SERVES 4   I sometimes forget just how delicious braised chicken can be. When you make this, your kitchen fills with a wonderful fragrance. Serve with Pommes Puree (page 278) and you have a truly satisfying meal.

2	tablespoons vegetable oil, plus more as needed
8	skin-on, bone-in chicken thighs, trimmed of excess fat and skin
	Kosher salt and freshly ground black pepper
3	garlic cloves, sliced
1½	tablespoons finely chopped fresh rosemary
1	cup dry white wine
1½	cups chicken broth, preferably Roasted Chicken Stock (page 108)
2	tablespoons chopped fresh parsley
	Fresh lemon juice to taste
	Fleur de sel

Heat the oil in a large skillet over medium-high heat. Season the thighs with salt and pepper and cook them skin side down without moving them until the skin is crisp and golden, 6 to 8 minutes. If your pan can't accommodate all 8 with space in between, sear the chicken in batches. Use a spatula to flip the chicken over carefully and sear the other side for 2 to 3 minutes. Remove the thighs from the pan and pour off all but about 1 tablespoon of the fat. Lower the heat to medium, add the garlic, and cook, stirring, until fragrant and lightly colored (don't let it brown), about 2 minutes. Add the rosemary and cook for another minute. Add the wine, bring to a boil, and cook until the wine reduces by about three quarters. Add the broth.

Return the chicken to the pan, cover with the lid slightly ajar, and simmer, stirring occasionally, until the chicken is cooked through and fork-tender and the liquid in the pan has reduced by about two thirds, about 30 minutes. Transfer the chicken to plates or a serving platter and keep warm. If necessary, return the sauce to the heat to reduce further. Stir the parsley and lemon juice into the sauce in the pan and pour the sauce over the chicken. Sprinkle with a little fleur de sel and serve.

MAKE AHEAD: *The chicken can be made 2 days ahead (without the parsley and lemon juice) and refrigerated, covered. Reheat it over low heat, partially covered, until heated through, about 10 to 15 minutes. Add the parsley and lemon juice just before serving.*

Poulet au Pain

Warm fresh-baked bread and tender roasted chicken: two of the most comforting foods in the world, right? In this recipe, you put them together, wrapping a whole chicken in bread dough. Because the meat cooks so gently, it's amazingly tender and juicy, which is good, because you also have the crackerlike bread to dunk into those juices. Once the chicken is cooked and cooled, it's easy to transport. Bring it on a picnic and let people pull it apart with their hands.

3	cups all-purpose flour, plus more as needed
1½	teaspoons kosher salt, plus more as needed
½	teaspoon sugar
12	tablespoons (1½ sticks) unsalted butter, cut into pieces
1	tablespoon olive oil
2	celery stalks, peeled and chopped
1	medium carrot, peeled and chopped
1	medium onion, chopped
1	tablespoon chopped fresh rosemary
1	3- to 3½-pound chicken, giblets and excess fat and skin removed, bird patted dry
	Freshly ground black pepper
1	large egg, beaten

To make the bread dough, combine the flour, salt, and sugar in the bowl of a stand mixer fitted with the paddle attachment. Add the butter and mix with the paddle, stopping the mixer occasionally to break up bigger chunks of butter with your hand. Add ½ cup water and continue mixing until the dough begins to come together. At this point, turn off the mixer and switch to the dough hook (scraping all the dough off the paddle first, of course). Knead the dough with the hook until it comes together in one mass, 1 to 2 minutes. Turn the dough out onto a lightly floured surface and continue to knead it by hand, pushing it away from you with the heel of your hand, folding it over, giving it a quarter turn, and pushing it away again until it feels nice and elastic. If the dough is very sticky, add a little more flour to it as you knead. Wrap the dough in plastic wrap and refrigerate it for at least 30 minutes.

Meanwhile, heat the olive oil in a medium skillet over medium heat. Add the celery, carrot, onion, rosemary, and a pinch of salt and cook, stirring occasionally, until the vegetables are just tender but not colored, 8 minutes. Let cool.

Clip the chicken wings off at the body and save for making stock or discard. Season the chicken liberally inside and out with salt and pepper. Stuff the bird with the cooled vegetables and tie the legs together with kitchen twine.

Heat the oven to 400°F. On a very lightly floured surface, roll the dough out to 1/8 inch thick; this will take some muscle. If the dough is very stubborn, let it rest for a few minutes before trying to roll it some more. Put the chicken on the dough breast side down and wrap the dough up and around the bird, encompassing it completely and overlapping the dough. (If there is a lot of overlap, trim the dough.) Pinch the seams together to keep them closed. Turn the bird over and put the bird seam side down on a baking sheet.

Brush the dough all over with the egg and sprinkle it lightly all over with salt. Bake until the chicken is cooked through and the bread is a lovely golden brown, 1 to 1 1/2 hours, depending on the size of the chicken (an instant-read thermometer inserted through the crust into the breast should read 170°F). Let cool for at least an hour, preferably 2, before tearing it apart and serving.

MAKE AHEAD: *You can refrigerate the dough-wrapped chicken, covered in plastic wrap, for a day before cooking it.*

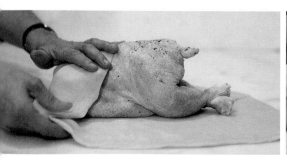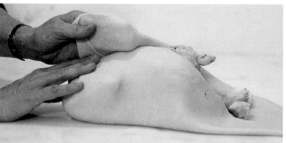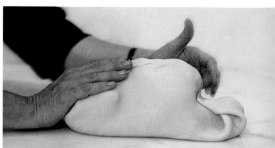

Cornish Game Hen Cacciatore
with Creamy Mascarpone Polenta

Cornish game hens (also called Rock Cornish hens) are basically miniature chickens, each about 1½ pounds. While they're great to roast whole—kids especially love them—they also braise beautifully and in less than half the time of full-sized chicken pieces. What results is juicy, tender meat and a deeply flavored sauce that's wonderful served over a bowl of creamy polenta.

2   Cornish game hens
2   tablespoons extra-virgin olive oil
1   onion, thinly sliced
1   red bell pepper, stemmed, seeded, and thinly sliced
2   hot Italian peppers, stemmed, seeded, and thinly sliced
3   garlic cloves, very finely chopped
5   plum tomatoes, seeded and chopped
½   cup dry red wine
1½ cups chicken broth, preferably Roasted Chicken Stock (page 108)
    Kosher salt and freshly ground black pepper
    Creamy Mascarpone Polenta (page 286)
1   tablespoon chopped fresh parsley
    Fleur de sel

Using a sharp chef's knife, cut the hens into 6 bone-in pieces each: breasts, legs, and thighs. Remove the thighbones, if you like, though it's fine to leave them in for a more rustic dish. (Use what is left over—wings, backbones, and possibly thighbones—to make the stock, if you like.)

In a large deep skillet, heat the olive oil over medium-high heat and place the chicken skin side down in the pan with some space between the pieces. Cook on one side until nicely browned and then turn the pieces over to brown on the other side, 6 to 8 minutes total. Remove the chicken from the pan. Lower the heat to medium and add the onion, bell pepper, hot peppers, and garlic to the pan. Cook, stirring, until the vegetables are soft and just lightly browned, 8 to 10 minutes. Add the tomatoes and wine to the pan, increase the heat to medium-high, and cook, stirring occasionally, until the wine has reduced by about half, 5 to 10 minutes. Return the chicken to the pan and continue cooking until the wine has reduced a little more. Add the broth, reduce the heat to a gentle simmer, and cook until the chicken is cooked through; the breasts should cook through in 6 to 7 minutes and the thighs and legs in 8 to 9 minutes. Remove the meat as it's cooked and reserve it. Continue cooking the liquid in the pan until it has reduced by about half; this should take about 30 minutes. Season to taste with salt and pepper and return the chicken to the pan briefly to reheat.

To serve, divide the polenta among four wide shallow bowls. Spoon the cacciatore sauce over it and then top it with the chicken pieces, evenly dividing them among the bowls. Finish with the chopped parsley and a sprinkle of fleur de sel.

How to Cut Up a Cornish Game Hen or Chicken

To cut up a Cornish game hen or chicken, cut the wings off at the body. Pull one leg away from the body to loosen it (you can do this by lifting the chicken up by the leg) and then slice through the skin that connects the thigh to the body to expose the inside of the thigh. Bend the whole leg away from the body until the thighbone pops from the hip socket. Separate the joint by cutting between the ball and socket. Cut the thigh away from the body by slicing as close to the body as possible. Cut the leg from the thigh by following the line of fat on the underside; it's a good guide to finding the joint that separates the two pieces. (You'll be cutting closer to the leg than you might think looks right.) To remove the breasts with the bone in, free the backbone by starting at the tail end and cutting through the ribs. Chop through the collarbone to take off the back completely. You will have the whole breast. To cut it into 2 pieces, cut down through the breastbone with some force.

CORNISH GAME HEN CACCIATORE (PAGE 218)

CREAMY MASCARPONE POLENTA (PAGE 286)

Seared Duck Breasts with Spiced Cherries

SERVES 4

Duck is one of my favorite things to eat, especially when it's got some nice crispy skin on it. Though I cook it year-round, the accompaniments in this dish celebrate early summer, specifically the arrival of fresh cherries in June and July. I stew the cherries with fragrant warm spices before serving them on sliced duck breasts. The sweet, tangy topping is a perfect foil for the rich, gamy meat. I like to serve the duck with Pommes Puree (page 278) or Creamy Mascarpone Polenta (page 286). Or try it with Braised Tuscan Kale (page 276). To make serving it all go smoothly, I make the cherries in advance.

FOR THE CHERRIES

1	tablespoon black peppercorns
1	cinnamon stick
1	star anise
1	clove
1½	pounds sweet cherries, pitted
¼	cup sugar
½	cup dry red wine
¼	teaspoon red wine vinegar

FOR THE DUCK

4	boneless, skin-on Pekin duck breasts or 2 Moulard duck breasts
	Kosher salt and freshly ground black pepper

FOR SERVING

	Fleur de sel
2	tablespoons chopped fresh chives
1	tablespoon pulled-apart chive blossoms (optional)

TO MAKE THE CHERRIES: Tie the peppercorns, cinnamon stick, star anise, and clove in a cheesecloth sachet (see page 224). In a medium saucepan, combine the cherries, sugar, red wine, and sachet and bring to a simmer over medium-low heat. Reduce the heat to low and cook, stirring occasionally, until the liquid is reduced to a syrup and the cherries are quite soft, 45 minutes to an hour. Remove and discard the spice sachet, stir in the red wine vinegar, and remove the cherries from the heat. (You can serve the cherries warm or at room temperature.)

TO MAKE THE DUCK: Season the duck breasts with salt and pepper. Heat a large skillet over medium heat. Add the duck breasts skin side down and cook for a few minutes to brown the skin. Reduce the heat to medium-low and continue cooking to render more fat and further crisp and brown the skin, about 12 minutes more. Pour or spoon off some of the accumulated fat and turn the breasts over to finish cooking on the other side. (To check for doneness, use an instant-read thermometer; 135° to 140°F is right for medium-rare, which is how I like it.) Transfer the cooked breasts to a plate or platter and let them rest for 6 to 8 minutes in a warm place.

TO SERVE: Slice the duck and divide it among four plates and top with the spiced cherries. Finish with a pinch of fleur de sel and a sprinkling of chopped chives and chive blossoms, if you have them.

MAKE AHEAD: *The spiced cherries will keep for up to a week, covered and refrigerated.*

How to Tie a Cheesecloth Sachet

Occasionally I call for tying herbs, spices, or aromatics in a cheesecloth sachet. I do this so that after the herb or spice has given up its flavor to the soup, braise, or marinade, it can be easily retrieved, leaving no physical trace behind. To make a sachet, cut a large single-layer square of cheesecloth (it should be large enough so that when you place your ingredients in the center of it, you can pull up the edges with room to tie). To remove any loose fibers from the cloth, rinse it under water and squeeze it dry. Lay it on your work surface and pile the aromatic ingredients in the center. Gather the edges like a beggar's pouch and tightly wrap some kitchen twine around the top where the cloth is gathered to keep it closed. If you're going to submerge the sachet in a large pot, consider leaving a tail on the twine so you can tie the sachet to the handle of the pot once you have added it. This trick makes finding and collecting the sachet a snap.

Duck Confit

SERVES 4   With tender meat and amazingly crisp skin, what's not to love about duck confit? You can buy it, but confiting—curing with a mixture of salt and sugar and spices and then cooking the meat slowly in its own fat—is one of those old-fashioned techniques that is truly rewarding. Nothing tastes quite like it. For ideas on how to use duck confit, see page 227, or follow the recipe on page 228.

Duck and duck fat can be ordered from Hudson Valley Foie Gras (www.hudsonvalleyfoiegras.com) or from D'Artagnan (www.dartagnan.com).

8	duck legs or 2 whole ducks
1½	teaspoons dried thyme
1½	teaspoons fennel seeds
1½	teaspoons black peppercorns
1½	teaspoons coriander seeds
1	bay leaf
1	cup kosher salt
½	cup sugar
6–8	cups duck fat

If using duck legs, trim the excess fat and skin. If using whole ducks, cut off the legs and cut away each half breast. Trim any excess skin and fat from the legs and carcasses and save for rendering, if you like. (To render the fat, put the skin and fat in a small saucepan and gently heat over low heat until the clear fat is released and the skin is golden and crisp; this will take about 1½ hours. Strain the fat and use it for your confit—you will need more than this amount—and save the cracklings to eat or serve over a salad.)

Grind the thyme, fennel, peppercorns, coriander, and bay leaf together in a spice grinder or a coffee grinder dedicated to spices and combine the ground spices with the salt and sugar. (This makes more than you will need for the confit, but it keeps well and is delicious sprinkled on roasts of all kinds.)

Put the legs and the breasts, if using, in a baking dish and sprinkle them with about ½ cup of the curing mixture. Cover with plastic wrap and refrigerate for at least a few hours, preferably overnight.

Heat the oven to 250°F. In a pot large enough to hold the duck pieces, heat the duck fat over medium heat to melt it. Pat the duck dry and slide the pieces into the melted fat. The fat should completely cover the duck. (If not, you can add more melted duck fat or even vegetable oil to cover.)

Cook in the oven until the meat is very tender but not falling apart, 3 to 4 hours. (When the thighbones loosen fairly easily from the legs, the meat is cooked.) Allow the duck to cool in the fat at room temperature.

Remove the duck pieces from the pot while the fat is still liquid (though cool) and transfer them to a parchment-lined baking sheet. Wrap the baking sheet well in plastic and refrigerate it. The duck confit will easily keep for a week this way. For longer storage, see below.

You can reuse the fat that's left behind. To do this, gently melt the fat, strain it through a fine-mesh strainer, leaving any solids behind, and store it in the refrigerator. You can then use it one or two more times for confit. (After a couple of reuses, the curing mixture left behind will make the fat too salty.)

To prepare the confit for serving, heat the oven to 350°F. Melt a tablespoon or two of the duck fat from the confit in a large skillet (or use vegetable oil) over medium-high heat. Add as many pieces of confit as will fit without touching, skin side down, and crisp the skin in the hot fat for about 3 minutes. Turn the legs over and transfer to a baking sheet. Repeat with any remaining pieces, if necessary, pouring off the fat between batches if there is too much. Finish heating the confit in the oven for about 5 minutes.

MAKE AHEAD:

▌ *Traditionally duck confit was kept in the fat to preserve it for months at a time. Stored this way, the duck flavor continues to intensify. If you want to store the duck in the fat, keep it submerged and refrigerated, and it will last a few weeks in the solid fat. (You may want to divide the pieces among smaller heatproof containers before refrigerating them.) To remove a piece, gently heat the pan in a low oven or on the stove to melt the fat enough so you can carefully remove the pieces without tearing the skin or meat.*

▌ *Duck that is not stored in fat is a little more susceptible to spoilage and should be used within a week.*

Delicious Ideas for Duck Confit

You can serve a duck confit leg with just about anything, and people will love you for it. Try it with roasted or sautéed potatoes and some garlicky braised greens (like Braised Tuscan Kale, page 276) for a hearty wintertime dish. Or serve a crisped leg with green salad for a bistro-style lunch. (The spiced cherries on page 222 or the spiced prunes on page 12 make a delicious accompaniment.) You can also pull apart the tender meat and use it in a risotto or pasta, or even as a topping for a brioche pizza (page 48). If you're not going to use the skin, don't throw it away. Remove it and crisp it up on its own. Those cracklings make a great garnish or a treat for the cook.

Crisped Duck Confit with Kumquat Marmalade

SERVES 4 AS A
MAIN COURSE OR 8
AS A FIRST COURSE

I serve crispy pieces of duck confit with all kinds of accompaniments, changing them with the seasons. In winter, I brush the duck with kumquat marmalade—a yummy take on duck à l'orange—and serve it over a smooth and delicate parsnip puree. This recipe makes more marmalade than you will need here, but it keeps well and is delicious with cheese or spread on bruschetta topped with a little ricotta. If you can't find kumquats, you can make the marmalade with oranges instead, or you can use a good-quality purchased orange marmalade.

1   pound kumquats or oranges, quartered lengthwise, seeds removed

½   cup fresh orange juice

½   cup sugar

8   pieces purchased or homemade Duck Confit (page 225),
      crisped as directed on page 226
      Parsnip Puree (page 285; follow the recipe for Turnip Puree
      using the same amount of parsnips)

2   tablespoons fresh parsley leaves

2   tablespoons celery leaves

1   teaspoon extra-virgin olive oil
      Fresh lemon juice

To make the kumquat marmalade, combine the kumquats with the orange juice, sugar, and ½ cup water in a wide saucepan and simmer over low heat until the liquid has reduced slightly and thickened and the kumquat skins are very tender, 30 minutes to 1 hour. Let cool and refrigerate until ready to use.

Just before serving, brush the skin side of the warm, crisped duck with some of the kumquat marmalade. Divide the parsnip puree among four or eight plates and top with a piece or two of the duck. Toss the parsley and celery leaves with just enough olive oil to barely moisten the leaves and a few drops of lemon juice and place a little salad on each plate, along with a few drops of the kumquat marmalade.

MAKE AHEAD: *The kumquat marmalade can be made a couple of weeks ahead and kept refrigerated, in an airtight container.*

Spice-Rubbed Roast Goose

With its deep rich flavor and crisp mahogany skin, a roast goose is the perfect choice for a special winter meal like Christmas or, more radically, Thanksgiving. Many butchers and specialty food markets stock geese for the holidays. And if you can roast a turkey, you can roast a goose. The only difference is that a goose renders more fat as it cooks. If you cook the goose on top of potatoes, they will become sinfully delicious, just the right accompaniment to the bird. Counter all that richness with a crisp salad. Or you can just give in to the opulence and serve the goose with Pearl Onions au Gratin (page 277). This spice rub is also delicious on chicken, duck, and turkey.

Strain any leftover goose fat through a fine-mesh strainer into a jar and use it for pan-frying potatoes. Refrigerated, it will keep for up to 6 months.

D'Artagnan (www.dartagnan.com) carries all kinds of birds, including goose, Pekin duck, squab, and pheasant.

1	goose, 10–12 pounds, trimmed of any excess fat
1	tablespoon ground cayenne
1	tablespoon ground cumin
1	tablespoon ground coriander
1	tablespoon ground cardamom
¼	cup kosher salt
1	tablespoon vegetable oil
2	white onions, chopped
2	celery stalks, peeled and chopped
1	carrot, peeled and chopped
4	fresh thyme sprigs
	Zest of 2 oranges
2	bay leaves
2	pounds fingerling potatoes, washed

Heat the oven to 350°F. Rinse the goose inside and out and pat it dry. Combine the spices with the salt and sprinkle this all over the bird, inside and out.

In a large skillet, heat the oil over medium heat. Add the onions, celery, and carrot and cook, stirring occasionally, until lightly browned. Add the thyme, zest, and bay leaves. Set aside to cool, then fill the cavity of the goose with the cooled vegetables.

Spread the fingerlings out in a large roasting pan. Truss the goose and set it right on top of the potatoes. Roast for 1 hour; rotate the pan once during cooking. At this point the potatoes should be nice and tender (if not, continue cooking until they are). Transfer the goose to a baking sheet and use a slotted spoon to transfer the potatoes from the pan to a baking dish; cover them with a little of the fat to keep them nice and moist and keep them in a warm place. Pour off most of the accumulated fat in the pan—there will be a lot of it—but leave some on the bottom so the juices don't burn. Return the goose to the pan and continue cooking until an instant-read thermometer inserted into the thigh reads about 175°F; the time this takes will vary, depending on the size of your goose, but will probably be another 10 to 30 minutes. Allow the bird to rest for 20 to 25 minutes in a warm spot before carving. If necessary, reheat the potatoes gently before serving with the goose.

MAKE AHEAD: *The spice rub will keep in an airtight container for up to 6 months.*

Notes

from the butcher: beef, pork, and lamb

SLOW-ROASTED BEEF TENDERLOIN WITH THYME   236

FRESH HERB BUTTER   239

WILD MUSHROOM BUTTER   240

BLUE CHEESE BUTTER   242

A-9 STEAK SAUCE   243

SEARED STEAKS WITH CHEESE SAUCE AND ROASTED ONIONS   244

RED WINE–BRAISED SHORT RIBS   246

PORK CHOPS WITH CARAMELIZED APPLES, CELERY, AND SPICED WALNUTS   249

RACK OF LAMB WITH FRESH MINT GREMOLATA   252

LAMB STEW WITH SWEET POTATOES AND BARLEY   253

BRAISED LAMB SHANKS WITH WINTER ROOT VEGETABLES   255

Y^{ou} know the phrase "like a kid in a candy shop"? For me it's "a kid in a butcher shop." Some of my favorite childhood memories involve Taylor's Market, where my mom went to buy our meat. She often took me with her, and with so many kids in the house, it was one of the few times she and I could be alone, so I tagged along happily. Her order was almost always the same: hamburger, maybe a skirt steak, and, when we could afford it, London broil. I felt totally comfortable there, listening to my mother chat with the butcher and the other people in line, looking at the various cuts on display in the case, inhaling the aroma of fresh-cut beef, and knowing dinner was going to be good that night. Sit me down in front of a medium-rare steak and some French fries, well seasoned and still hot from the oil, and I am a very happy girl indeed. Beef and blood and salt and memory: that's what I'm talking about.

My fondness for meat and for that comfortable neighborhood experience led me to open my own butcher shop. In front it's a casual, bistro-style restaurant, and in the back, a glass-fronted refrigerator case is stocked with links of homemade sausages and hot dogs, pork and chicken, and beautifully marbled cuts of beef. On a butcher-block table is an ever-changing selection of homemade preserves, chutneys, baguettes, and nut butters. Often there's a big jar of kosher dills, because when my mom and I went to Taylor's, I always got a pickle, wrapped in butcher paper, to savor on the way home.

Unfortunately, where most people live, a dedicated butcher shop is only a memory, which is really too bad. The good news is that in many parts of the country, you can now buy your meat directly from the farm where the animals are raised. That's what I do, because I like to know what they ate and how they were treated. I always try to buy grass-fed beef, for example. Grass feeding is a far more natural way to raise cattle; it's better for the environment and our bodies, and the meat has more flavor. You can sometimes find locally raised meat products at supermarkets. Your nearby farmers' market may also sell local meat products, and you can probably find a farm near you by searching on the Internet. Many will also ship their products. You will pay more for such meat, but I believe it's worth it. If your budget is tight, eat less, not lesser-quality, meat.

SEARED STEAKS WITH CHEESE SAUCE AND ROASTED ONIONS (PAGE 244)

Slow-Roasted Beef Tenderloin with Thyme

This dish is perfect for company. Roasting the meat low and slow reduces any risk of overcooking while making it especially tender and juicy. I love the buttery texture of beef tenderloin, but its flavor can usually use a boost, which explains the ample thyme in the pan and the red wine sauce on the side. The sauce, by the way, not only is simple but can mostly be made in advance. Serve the tenderloin with Potatoes Mousseline (page 279) and Spinach Amandine (page 282). They don't call these classics for nothing.

1 beef tenderloin (about 6 pounds), trimmed of excess fat and sinew
Kosher salt and freshly ground black pepper
About 25 fresh thyme sprigs
2 tablespoons extra-virgin olive oil
Red Wine Sauce (optional; recipe follows)

Heat the oven to 250°F. Season the beef generously with salt and pepper. Fold the thin tailpiece of the tenderloin under to create a roast of even thickness. Using twine, tie the beef at regular intervals to help it keep its shape during cooking. Tuck the thyme beneath the twine all the way around the beef, spacing the sprigs about 2 inches apart. Brush with the olive oil. Put the beef in a roasting pan and roast until an instant-read thermometer inserted in the thickest part reads 130°F for medium-rare, 1³/₄ to 2 hours.

Transfer to a carving board, tent with foil, and let rest for 20 to 25 minutes. Just before serving, carve into ¹/₂-inch slices. Serve with the red wine sauce, if desired.

MAKE AHEAD: *The tenderloin is delicious at room temperature, which means you can make it ahead and serve it sliced as part of a holiday buffet, if you like.*

Red Wine Sauce

MAKES ABOUT 1¼ CUPS; SERVES 6 TO 8

This easy sauce is deeply flavored, with a lovely body, thanks to the shallots and the time it spends on top of the stove reducing. You can make it almost completely ahead, so it's at the ready when it's time to serve the meat. It's important to use a low-sodium broth, since reducing intensifies all flavors, including salt.

5 tablespoons unsalted butter

²/₃ cup thinly sliced shallots (4–5 shallots, depending on size)

2 cups full-bodied dry red wine, such as Merlot

2 tablespoons red wine vinegar, plus more to taste

6 fresh thyme sprigs

4 cups low-sodium beef broth

Kosher salt and freshly ground pepper

Melt 2 tablespoons of the butter in a large skillet over medium-low heat. Cook the shallots, stirring occasionally, until they're soft and translucent, 10 to 12 minutes. Turn the heat to high, add the wine and vinegar, and boil until reduced to a syrupy consistency (about ¼ cup), about 10 minutes. Add 5 of the thyme sprigs and beef broth and reduce to 1 cup, about 20 minutes. Strain the sauce through a fine-mesh strainer. If not using right away, let the sauce cool, cover, and refrigerate.

Just before serving, reheat the sauce with the remaining thyme sprig over medium heat. When it's hot, whisk in the remaining 3 tablespoons butter. Taste and add a few drops of vinegar to brighten the flavor, if necessary. Season to taste with salt, if necessary, and a little pepper.

MAKE AHEAD: *You can make the sauce up to the point of adding the 3 tablespoons butter days ahead of serving it. Refrigerate it, covered with plastic wrap, and whisk in the butter when you reheat it.*

How to Cook a Steak

I love the physicality of cooking, of using all my senses when I am in the kitchen. This is particularly true when I'm cooking something as seemingly simple as steak: I make sure that the meat is well seasoned before it hits the pan and I hear the sizzle that signals the pan was properly heated. I smell that one side is getting nicely browned before I turn the steak over and confirm it with a glance. I press on the steak with my finger to feel if the muscle has tightened somewhat but not too much, to give me a nice medium-rare. I slice the steak, taste a bit, and finish it with the tiniest pinch of fleur de sel.

My favorite cuts are rib eye, sirloin, and hanger steak, because unlike tenderloin, they all have that full meaty flavor you want in a steak. For my favorite way to cook steak, you'll need a heavy pan, salt, pepper, a little oil, lots of unsalted butter, a shallot, and some fresh thyme.

To start, season the steak liberally with kosher salt (never table salt) and freshly ground black pepper (never preground). Next, heat your heaviest pan over medium-high heat. (A thin pan can heat unevenly and burn the steak.) When the pan is hot, add just enough grapeseed or canola oil to coat the bottom. (Or, if your steak has some nice bits of fat, you can render those in the pan and use it instead of, or in addition to, the oil.) When the oil is nice and hot, add the steak. (It's a good idea to have your kitchen fan on during all of this high-heat searing, unless you like the sound of your smoke alarm.)

Sear the steak on one side until it is well browned, 2 to 3 minutes. Be patient and leave the steak alone so that it has time to build a delicious crust. Turn the steak over to sear the other side. At this point, add a couple of tablespoons of unsalted butter to the pan, the leaves from a few sprigs of thyme, and 1 thinly sliced small shallot. Once the butter has melted, tilt the pan so you can spoon up some butter and pour it over the meat during the last few minutes of cooking. This basting is the key to an evenly cooked, flavorful steak.

The total cooking time for a 1¼-inch-thick steak cooked to medium-rare is 6 to 8 minutes. The more steaks you cook, the better you will become at recognizing the doneness that you prefer. Poke the steaks with your finger as they cook to get an idea of what they feel like as they move from raw to perfectly cooked. You can also take the temperature of a thick steak with an instant-read thermometer; 125° to 130°F is medium-rare.

Once the steak is cooked to your liking, remove from the pan and let it rest off the heat for at least 5 minutes before slicing or serving it. This is important. The resting period allows the juices to redistribute and the meat to relax, making each bite more tender and juicy. (To ensure that the steak is nice and hot when served, warm your dinner plates. You can also pop the steak very briefly under the broiler after its rest.) Pour any juices that have collected as the steak rested over the steak before serving and sprinkle each steak with a pinch of fleur de sel.

You can also top a steak with one of the flavored butters that follow.

Fresh Herb Butter

Speckled green and full of fresh herb flavor, this compound butter brightens up a summertime steak. You can cut the recipe in half and make just one stick of butter. While I love all these herbs, which make up the French herb mix called *fines herbes,* you can use just two or three. You can refrigerate half of the butter to use over the course of a week or so and freeze the other half for down the road. This is also a good way to preserve some of the fresh herbs from your garden.

This butter is especially versatile: it's as wonderful over steamed green beans and roasted potatoes or stuffed under the skin of a chicken as it is on steak.

16	tablespoons (2 sticks) unsalted butter, at room temperature
1	tablespoon chopped fresh chervil or parsley
1	tablespoon chopped fresh chives
1	tablespoon chopped fresh parsley
1	tablespoon chopped fresh tarragon
1	tablespoon fresh lemon juice
1	anchovy, well rinsed, patted dry, and finely chopped
1	teaspoon capers, rinsed, patted dry, and chopped
1	teaspoon kosher salt
1/2	teaspoon freshly ground black pepper

Combine all the ingredients in a bowl and mash and mix together until the ingredients are evenly distributed. Shape the butter into a fat log by rolling it up in waxed paper or parchment. (I find it easier to roll the soft butter in paper, but you can also use plastic wrap.) Twist the ends of the paper tightly as if you were making a sausage and tuck them under to keep them from unraveling and to make a neat little package. Refrigerate until firm.

To use on steak, top a resting steak with a good 1/2-inch slice of the cold butter; this way, some of the butter will melt before serving, but not all.

MAKE AHEAD: *Having an herb butter on hand means you can always cook up something delicious even at a moment's notice. The logs will keep for up to 2 weeks in the refrigerator and freeze beautifully for up to 4 weeks. To freeze, cut whatever portion you would like to freeze and wrap it well in plastic wrap.*

Wild Mushroom Butter

The more flavorful your mushrooms, the more flavorful the butter. I love it spread on crostini and topped with a poached egg as well as on steak.

1 tablespoon extra-virgin olive oil

4 ounces wild mushrooms, preferably an assortment, finely chopped (about 2 cups)

1 small shallot, finely chopped

1 garlic clove, finely chopped

Kosher salt and freshly ground black pepper

16 tablespoons (2 sticks) unsalted butter, at room temperature

2 teaspoons chopped fresh parsley

1 teaspoon chopped fresh thyme leaves

1/2 teaspoon fresh lemon juice

Heat the olive oil in a large skillet over medium-high heat. Add the mushrooms and cook without stirring for a couple of minutes to let them brown. Stir in the shallot and garlic and cook, stirring occasionally, until the mushrooms are tender and well browned and the liquid they release has evaporated from the pan, 6 to 8 minutes. Season to taste with salt and pepper and let cool.

In a bowl, combine the cooled mushrooms with the butter, parsley, thyme, lemon juice, 1 teaspoon salt, and 1/2 teaspoon pepper. Mash and mix together until the ingredients are evenly distributed. Shape the butter into a fat log by rolling it up in waxed paper or parchment. (I find it easier to roll the soft butter in paper, but you can also use plastic wrap.) Twist the ends of the paper tightly as if you were making a sausage and tuck them under to keep them from unraveling and to make a neat little package. Refrigerate until firm.

To use on steak, top a resting steak with a good 1/2-inch slice of the cold butter; this way, some of the butter will melt before serving, but not all.

MAKE AHEAD: *The logs will keep for up to 2 weeks in the refrigerator and freeze beautifully for up to 4 weeks. To freeze, cut whatever portion you would like to freeze and wrap it well in plastic wrap.*

Blue Cheese Butter

Blue cheese and steak is one of the best flavor combinations ever. Mixing the cheese with butter mellows its flavor, smooths its texture, and makes it melt beautifully on a hot steak.

16 tablespoons (2 sticks) unsalted butter, at room temperature
4   ounces good-quality blue cheese, such as Roquefort or Gorgonzola, rind removed
¼   cup finely chopped fresh chives
1   teaspoon freshly ground black pepper
    Kosher salt

Combine all the ingredients except the salt in a bowl and mash and mix together until the ingredients are evenly distributed. Taste and season with salt; the amount will vary depending on the saltiness of your cheese, but about ½ teaspoon salt usually does the trick. Shape the butter into a fat log by rolling it up in waxed paper or parchment. (I find it easier to roll the soft butter in paper, but you can also use plastic wrap.) Twist the ends of the paper tightly as if you were making a sausage and tuck them under to keep them from unraveling and to make a neat little package. Refrigerate until firm.

To use on steak, top a resting steak with a good ½-inch slice of the cold butter; this way, some of the butter will melt before serving, but not all.

MAKE AHEAD: *The logs will keep for up to 2 weeks in the refrigerator and freeze beautifully for up to 4 weeks. To freeze, cut whatever portion you would like to freeze and wrap it well in plastic wrap.*

A-9 Steak Sauce

One year I had a contest among my cooks to see who could come up with the best steak sauce. This recipe won. It's got the tangy flavor you look for in a steak sauce, plus a deep, earthy sweetness from the molasses and raisins, but it also has a brightness you don't get from the bottle, thanks to the fresh orange juice and zest. The ingredient list is long, but most of it comes from a jar or bottle, so there's little prep work. It's also delicious as a barbecue sauce brushed onto ribs or chicken just before they come off the heat.

2	teaspoons grapeseed or canola oil
1	small red onion, chopped (about ¾ cup)
2	garlic cloves, chopped
1	tablespoon sugar
⅓	cup apple cider vinegar
2½	tablespoons balsamic vinegar
2	cups ketchup (I like Heinz)
1	orange
¼	cup raisins
2	tablespoons molasses
1	tablespoon Worcestershire sauce
1	tablespoon Dijon mustard
1	bay leaf
¼	teaspoon freshly ground black pepper
¼	teaspoon crushed red pepper flakes
¼	teaspoon coriander seeds
¼	teaspoon caraway seeds

Heat the oil in a medium saucepan over medium heat. Add the onion and garlic and cook, stirring occasionally, until tender and lightly colored, about 5 minutes. Add the sugar and continue to cook until the onion is quite brown, another 5 minutes. Add the cider and balsamic vinegars and cook until reduced by about half. Add the ketchup. Using a rasp-style (Microplane) grater, finely zest about a quarter of the orange and add the zest to the pan as well as the juice from ¼ of the orange. Add the remaining ingredients and cook at a low simmer, stirring every once in a while, until all the flavors have melded and the sauce has reduced slightly, 1½ to 2 hours for best flavor. Puree in a blender or food processor and pass through a fine-mesh strainer.

MAKE AHEAD: *This will keep for a month in a jar in the refrigerator, and probably longer.*

Seared Steaks with Cheese Sauce and Roasted Onions

SERVES 4

At heart, this is a Philly cheesesteak sandwich but without the bread and made refined enough to serve for dinner. The cheese sauce, which takes minutes to make, is also a good fondue, with cubed pieces of seared beef and toasted bread, similar to the recipe on page 37. (See the photo on page 234.)

1	cup heavy cream
8	ounces aged Mimolette (see page 165), Gouda, or Edam, finely grated
	Kosher salt and freshly ground white pepper
5	tablespoons unsalted butter
2	small sweet onions, such as Vidalia, trimmed of roots and tops and sliced in half from top to bottom
½	teaspoon chopped fresh thyme leaves
	Freshly ground black pepper
4	ounces mushrooms, preferably chanterelles or other wild mushrooms, trimmed and cut or broken into pieces if large
¼	cup chicken broth, preferably Roasted Chicken Stock (page 108)
4	thick sirloin steaks, each about 6 ounces
2	tablespoons grapeseed or canola oil
1	small shallot, thinly sliced
	Fleur de sel

Heat the oven to 350°F. To make the cheese sauce, bring the heavy cream to a simmer in a medium saucepan over medium heat. Add the cheese and stir until all the cheese has melted into the cream. If you have grated the cheese finely on a rasp-style (Microplane) grater, the sauce should be quite smooth; if it's lumpy, pass it through a fine-mesh strainer to remove any lumps. Season to taste with salt and white pepper and keep off the heat until just before serving.

In a medium ovenproof skillet over medium-high heat, melt 2 tablespoons of the butter. Add the onions cut side down and cook them undisturbed until well browned, about 5 minutes. Turn the onions over and cook the other side for 1 to 2 minutes. Add a pinch of the thyme leaves and ¼ cup water to the pan, transfer the pan to the oven, and roast the onions, basting them occasionally with the butter and water, until very tender but still holding their shape, about 20 minutes. Remove the onions from the pan and drain on paper towels. Season with salt and black pepper and set aside in a warm spot.

Meanwhile, melt 1 tablespoon of the butter in a clean skillet over medium-high heat. Add the mushrooms and cook, stirring occasionally, until they are nicely browned and almost tender. Add the chicken broth and continue to cook, stirring occasionally. As the mushrooms cook, the broth will reduce and form a glaze, coating the mushrooms. Season well with salt and black pepper and reserve.

Season the steaks with salt and black pepper. Heat the oil in a large ovenproof skillet over medium-high heat until the pan is quite hot. Sear the steaks on one side without moving them until that side is well browned, 2 to 3 minutes. Turn the steaks over to sear the other side. (It's a good idea to have your kitchen fan on during all of this high-heat searing, unless you like the sound of your smoke alarm.) After the other side has been searing for about 1 minute, add the remaining 2 tablespoons butter, the shallot, and the remaining thyme to the pan. Once the butter has melted, tilt the pan so you can spoon up some butter and baste the meat with the butter during the last few minutes of cooking. The total cooking time for medium-rare (125° to 130°F on an instant-read thermometer) is 6 to 8 minutes. (Alternatively, you can finish the steaks in the 350°F oven.) Transfer the steaks to a plate or platter and let them rest for 6 to 8 minutes. If necessary, gently reheat the sauce, the mushrooms, and the onions.

To serve, divide the steaks among four plates and top with the mushrooms and any juices from the meat that have collected on the plate or cutting board. Spoon the sauce on the plate and lay the roasted onion down on each plate cut side up. Sprinkle both the onion and the steak with a pinch of fleur de sel.

MAKE AHEAD: *You can make the cheese sauce days ahead of serving this and refrigerate, covered with plastic wrap. It will solidify in the refrigerator, but all you need to do to bring it back to life is warm it gently. If it gets grainy, stir in a little bit of milk and whisk until it is smooth.*

Red Wine–Braised Short Ribs

SERVES 6 Though this recipe is a pretty traditional take on classic braised short ribs, I cook them longer and at a lower temperature than most recipes call for, which makes them so tender the meat practically melts in your mouth. The deeply flavored sauce is easy to make by simply simmering the braising liquid until it is very much reduced, which intensifies its flavor and thickens it, too. A pat of butter and a little thyme swirled in just before serving are all it needs. This is a great dish for company, because you can make it a day or two ahead and it only tastes the better for it. The trick to making short ribs is not to take them out of the oven until you can easily pull the meat away from the bone with a fork.

	Kosher salt and freshly ground black pepper
6–8	pounds meaty, bone-in short ribs (see page 248)
2	tablespoons grapeseed or canola oil, plus more if needed
1	large onion, chopped
3	celery stalks, peeled and chopped
1	large carrot, peeled and chopped
1	head garlic, separated into individual cloves and peeled
1	750-ml bottle dry red wine
6	fresh thyme sprigs
4	bay leaves
1	tablespoon black peppercorns
1	tablespoon coriander seeds
1	tomato, chopped
6	cups low-sodium beef broth or chicken broth, preferably Roasted Chicken Stock (page 108)
1	tablespoon unsalted butter
1½	tablespoons coarsely chopped fresh thyme leaves

Heat the oven to 275°F. Sprinkle a good amount of salt and some pepper all over the ribs. Heat the oil in a large skillet over medium-high heat. Brown the ribs, in batches if necessary, on all sides. Be sure there is room around the ribs so that they sear instead of steam, and be patient, turning them only after they have browned on one side; the browning step should take 10 to 12 minutes total.

As the ribs are browned, transfer them to a deep baking dish or Dutch oven large enough to accommodate the meat and braising liquid. Leave about 2 tablespoons of the rendered fat in the skillet and pour off any excess. Return the pan to medium-high heat and add the onion, celery, carrot, and garlic. Cook, stirring, until the vegetables are tender and nicely browned, about 8 minutes. Add the red wine, thyme sprigs, bay leaves, peppercorns, coriander, and tomato and cook, stirring occasionally, until the liquid is reduced by half, about 15 minutes. Add the broth, bring to a boil, and pour the liquid over the ribs in the baking dish. Cover the dish with aluminum foil and cook in the oven until fork-tender, 4 to 5 hours; some of the meat may fall off the bones, which is okay, though the ribs look more dramatic on the plate if still on the bone.

Let the meat cool in the braising liquid until it is almost room temperature. Transfer the ribs, meat side down, to another baking dish. Strain the braising liquid through a fine-mesh strainer into a large saucepan. Ladle some of the braising liquid over the ribs to keep them moist; you want about $1/2$ inch of liquid in the dish. If serving the ribs immediately, spoon off any fat you can see on the surface of the braising liquid. If not serving right away, refrigerate the ribs and the braising liquid separately, covered with plastic wrap, until ready to serve. You can then remove the fat that has solidified on top of the liquid once cooled, which is easier and more thorough.

To serve, heat the oven to 300°F. Bring the defatted braising liquid to a simmer over medium heat and cook, skimming occasionally, until reduced to about $1^1/2$ cups, about 30 minutes. (If the reduction is done before the meat is sufficiently heated, just take it off the heat.) You don't want to let the liquid come to a rolling boil, but you do want to see tiny bubbles coming to the surface. Meanwhile, gently reheat the ribs in the oven for 20 to 30 minutes. Just before serving, whisk the butter and chopped thyme leaves into the reduced braising liquid. Divide the ribs among six plates and top with the sauce.

Buying Short Ribs

Short ribs are the meaty ends of the ribs of a cow. You'll find them cut in one of two ways: parallel to the bones (English style; shown below), so you get rectangles of meat sitting on top of a single bone, or across the bones (flanken style), which are thinner strips of meat containing multiple bone segments. You can use either kind for most braises, but I much prefer the English-style ribs, which are more widely available. (I don't understand why anyone would prefer flanken, with all that bone and so little meat.) Often, however, the ribs are not labeled as such, so you'll need to take a look at them or ask your butcher. Because the bones add a ton of flavor to the sauce, avoid boneless short ribs. Ideally, buy them from a butcher. If you buy them prepackaged, it's difficult to tell where one rib starts and another ends, and you can wind up with some nice meaty ribs and some that are so thin they're almost all bone. If you can only buy prepackaged, get a little extra to be sure that everyone will have a big, good-looking rib on his or her plate. Don't go crazy trimming short ribs. Cut away any really thick pieces of fat on the surface, but leave that internal layer alone; most of it cooks away, and what's left softens and also holds the meat to the bone. You should leave on the silverskin that connects the meat to the bone, too.

Pork Chops with Caramelized Apples, Celery, and Spiced Walnuts

Meaty chops, crisp celery, crunchy nuts, and tender apples: each bite of this dish is a little different from the last, a mingling of peppery flavors, sweet heat, and toasty goodness. Serve the chops with Turnip Puree; its smooth feel and earthy flavor add to the symphony of tastes and textures.

2 tablespoons plus 1 teaspoon grapeseed or canola oil

4 pork chops, each about 1½ inches thick
  Kosher salt and freshly ground black pepper

1 dense apple, such as Honeycrisp or Granny Smith, cored and
  cut into 12 wedges

1 tablespoon sugar

2 teaspoons unsalted butter

¼ teaspoon chopped fresh thyme

2 small celery stalks, peeled and sliced very thinly on the diagonal
  (save any tender leaves and use those, too)

¼ cup whole fresh parsley leaves

1 teaspoon extra-virgin olive oil, plus more if needed
  Fresh lemon juice
  Spiced Walnuts (recipe follows)
  Turnip Puree (optional, page 285)
  Fleur de sel

Heat the oven to 350°F. Heat 2 tablespoons of the grapeseed oil in a large skillet over medium-high heat. Season the pork chops well with salt and pepper. Add them to the pan and cook without moving them until well browned on one side. Turn the chops over and cook the other side for 1 to 2 minutes. Transfer the pan to the oven and finish cooking the chops, 5 to 6 minutes. The pork chops are done when they're still a little pink inside and an instant-read thermometer reads between 140° and 145°F. Transfer the chops to a plate or platter and let them rest in a warm spot for 5 to 6 minutes before serving.

While the pork finishes cooking, caramelize the apples. Toss the apple wedges with the sugar. Heat the remaining 1 teaspoon grapeseed oil in a medium skillet over medium-high heat. Add the apples in a single layer and cook on one side undisturbed until golden brown, 3 to 4 minutes. Flip the apples over and cook the other side until

nicely browned. Add the butter and swirl it around in the pan to melt it. Add the thyme and finish with a pinch of salt.

To serve, toss the celery, celery leaves, and parsley with the olive oil and a squeeze of lemon juice; you want them just barely moistened. Toss the nuts in and season with salt and pepper. If serving the chops with the turnip puree, put some of the puree down on the center of four warm plates. Put a chop on top of the puree and top with a few apple slices and then the celery salad. Finish each plate with a pinch of fleur de sel.

MAKE AHEAD: *You can toss the celery with the celery leaves and parsley and keep the salad refrigerated for a few hours. Dress it at the last minute.*

Spiced Walnuts

MAKES ABOUT ½ CUP

These tasty, sweet and spicy nuts are a delightful addition to any green salad, so consider making a double batch.

½	cup walnuts
¼	teaspoon grapeseed or canola oil
¼	teaspoon sugar
¼	teaspoon ground cayenne
	Kosher salt

Heat the oven to 350°F. Toss the walnuts with the oil, sugar, cayenne, and a good pinch of salt. Spread them out in a single layer on a baking sheet and bake, shaking the pan occasionally, until toasted and fragrant, 5 to 10 minutes. They'll crisp a little more as they cool.

MAKE AHEAD: *If you can keep yourself from eating these addictive nuts, you can make them a couple of days ahead. Store them in an airtight container when they have completely cooled.*

Rack of Lamb with Fresh Mint Gremolata

SERVES 6 TO 8   This bright accompaniment, a riff on traditional gremolata (the mix of lemon zest, garlic, and fresh parsley that complements osso buco), dresses up an otherwise straightforward roasted rack of lamb. If you want to give the gremolata an even deeper flavor, add a very finely minced anchovy. Serve the lamb with cucumber and fennel salad (page 72). When the weather is warm, feel free to go with grilled lamb chops, kebabs, or boneless leg of lamb instead of a roast.

1   cup coarsely chopped fresh mint leaves

½   cup golden raisins, plumped in hot water for at least 10 minutes
      and drained

½   cup pine nuts, toasted in a dry skillet or in the oven until golden brown

2–3   garlic cloves, very finely chopped

      Finely grated zest of 1 lemon

      Crushed red pepper flakes

½   cup extra-virgin olive oil, plus more for searing the lamb

      Kosher salt and freshly ground black pepper

3   racks of lamb (7–8 chops each), trimmed and frenched,
      at room temperature

In a small bowl, combine the mint, raisins, pine nuts, garlic, lemon zest, and a pinch of red pepper flakes. Whisk in the olive oil and season to taste with salt and pepper.

Heat the oven to 350°F. Season the lamb well on all sides with salt and pepper. Heat a large, heavy skillet over medium-high heat. Add about 2 tablespoons olive oil and wait for the oil to get very hot. In batches if necessary, sear the lamb racks on all sides until well browned; it should take at least 5 minutes to get the meat nicely caramelized all over. Put the browned racks bone side down on a heavy baking sheet and finish cooking them in the oven until an instant-read thermometer inserted in the thickest part of the meat reads 125° to 130°F (for lamb that is rare and just on its way to medium-rare), 20 to 25 minutes. Let the lamb rest for 8 to 10 minutes before slicing it into chops. Divide the chops among warm plates and drizzle a few tablespoons of the gremolata over the meat.

MAKE AHEAD: *You can make the gremolata a day or two ahead and keep it refrigerated, covered.*

Lamb Stew with Sweet Potatoes and Barley

SERVES 6   Here's everything you would want to eat on a cold winter or early spring evening: lamb, sweet potatoes, and barley simmered in a deep, dark, and rich sauce of red wine, beef broth, and fragrant warm spices. To add color and a burst of flavor, you can top individual servings of this stew with a tiny salad made of lightly dressed whole leaves of fresh, delicate herbs.

1	tablespoon ground cumin
1	teaspoon ground ginger
1	teaspoon ground cardamom
1/2	teaspoon ground cinnamon
1/2	teaspoon crushed red pepper flakes
2	tablespoons grapeseed or canola oil, plus more as needed
2	pounds boneless leg of lamb, trimmed of excess fat and sinew, cut into 1- to 2-inch chunks
	Kosher salt and freshly ground black pepper
2	medium carrots, peeled and diced
1	medium onion, diced
2	celery stalks, peeled and diced
3	garlic cloves, sliced
1	cup dry red wine
4	cups beef broth
15	prunes
1/2	cup raisins, preferably golden
1	pound sweet potatoes, peeled and diced
1	cup barley

In a small bowl, combine the cumin, ginger, cardamom, cinnamon, and red pepper flakes.

Heat a large Dutch oven or similar braising pot over medium-high heat. Add the oil and let it heat up. Add the meat and let it brown very deeply on one side before turning it to brown all sides; this browning step, crucial for great flavor, can take as long as 10 to 15 minutes. Be sure there is space between the pieces or the lamb will steam instead of brown; sear the lamb in batches if necessary.

Transfer the lamb to a platter or baking sheet as it browns and season it well with a few pinches of salt and a few grinds of pepper.

Add a little more oil to the pot, if needed, then add the carrots, onion, celery, and garlic. Season with a good pinch of salt and cook, stirring up the browned bits on the bottom of the pot. Reduce the heat if necessary and cook until the vegetables are lightly browned, 3 to 4 minutes. Add the spice mixture and red wine, stir, and cook over medium heat until the wine has reduced by about half. Add the beef broth and return the lamb to the pot, nestling it into the liquid. Cover the pot with the lid slightly askew and cook over medium-low heat for 1 hour. Add the prunes and raisins, cover, and cook for another 30 minutes. Add the sweet potatoes, barley, and 3 cups water to the pot, cover, and cook until the potatoes, lamb, and barley are tender, another 45 minutes to an hour, adding up to 1 cup more water if needed. Season to taste with salt and pepper. Serve in bowls, topped with herb salad, if you like.

MAKE AHEAD: *Like all stews and braises, this tastes better when made a day or two ahead. Reheat it gently to keep the meat tender.*

Fresh Herb Salads

When I am serving rich pieces of meat, I like to garnish the plate with a tiny salad made of delicate fresh herb leaves, what the French call *fines herbes:* tarragon, parsley, chervil, and chives. Simply combine equal parts of whole leaves from these herbs (with the chives cut into similar-sized pieces) and gently toss them with the tiniest bit of olive oil (a teaspoon or two per ½ cup herbs) and a few drops of lemon juice. A tablespoon or two of this salad offers a lively counterpoint to the deep, and often sweet, flavors on the plate. Of the four herbs, chervil may not always be available; if that's the case, just use the other three herbs.

Braised Lamb Shanks with Winter Root Vegetables

SERVES 6

I love the way a big lamb shank looks on the plate. You see that hulking cut with the bone sticking up high—think Fred Flintstone—and you know you're in for some hearty eating. One bite of the tender braised meat and you fall hard for its elegant texture and mild flavor. I don't cook the earthy root-cellar vegetables along with the meat, because they would lose their individual character. Instead, I glaze them separately on top of the stove. I like to use different vegetables for a mix of colors and flavors.

- 6   lamb shanks, each about 1½ pounds, preferably frenched (see page 257)
  Kosher salt and freshly ground black pepper
- 2   tablespoons grapeseed or canola oil, plus more as needed
- 1   large carrot, peeled and chopped
- 1   large celery stalk, chopped
- 1   medium onion, chopped
- 4   garlic cloves, chopped
- ½   750-ml bottle dry red wine
- 6   cups chicken broth, preferably Roasted Chicken Stock (page 108)
- 2   bay leaves
- 1   fresh rosemary sprig
- 1   teaspoon black peppercorns
- 4   tablespoons (½ stick) unsalted butter, plus more as needed
- 10   cups peeled, cut-up root vegetables, such as carrots, beets, potatoes, parsnips, celery root, and rutabaga (the pieces should be about the same size but will look better varied in shape, such as large cubes, wedges, and sticks)
- ¼   cup chopped fresh parsley
  Fleur de sel

To braise the lamb shanks, heat a large Dutch oven or similar large braising pot over medium-high heat. Season the lamb well with salt and pepper. Add the grapeseed oil and let it heat up. In batches, so as to have space between the shanks, brown the shanks well on all sides, 10 to 12 minutes. Transfer the lamb to a platter or baking sheet when it has browned.

Add a little more oil to the pot, if needed, then add the chopped carrot, celery, onion, and garlic. Season with a good pinch of salt and cook, stirring and reducing the heat if necessary, for 3 to 4 minutes; you want the vegetables just tender and not colored. Add the red wine, stir, and cook over medium-high heat until the wine has reduced by about half. Add the chicken broth, bay leaves, rosemary, and peppercorns and return the lamb to the pot, nestling it into the liquid. Cover the pot with the lid slightly askew and cook over medium heat until the meat is fork-tender, $2^{1}/_{2}$ to 3 hours.

Transfer the lamb to a baking sheet. Strain the braising liquid by passing through a fine-mesh strainer into a saucepan; pour half of the liquid over the lamb to keep it moist and flavorful as it cools to room temperature. Remove any visible fat from the remaining liquid; this is easier to do after the liquid has cooled and the fat has congealed, so if not serving right away, refrigerate both the lamb shanks and the braising liquid.

To cook the root vegetables, divide the 4 tablespoons butter between two large skillets (you can cook them in stages in one pan, but that takes longer). Add $^{1}/_{4}$ cup water to each. Cook the vegetables in batches separately in the butter and water, stirring occasionally and adding more water and (less often) more butter as needed. (You can cook those with similar cooking times together, but if using red beets, cook them alone, and last, so they don't turn the other vegetables pink.) As each vegetable becomes tender, transfer it to a baking sheet with a slotted spoon and add a new vegetable to the pan. Once cooked, you can combine the vegetables, but keep the beets, if using, separate.

To serve, reheat the lamb gently in a 250°F oven if necessary. If you have not removed the fat from the braising liquid, do so now. Bring the liquid to a simmer over medium-high heat and cook it, skimming the surface as needed, until reduced to a glaze. Reheat the vegetables in a little butter and water if necessary. (Reheat beets, if using, in a separate small pan.) Toss gently with the parsley and season to taste with salt and pepper. Divide the vegetables, including any beets, among six wide bowls and top each with a lamb shank, bone side up. Drizzle the reduced sauce over the lamb and finish with a pinch of fleur de sel.

MAKE AHEAD:

I *The lamb tastes even better if made a day or two ahead, covered, refrigerated, and gently reheated.*

I *You can also cook all the vegetables a day ahead, cover, refrigerate, and reheat them gently to serve.*

A Better-Looking Lamb Shank

Though it's not vital to the flavor of the dish, lamb shanks that have been frenched—trimmed to expose a good amount of the bone—look more elegant on the plate. Some markets sell lamb shanks already frenched, but it's not difficult to do yourself if you have a sharp, flexible knife. To french a lamb shank, cut around the meat at the narrower end to release the meat from the bone. Next, cut along the exposed bone and snip the tendons holding the meat to the bone. Go almost all the way down the other end of the shank, exposing the bone but keeping the meat attached at the end. Grab the loosened meat and pull it down toward the meaty end of the bone, essentially turning it inside out in the process to make a ball. Tie the meat twice around with butcher twine to help it hold its new shape and scrape the exposed bone clean with the knife.

Notes

B&G COLESLAW   264

B&G PICKLES   267

STEAM-ROASTED ASPARAGUS WITH FRESH HERB VINAIGRETTE   268

GINGER-GLAZED CARROTS   269

CORN OFF THE COB   270

CORN BLINI   271

OLIVE OIL–GLAZED BABY VEGETABLES   272

ROASTED FENNEL AND GREEN BEANS   275

BRAISED TUSCAN KALE   276

PEARL ONIONS AU GRATIN   277

POMMES PUREE   278

POTATOES MOUSSELINE   279

POMMES FRITES   280

SPINACH AMANDINE   282

ROASTED WINTER SQUASH WITH MAPLE SYRUP
AND SAGE CREAM   283

TOMATO JAM   284

TURNIP PUREE   285

CREAMY MASCARPONE POLENTA   286

BEN'S WILD RICE SALAD   287

You may have noticed that potatoes show up a lot in my cooking, in soups, salads, and gnocchi. It should be no surprise that with a name like Lynch, I love them. Growing up, we ate baked potatoes often. My mom was busy, and few things are easier (or cheaper) for feeding a bunch of kids than throwing spuds in the oven. They satisfied me, but I can't say the same for her mashed potatoes, which came from a box. Incongruously, she added sautéed onions. If you're going to the trouble of peeling and cooking an onion, why would it be any more bother to peel a potato?

My version of mashed potatoes is so far removed from hers that I refuse to call them mashed potatoes. To make "Pommes Puree," I pass the potatoes through a mesh strainer, which makes them fabulously smooth and silky. My mom would look at me as if I were crazy if she saw me doing this, so I guess that makes us even. Potatoes Mousseline also begin as mashed potatoes but are lightened with whipped cream and baked in a gratin dish. And who can resist potatoes when they're fried? I can't, which is why I tell you how to make French fries and potato chips, both of which are incredibly easy.

I do know that there's a world beyond potatoes, though. I'm the one with the overflowing bags at the Copley Square farmers' market. Buying locally just makes sense: if the vegetable already tastes delicious, there's not much I need to do to it. For example, my method for cooking asparagus—steam-roasting it on a baking sheet in the oven—lets its sweet green flavor shine through. Pour a little vinaigrette over it and you've got a perfect springtime side dish.

You'll find recipes for other vegetables—carrots, kale, corn—but what you won't find are recipes for rice, which I find boring. An exception is Ben's Wild Rice Salad. Then again, wild rice isn't technically a rice (it's a marsh grass), and its nutty flavor and meaty texture make it a hell of a lot more interesting than white rice. (And, yes, I know: risotto is rice, but it's completely different from white rice.)

Most of my salads can double as side dishes, too, especially the cucumber and fennel salad on page 72, which is great alongside roasted or braised chicken, steak, salmon, and (my favorite with it) lamb. Of course, that salad features tiny roasted potatoes, too. And why not?

POMMES FRITES (PAGE 280)

B&G Coleslaw

I always serve this signature slaw from my restaurant B&G Oysters alongside my lobster rolls (page 200), but it's also great with barbecued ribs and chicken.

1	medium head green cabbage, cored and shredded
1	carrot, peeled and grated
1	small red onion, thinly sliced
1	cup Lemon Aïoli (page 47) or 1 cup Hellmann's mayonnaise mixed with 1 teaspoon fresh lemon juice
2½	tablespoons apple cider vinegar, plus more if needed
1½	tablespoons sugar
1½	teaspoons kosher salt, plus more if needed
½	teaspoon Dijon mustard
	Freshly ground black pepper

In a large bowl, toss the cabbage, carrot, and onion together. In a small bowl, whisk together the aïoli, vinegar, sugar, salt, mustard, and pepper to taste. Toss this dressing well with the vegetables and chill. Before serving, taste and add more vinegar or salt if necessary, as coldness can mute the flavors a bit.

MAKE AHEAD: *You can shred the cabbage and grate the carrot a day ahead. Store them separately, covered, in the refrigerator.*

B&G Pickles

Quick pickling is just a matter of pouring hot seasoned liquid (mostly vinegar) over vegetables.

6	pickling cucumbers, sliced about ⅛ inch thick
2½	cups apple cider vinegar
1	cup sugar
1½	tablespoons kosher salt
3	tablespoons pickling spices, tied in cheesecloth to make a sachet (see page 224)

Put the cucumbers in a clean, heatproof bowl large enough to easily accommodate a quart of liquid. Combine the vinegar with ¾ cup water in a medium saucepan. Add the sugar, salt, and pickling spices and bring to a simmer to dissolve the sugar. While the liquid is still hot, pour it over the cucumbers and cover with a small plate to keep the cucumbers submerged. Allow to cool to room temperature before storing, covered with plastic wrap, with the sachet in it, in the refrigerator.

MAKE AHEAD: *These pickles will keep for up to 2 weeks in an airtight container in the refrigerator.*

Homemade Potato Chips

I make my own potato chips to serve with my signature lobster BLT (see page 200). They're so good and ridiculously easy to make. You don't need a lot of oil, because you fry the potatoes in batches. And unlike French fries, which need to be fried twice to cook them through without burning on the outside, thin potato chips need just a single dip. All you have to do is slice a russet (I peel it first) 1/16 inch thin on a mandoline. (You really do need a mandoline, but a cheap Japanese model is fine—no need to spend a fortune on one.) Separate the slices, lower them into oil heated to 300°F, and fry until golden brown, 4 to 6 minutes. For safety's sake, fill the pan only to the halfway point with the oil. Use a Chinese skimmer or other slotted spoon to retrieve the chips and drain them on a stack of paper towels. Salt to taste and enjoy.

Steam-Roasted Asparagus with Fresh Herb Vinaigrette

SERVES 4   This method combines the ease of roasting—the stalks are laid out on a baking sheet—with the benefits of steaming: a bright green unblemished look and pure asparagus flavor. A vinaigrette made with a mix of chervil, chives, parsley, and tarragon adds the right touch without overwhelming the asparagus. For a pretty presentation, reserve some whole leaves of the herbs to sprinkle over the asparagus just before serving.

1   bunch asparagus
¼   cup extra-virgin olive oil
      Kosher salt and freshly ground black pepper
1   shallot, finely chopped
1   tablespoon Dijon mustard
2   teaspoons white wine vinegar, preferably Chardonnay
¼   cup grapeseed oil or mild olive oil
¼   cup chopped mixed fresh tender herbs, preferably chives, chervil,
         parsley, and tarragon
      Fleur de sel

Heat the oven to 350°F. To cook the asparagus, line a baking sheet with parchment paper. Lay the asparagus on the parchment and toss the spears with the olive oil. Season well with salt and pepper. Cover the asparagus with another piece of parchment and put them in the oven to steam-roast until their color is bright green and they are tender, 6 to 12 minutes, depending on thickness; check by biting into a spear.

Meanwhile, make the vinaigrette by combining the shallot, mustard, and vinegar in a small bowl. Whisk in the grapeseed oil. Just before serving, whisk in the herbs and season with salt. Drizzle the vinaigrette over the asparagus while it's still warm and finish with a sprinkling of fleur de sel.

MAKE AHEAD:

▌ *The asparagus can be served warm or at room temperature, so you can cook it a little ahead of serving.*

▌ *The vinaigrette will hold for a day refrigerated, but don't add the chopped herbs until just before serving, as they will darken in color and won't taste as fresh.*

Ginger-Glazed Carrots

SERVES 4 The bright flavor of these carrots is welcome next to any braised or roasted dish. Try them with roasted chicken that's been rubbed with the spice rub on page 229.

3   large carrots, trimmed and peeled
1   tablespoon yellow mustard seeds
2   tablespoons unsalted butter
1   tablespoon honey
1   teaspoon finely grated ginger, preferably grated on a rasp-style (Microplane) grater (see page 21)
¼   teaspoon crushed red pepper flakes
½   teaspoon kosher salt
    Freshly ground black pepper
2   scallions, trimmed and very thinly sliced on a diagonal

Bring a medium saucepan of water to a boil. Have ready a medium bowl full of ice water. Cut the carrots into 1½- to 2-inch lengths and cut the lengths into quarters and thirds, depending on thickness. Cook the carrots in the boiling water until just tender (taste one to see), 6 to 8 minutes. Using a Chinese skimmer or other slotted spoon, transfer the carrots to the ice water to halt the cooking. Drain well.

Heat the mustard seeds in a medium dry skillet over medium heat, shaking the pan occasionally, until slightly toasty-smelling, about 2 minutes. Add the butter and honey to the pan. When the butter is melted, add the ginger, crushed red pepper flakes, salt, and a few grinds of pepper and stir to combine. Add the carrots and toss them well with the butter and flavorings. Garnish with the scallions just before serving.

MAKE AHEAD: *You can blanch the carrots a day ahead of finishing the dish and store them, covered with plastic wrap, in the refrigerator.*

Corn Off the Cob

SERVES 4

I love corn in season, but I get tired of eating it on the cob. By taking it off the cob, cooking it in a lot of butter, and pureeing some of the corn, I keep that summer-corn goodness while making the dish a little more refined. For something amazing to serve alongside a piece of spice-rubbed salmon, pork, beef, or lamb, put a big spoonful of my easy-to-make Tomato Jam (page 284) alongside this corn; you won't know what hit you.

5 large ears corn, shucked, silk removed
5 tablespoons unsalted butter
1 small onion, diced (about 1/2 cup)
   Kosher salt
1 tablespoon chopped fresh chives
   Freshly ground black pepper

Remove the kernels from the cob by slicing straight down the cob with a sharp chef's knife, turning the ear and repeating until most of the kernels are off the cob. (This is easier and neater to do if you cut the cobs in half crosswise first.)

In a large skillet, melt 3 tablespoons of the butter over medium-low heat. Add the onion and a pinch of salt and cook, stirring occasionally, until tender but not colored, about 6 minutes. Add the corn and 2 tablespoons water and cook for just a few minutes, until the corn is tender. Puree about half of the corn in a food processor and stir it back into the pan, along with the remaining 2 tablespoons butter. Stir in the chives, season to taste with salt and pepper, and serve.

Corn Blini

MAKES 20 TO 25
SMALL PANCAKES Full of fresh corn flavor and as light as air, these little pancakes are a delightful accompaniment to the lobster on page 202. Or serve them as an hors d'oeuvre, topped with a little Citrus-Cured Salmon (page 41) and a dollop of crème fraîche or a bit of Tomato Jam (page 284).

1	ear corn, shucked, silk removed
$2/3$	cup whole milk
1	medium Yukon Gold potato, peeled
3	large egg whites
2	tablespoons all-purpose flour
$1/2$	teaspoon kosher salt
$1/4$	teaspoon freshly ground white pepper
	Grapeseed or canola oil for cooking the blini

Snap the corncob in half. Remove the kernels from the cob by slicing straight down the cob with a sharp chef's knife, turning the ear and repeating until most of the kernels are off the cob. Reserve half of the kernels and put the rest, plus the cob, in a small saucepan with the milk. Bring to a gentle boil, turn off the heat, and let steep in the milk for at least 30 minutes, though longer is fine. Remove and discard the cob and puree the milk and kernels.

In a small saucepan, boil the potato until fork-tender, about 30 minutes. Let it cool briefly, then rice it into a large bowl. Whisk the egg whites until frothy and full. Fold the egg whites, corn puree, flour, salt, and white pepper into the potato. Refrigerate until ready to use.

To serve, heat a tablespoon of oil in a nonstick skillet or griddle over medium-high heat. Once the pan is hot, spoon a couple tablespoons of batter per pancake into the skillet to make four pancakes, each about $2^1/2$ inches across (you may have to spread the batter into a circle with the back of a spoon). Let cook until bubbles begin to appear, at which time add 5 or 6 of the reserved corn kernels to each pancake. Cook until golden brown on one side. Flip and cook the other side. Transfer the blini to a paper-towel-lined plate and pat lightly with a paper towel to absorb any excess oil. Continue making pancakes until all the batter is used and serve.

MAKE AHEAD: *The batter will hold for up to a day, covered with plastic wrap and refrigerated, but is best used within a couple of hours of making it. Give it a gentle stir before using it.*

Olive Oil–Glazed Baby Vegetables

SERVES 4 These tender, colorful, glistening baby vegetables make just about any plate look pretty, but I especially like to serve them with the sea scallops (page 198), because the hazelnuts and tangy herb sauce that go with the scallops really complement these vegetables, too.

½ cup extra-virgin olive oil

1 fresh thyme sprig, preferably lemon thyme

4 cups mixed baby vegetables, such as carrots, artichokes, onions, fennel, zucchini, and summer squash, all cut to about the same size (if you don't have baby vegetables, cut larger ones into 1- to 1½-inch pieces)

2 medium celery stalks, peeled and cut into matchsticks

Kosher salt and freshly ground black pepper

Combine the olive oil with 1 cup water in a large skillet and heat over medium-high heat. Add the thyme and then the vegetables in stages, starting with the heartier ones, like fennel, carrots, and onions. Bring the liquid to a boil, cover the pan with a lid or, even better, parchment paper laid directly on the vegetables, and cook the vegetables for about 10 minutes, tossing occasionally. You're not trying to color the vegetables, so adjust the heat accordingly. Add the more tender vegetables, such as zucchini and summer squash, as well as the celery and continue cooking until all of the vegetables are tender, another 5 minutes or so. Remove the vegetables to a serving dish with a slotted spoon, drizzle with a little of the flavorful oil from the pan, and keep warm. Season to taste with salt and pepper.

Roasted Fennel and Green Beans

SERVES 4

I am a big fan of raw fennel and like to shave it into salads and side dishes. But fennel is also fabulous roasted; it still has some of its faintly licorice flavor, but also a toasty sweet undertone. If you can find baby fennel, use it in place of larger, more mature bulbs. If it's very small, you can roast it whole. This is excellent with grilled salmon.

1	medium fennel bulb
2	tablespoons plus 1 teaspoon mild vegetable oil, preferably grapeseed oil
	Kosher salt and freshly ground black pepper
¼	pound green beans, preferably haricots verts, trimmed
2	tablespoons dried currants, plumped in hot water until soft and drained
1	tablespoon finely chopped shallot
2	teaspoons white wine vinegar, preferably Chardonnay
	Leaves from 2 fresh tarragon sprigs

To roast the fennel, heat the oven to 350°F. Trim the fennel bulb of its stalk, cut it in half, and cut away the tough core. Slice the fennel lengthwise about ¼ inch thick. In a small roasting pan or ovenproof skillet, toss the fennel with 1 teaspoon of the oil. Season with a pinch of salt and a few grinds of pepper and roast until tender and golden, 15 to 20 minutes.

Meanwhile, bring a small saucepan of salted water to a boil and have ready a medium bowl filled with ice water. Boil the green beans until tender, 4 to 6 minutes, depending on thickness, and transfer them with a slotted spoon to the ice water to halt the cooking. Drain and reserve.

To make the vinaigrette, combine the currants, shallot, and vinegar. Slowly whisk in the remaining 2 tablespoons oil and season with a little salt and pepper.

To serve, toss the fennel and green beans with enough of the vinaigrette to moisten them well. Add the tarragon and toss again. Serve warm or at room temperature.

MAKE AHEAD: *You can roast the fennel, blanch the green beans, and make the vinaigrette up to 1 day ahead of serving. Refrigerate the fennel and beans separately, covered with plastic wrap, then let the beans come to room temperature and warm the fennel in a low (200°F oven) before combining.*

Braised Tuscan Kale

Kale—particularly Tuscan kale, which is also called black kale or cavolo nero—has a hint of bitterness, which is why I like to serve it with rich, almost sweet dishes. It is good alongside the lamb shanks (page 255), especially if you don't feel like cooking all the other vegetables that go with that dish. If you can't find Tuscan kale, use regular kale or collard greens.

2	tablespoons extra-virgin olive oil
2	garlic cloves, thinly sliced
1	small shallot, thinly sliced
¼	teaspoon crushed red pepper flakes
	Kosher salt
1	pound kale, preferably Tuscan, trimmed and sliced into ½-inch-wide strips
	Freshly ground black pepper
	Fresh lemon juice

Heat the olive oil in a large skillet over medium heat. Add the garlic, shallot, crushed red pepper, and a pinch of salt and cook, stirring, until fragrant but not browned, 1 to 2 minutes. Add the kale and ¼ cup water and cook, stirring occasionally and turning the greens over in the pan to wilt them, until tender, 15 to 20 minutes. You may need to add more water, depending on how hearty your greens are. Season well with salt and pepper and finish with a few drops of lemon juice.

MAKE AHEAD: *You can hold the cooked kale in the pan off the heat for 30 minutes or so and then reheat it just before serving.*

Pearl Onions au Gratin

SERVES 8   This is a great dish to serve with a big roasted bird, such as Spice-Rubbed Roast Goose (page 229) or a turkey.

  2   pounds red or white pearl onions
  3   thick strips bacon, finely diced
  1   tablespoon unsalted butter
  2   small shallots, finely chopped
  2   garlic cloves, minced
1$\frac{1}{2}$ cups heavy cream
      Kosher salt and freshly ground black pepper
  $\frac{3}{4}$ cup panko (Japanese bread crumbs; see page 209) or coarse
        dry bread crumbs
  2   tablespoons finely chopped fresh parsley

Heat the oven to 350°F. Bring a large pot of water to a boil. Add the onions and cook for 5 minutes. Drain and rinse under cold water. Use a sharp knife to trim off the root ends, then pinch the onions to remove the skins.

In a medium deep skillet, cook the bacon over medium-high heat until the fat is rendered, 3 to 4 minutes. Pour the bacon fat into a heatproof cup and reserve 1$\frac{1}{2}$ teaspoons. Drain the bacon on paper towels.

Add the butter to the skillet along with the shallots and garlic. Cook over medium heat, stirring, until softened, about 3 minutes. Add the cream and simmer until reduced by half, about 10 minutes; season with salt and pepper.

Transfer the pearl onions to a large shallow baking dish and cover with the cream mixture. In a small bowl, toss the panko with the bacon, parsley, and the reserved bacon fat. Season lightly with salt and pepper. Spread the crumb mixture over the onions, bake until the crumbs are toasted and the cream is bubbling, about 30 minutes, and serve.

MAKE AHEAD:

▮ *The onions can be blanched and peeled up to a day ahead. Refrigerate them, covered with plastic wrap, but bring them to room temperature before baking.*

▮ *You can also crisp the bacon a day ahead, though it sure is tough not to eat it.*

Pommes Puree

Pommes Puree is a fancy version of mashed potatoes. The secret to the silky texture is forcing the mash through a fine-mesh strainer after you rice them. You won't go to that trouble for an everyday meal, and the potatoes are still tasty without this step. But the texture of the strained potatoes is so exceedingly smooth and luscious that you have to try it for a special dinner. This recipe is easily multiplied.

2–2¹/₂   pounds Idaho potatoes (russets), whole and unpeeled
            Kosher salt
16   tablespoons (2 sticks) unsalted butter, cut into large pieces
1   cup heavy cream
            Freshly ground white pepper

Put the potatoes in a medium pot of salted water. Bring to a boil and cook until very tender (a cake tester or toothpick will pull out easily), 30 to 40 minutes. Drain the potatoes and allow them to cool just until you're able to handle them. Peel the potatoes while still quite hot (the skin will come off easily), put them in a potato ricer, and rice them into a large bowl.

Meanwhile, heat the butter and cream together over low heat until the butter melts. Using a wooden spoon, stir this mixture into the potatoes. Continue mixing until all the lumps are gone, but don't overmix or the potatoes will become gluey.

You can serve them as is, which is nice and homey. Or, for an incredibly smooth puree, pass the potatoes through a fine-mesh strainer. Either way, taste and season with salt and a few grinds of white pepper before serving.

MAKE AHEAD: *These are definitely best if served right away, but you can make them a few hours ahead and carefully reheat them over low heat.*

Potatoes Mousseline

SERVES 6 TO 8 This is a great dish for entertaining, because you can make it completely ahead and pop it in the oven just before serving. The potatoes are lightened by the addition of whipped cream, and a quick flash under the broiler creates a golden brown crust that people fight over.

8	tablespoons (1 stick) unsalted butter, melted
3–3½	pounds Idaho potatoes (russets), whole and unpeeled
	Kosher salt
¾	cup whole milk
1	cup heavy cream, whipped to soft peaks
	Freshly ground black pepper

Heat the oven to 250°F. Brush a 9-x-13-inch baking dish with some of the melted butter.

Put the potatoes in a large saucepan and cover with well-salted cold water. Bring to a boil and cook until tender (a cake tester or toothpick will pull out easily), about 30 minutes. Drain the potatoes and allow them to cool just until you're able to handle them. Peel the potatoes while still quite hot (the skin will come off easily) and rice them into a large bowl. Stir in the milk and half of the remaining melted butter with a wooden spoon.

Whisk the whipped cream a few times to fluff it up and then gently stir about one third of it into the potato mixture, lightening it with the whisk. Using a rubber spatula, fold in the rest of the whipped cream. Season well with salt and add a few grinds of pepper.

Transfer the potatoes to the baking dish. Spread evenly and drizzle with the remaining butter. Bake the mousseline for 30 minutes, until heated through. Just before serving, heat the broiler to high and broil the potatoes until lightly browned, 2 to 4 minutes.

MAKE AHEAD: *You can drizzle the riced potatoes with butter, cover with plastic wrap, and refrigerate them for up to 12 hours. Let the potatoes come to room temperature for about 30 minutes before baking.*

Pommes Frites

The key to crisp, perfectly browned French fries is to fry them twice, first to cook the interior, then to brown and crisp the exterior. (See the photo on page 262.) In a perfect world, all French fries would be made with duck fat, but grapeseed oil works well, too, because of its high smoke point. (Peanut oil is also good for frying.) I like to enliven the fries with some fresh herbs sprinkled over them and serve them with mayonnaise or, even better, a flavored aïoli (page 20 or page 47) instead of ketchup. For a classic pairing, offer some pommes frites with the mussels on page 192.

About 2 quarts grapeseed oil
6 Idaho potatoes (russets), preferably long ones, peeled and soaked
  in cold water
Kosher salt
2 tablespoons fresh fines herbes (see page 254)

Pour enough oil into a large, heavy pot to fill it just over halfway. Begin heating the oil over medium heat as you prepare the potatoes. Line a baking sheet with paper towels.

Remove the potatoes from the water and dry them well. Square off the potatoes by cutting the rounded edges. (This makes them easier to slice and more uniformly shaped.) Cut into $\frac{1}{3}$-inch-thick slices, stack a few slices, then cut the slices into $\frac{1}{3}$-inch-wide sticks.

When the oil reaches 325°F on a candy/fry thermometer, fry the potatoes in batches for 3 minutes (they will not look cooked but will be tender). Increase or decrease the heat as needed to maintain the oil at 325°F. Using a slotted spoon, preferably one with more slot than spoon, such as a Chinese strainer, transfer the potatoes to the lined baking sheet. Repeat this initial frying step with all the potatoes. Turn off the heat under the oil if not finishing the fries right away, but reserve it in the pot for the second frying.

When ready to serve, bring the oil to 375°F. Have ready another baking sheet lined with paper towels. If you're not eating the fries immediately (which is the best way), heat the oven to 300°F. Cook the potatoes in batches until golden brown, about 5 minutes. Transfer to the lined baking sheet and sprinkle with salt. Keep the potatoes warm in the oven, if you like, as you continue frying in batches. Just before serving, sprinkle the fries with the herbs.

MAKE AHEAD: *I like to give the potatoes their initial fry well before I plan to serve them, simply because the process feels much less arduous that way. The potatoes will hold at room temperature for 2 hours.*

Spinach Amandine

This spinach has a little cream in it for richness, but it is light and more green than creamy. Serve it with Potatoes Mousseline (page 279) and Slow-Roasted Beef Tenderloin with Thyme (page 236) for a special-occasion dinner. For the best flavor, don't use baby spinach.

½   cup sliced almonds
2   tablespoons extra-virgin olive oil
20   ounces fresh spinach (see headnote), stemmed, washed, and drained
    (about 8 cups, loosely packed)
½   cup heavy cream
    Kosher salt and freshly ground black pepper
1½   teaspoons almond oil (or walnut or hazelnut oil)

Heat the oven to 350°F. Put the almonds on a baking sheet or in an ovenproof skillet and toast them in the oven, shaking the pan once or twice, until fragrant and lightly browned on the edges, 3 to 5 minutes.

Heat the olive oil in a large nonstick pan over medium heat. Add a large handful of spinach, and as it wilts and makes room in the pan, add more spinach. When it's all just wilted, remove the spinach to a strainer. Pour off any liquid in the pan and wipe it clean. Press on the spinach with the back of a large spoon to release more liquid. Drain on paper towels and return to the pan. Add the heavy cream to the pan and cook until reduced by almost half. Add the spinach and toss to coat. Season with salt and pepper and keep on low heat until serving.

To serve, sprinkle each portion of spinach with the toasted almonds and drizzle with the nut oil.

MAKE AHEAD: *You can toast the almonds a couple of days ahead. Let them cool completely before storing them in an airtight container.*

Roasted Winter Squash with Maple Syrup and Sage Cream

SERVES 6   You can make this fall dish with whatever winter squash looks best at the market. A mix looks dramatic and tastes delicious, but you can use all butternut squash, and it will still be tasty.

About 4 pounds winter squash, preferably a mix of buttercup, delicata, butternut, and acorn, peeled (you can leave the tender skin on delicata) and cut into 1-inch-thick wedges or rings

3   tablespoons extra-virgin olive oil

1½   tablespoons brown sugar

Kosher salt and freshly ground black pepper

1½   tablespoons real maple syrup, plus more for drizzling

¾   cup heavy cream

15   fresh sage leaves, coarsely chopped

1   tablespoon unsalted butter

Sprigs of watercress for garnish

Shaved pecorino

Fleur de sel

Heat the oven to 350°F. In a large bowl, toss the squash with the olive oil and brown sugar. Season well with salt and pepper. Spread the squash pieces out on two large baking sheets, organizing them by type, and cook until tender when pierced with a skewer or toothpick and lightly caramelized but still holding their shape; the time will vary according to the size of the pieces and the variety, but start checking after 20 minutes or so and remove the pieces when they become tender. Arrange the squash on a large platter and drizzle with 1½ tablespoons maple syrup.

Meanwhile, in a small saucepan, bring the cream to a simmer with the sage and cook over medium heat until reduced by about half, 8 to 10 minutes. Remove from the heat and let stand for 5 minutes. Add the butter and season lightly with salt and pepper. Strain the cream into a heatproof cup. Drizzle it over the roasted squash, garnish with the watercress and pecorino shavings, drizzle a little bit of maple syrup over, and finish with a sprinkle of fleur de sel.

MAKE AHEAD: *The roasted squash and sage cream can be refrigerated separately, covered, overnight. Reheat the squash in a 350°F oven, loosely covered with foil; reheat the cream gently on the stove.*

Tomato Jam

When I gave this super-easy recipe to a friend to try, I asked her to report back on the yield. She couldn't give me one. Why? Because she ate too many spoonfuls of it right from the pan. This is the perfect recipe for late summer, when your tomato plants are weighted down with gorgeous ripe fruit. The jam keeps for a long time in the fridge and goes well with just about anything off the grill, from smoky-sweet barbecued ribs to burgers and butterflied leg of lamb. The sweet, silky tomatoes are also a great topping for salads, pizza, and crostini, especially when paired with some blue cheese. I could go on, but you get the idea: make this jam.

4½	pounds tomatoes
1	cup sugar
¼	cup white wine vinegar, preferably a good Chardonnay
	Kosher salt

Stem the tomatoes and coarsely chop them, removing most of their seeds; don't worry if some remain. In a wide, heavy pot or high-sided skillet over medium heat, combine the sugar, vinegar, and ¼ cup water. Cook, stirring occasionally, until the sugar has dissolved and the mixture begins to look syrupy. Add the chopped tomatoes and cook over medium-low heat, stirring occasionally, until the tomatoes cook to a jammy consistency, about 3 hours. Season to taste with salt.

MAKE AHEAD: *The jam will keep for a couple of weeks covered and refrigerated. Bring to a cool room temperature before serving.*

Turnip Puree

SERVES 4 I often pair meat and fish dishes with a rich and flavorful vegetable puree. You can vary this recipe using parsnips, carrots, sweet potatoes, celery root, or fennel in place of the turnips. You may need to adjust the amount of cream, using a little more or less, depending on the vegetable you choose, to get the consistency you want.

2 cups heavy cream
2 tablespoons unsalted butter (optional)
2 pounds turnips, peeled and cut into 1-inch cubes
  Kosher salt and freshly ground black pepper

Heat the cream and butter, if using, in a saucepan over medium heat. When the butter has melted, add the turnips and a pinch of salt. Reduce to a simmer and cover the turnips with a round of parchment paper set right on them in the pan. Cook until tender when pierced with a skewer, 30 to 45 minutes, depending on the age of the turnips. In a blender or a food processor, puree the turnips, then pass them through a fine-mesh strainer to get about 1 cup puree. Season with additional salt and a little pepper to taste, and serve.

MAKE AHEAD: *You can make vegetable purees a day ahead of serving them. Keep them refrigerated, covered, and reheat gently before serving.*

Creamy Mascarpone Polenta

"Oh, my god, this is so good" is what people say when they taste this polenta. Because it's so easy to make and goes so well with all kinds of roasts and braises, you will hear that refrain a lot. Get used to it. (See the photo on page 221.)

4 cups milk

1 cup cornmeal (I like Anson Mills coarse-ground)

6 tablespoons (¾ stick) unsalted butter

Kosher salt and freshly ground black pepper

A generous ½ cup mascarpone

In a large saucepan, bring the milk to a gentle boil. Pour the cornmeal slowly into the milk, whisking all the while to prevent clumping. Reduce the heat to a simmer, add 3 tablespoons of the butter, season with 2 teaspoons salt and a few good grinds of pepper, and let the polenta cook gently, stirring occasionally, until it's thick and the cornmeal is tender, about 45 minutes. Stir in the remaining 3 tablespoons butter and then the mascarpone and cook an additional 10 minutes or so, stirring occasionally. Season to taste with more salt and pepper, if needed, and serve.

MAKE AHEAD: *Polenta is best eaten soon after cooking, but it can hold over very low heat until the rest of the meal is ready; just remember to give it a stir now and again. Thin it with a little additional milk if necessary.*

Ben's Wild Rice Salad

SERVES 8 TO 10 Even I, an avowed rice hater, love this salad. Ben Elliott, a chef who has worked with me for years, created the recipe. He says he "just chops up a bunch of stuff and mixes it with the rice." And, in fact, that's about all there is to it. You can cook the rice the way Ben suggests or as your package directs; either way, you will need 2½ cups of cooked rice. This is yummy alongside some roasted chicken that's been rubbed with the spice mix on page 229.

8	ounces (1 cup) wild rice
	Kosher salt and freshly ground black pepper
1	red bell pepper, cut into medium dice (about 1 cup)
1	red onion, cut into medium dice
2	oranges, segmented as directed on page 187, juice reserved
2	tablespoons chopped fresh parsley
1	cup pine nuts, toasted in a dry skillet or oven until golden brown
1	large garlic clove, finely chopped (about 2 teaspoons)
½	cup golden raisins, plumped in hot water for 15 minutes and drained
1	cup feta cheese, preferably French, crumbled
1	teaspoon crushed red pepper flakes
1¼	cups extra-virgin olive oil
2	tablespoons sherry vinegar

To cook the rice, bring 2⅓ cups of water to a boil in a medium saucepan. Add the rice, stir, cover, reduce to a simmer, and cook until tender, 45 to 50 minutes. Remove from the heat and let stand, covered, for about 10 minutes. Fluff with a fork and season to taste with salt and pepper. Let the rice cool a little and then toss it with all the other ingredients, including reserved orange juice. Serve at room temperature or cool.

MAKE AHEAD: *You can make the rice salad ahead and refrigerate it, covered. For the best flavor, however, don't serve it cold straight out of the fridge. Let it warm up a little at room temperature. The cold will lessen the flavor a bit and may dry out the salad some, so taste the rice just before serving and add more salt, pepper, vinegar, and even a little oil, if need be.*

sweet treats

CREAMY VANILLA BREAD PUDDING   292

CHOCOLATE MOUSSE   296

OEUFS À LA NEIGE WITH STRAWBERRIES AND
VANILLA CRÈME ANGLAISE   297

YOGURT PANNA COTTA   300

BUTTER COOKIES   301

MY FAVORITE CHOCOLATE COOKIES   302

HOMEMADE APPLE BUTTER TART   304

WINTER CITRUS WITH CUMIN MERINGUE AND
WHIPPED CRÈME FRAÎCHE   307

PEACHES AND CREAM   310

For me, dessert is an all-or-nothing proposition. Much of the time, I skip this course when I'm out, because I fill up too much on dinner. At home, more often than not, I snap off a piece of really good dark chocolate to end a meal. But when I do give in to dessert, I go for it. I don't just serve bread pudding; I serve bread pudding topped with a fig sauce and a caramel sauce *and* chantilly whipped cream. Too much, you think? Wait till you try it.

When I create a dessert, I'm often inspired by what looks good at the farmers' market. I consider what flavors and textures excite and surprise me. I think about how to balance sweetness so the dessert has more than a single flavor note. And I look to the ingredients I love so much: fresh figs, peaches, cream, and (of course) chocolate.

I'm a sucker for classics like chocolate mousse and comforting desserts like bread pudding. My apple tart is a homey rendition made with homemade applesauce, and I like retro-chic dishes like oeufs à la neige. I've kept the attributes that make these treats so beloved while giving them a modern sensibility.

CHOCOLATE MOUSSE (PAGE 296)

Creamy Vanilla Bread Pudding

When I make this rich and comforting dessert at my restaurant, I keep a second pan in reserve for snacking, since my chefs are always stealing little spoonfuls. It's ridiculous how good the bread pudding is with two sauces and chantilly cream, but you don't have to go all out. As my chef-thieves will attest, the bread pudding is delicious straight from the pan. This pudding is more about the creamy custard than it is about the bread. I like the double whammy of using both the vanilla bean and the vanilla extract. If you don't have a vanilla bean, double the amount of extract and skip the vanilla-bean-steeping step.

3	cups heavy cream
1	vanilla bean (see headnote)
¼	teaspoon kosher salt
5	slices white bread (I like Pepperidge Farm White Sandwich Bread), cubed
4	large eggs
¾	cup sugar
1	teaspoon pure vanilla extract
	Fresh Fig Sauce (optional; recipe follows)
	Creamy Caramel Sauce (page 294)
	Chantilly Cream (page 295)

In a medium saucepan, heat the cream over low heat. Split the vanilla bean lengthwise with the tip of a paring knife and scrape the seeds out into the cream. Add the bean to the pot, too. Stir in the salt and heat the cream until warm to the touch. Take the pot off the heat and let the vanilla bean steep for 30 minutes to 1 hour.

Pile the bread cubes into a 9-×-13-inch baking dish, distributing them more or less evenly.

In the bowl of a stand mixer fitted with the whisk attachment or using a hand mixer, whisk together the eggs and sugar on medium speed until the mixture is light yellow in color and falls from the beater in thick ribbons, about 5 minutes. Add the vanilla extract.

Remove the vanilla bean pod from the cream mixture and reheat the cream over medium heat. Do not let it boil, but do let it get quite hot. Remove the cream from the heat and slowly pour 1 cup of it into the egg mixture, whisking constantly. Then pour the egg-cream mixture into the saucepan with the remaining cream and whisk it together. Strain the cream mixture through a fine-mesh strainer over the bread cubes in the baking dish. Give the pan a gentle shake to be sure all is distributed well and then let the bread absorb the custard for at least 30 minutes before baking. If baking the bread pudding right away, heat the oven to 350°F, with a rack in the center. If not, cover it with plastic wrap and refrigerate it.

When ready to bake, set the bread pudding dish in a larger roasting pan. Add hot water to the roasting pan until the water is halfway up the sides of the baking dish. Bake in the center of the oven until the custard is just firm, 50 minutes to 1 hour (begin checking earlier; give the pan a gentle shake and take it out of the oven when the custard is no longer jiggly). Let cool a bit.

Serve warm, at room temperature, or even cold. Put a serving in a large dish and top with fig sauce, caramel sauce, if using, and a dollop of chantilly cream.

MAKE AHEAD:

▌ *This tastes better the longer the bread soaks in the custard, so feel free to refrigerate it, unbaked, for as long as 24 hours.*

▌ *You can also bake the bread pudding a day or two ahead; let it cool at room temperature before covering it with plastic wrap and refrigerating it. Take it out before serving and let it warm up a bit; you'll taste the vanilla better if the pudding is not very cold.*

Fresh Fig Sauce

MAKES ABOUT 3½ CUPS

I love the sweet but not cloying flavor of fresh figs, their soft interior and tender skin. Black Mission figs, which have a purplish black skin, are my favorite, because of their small seeds. Look for fresh figs in summer and early fall. Choose those that are soft and supple, with no blemishes, and use them soon after buying. In spring, when figs may be hard to find, you can make this sauce using fresh cherries. This sweet, slightly boozy sauce is also delicious over vanilla ice cream.

1	cup brandy
1	cup sugar
1	cinnamon stick
1	pint ripe fresh figs, preferably Black Mission, halved or quartered if large

In a medium saucepan, combine the brandy, sugar, 1 cup water, and the cinnamon stick. Bring to a boil over medium-high heat and cook until reduced by half. Add the figs and cook, stirring occasionally, until the figs soften and absorb the flavor of the liquid, about another 10 minutes. Serve warm.

MAKE AHEAD: *You can make the sauce days ahead and keep it refrigerated. Reheat it gently before using it.*

Creamy Caramel Sauce

MAKES ABOUT 1½ CUPS

This caramel sauce is also fabulous drizzled over ice cream, grilled pineapple slices, a piece of warm apple tart, gingerbread cake, and spice-poached pears.

1	cup sugar
1	cup heavy cream

Combine the sugar with ¼ cup water in a medium saucepan. Dissolve the sugar over medium heat, stirring until the mixture is clear. Increase the heat to high and cook, swirling the pan to cook evenly but no longer stirring, until the caramel is a deep amber. (Check the color by carefully drizzling some onto a white plate.) Don't worry if the sugar hardens while cooking; simply stir it and continue cooking until it smooths out. Take the pot off the heat and carefully whisk in the cream. The caramel will sputter, so be careful, as it's very hot. Return the sauce to the heat and bring to a boil, whisking constantly until smooth, 2 to 3 minutes. Let cool a bit before serving, but serve warm.

MAKE AHEAD: *Homemade caramel sauce is a delicious treat to keep in the refrigerator, where it will last for months in an airtight container. Simply reheat it gently to serve.*

Chantilly Cream
MAKES ABOUT 1½ CUPS

One taste and you may never go back to regular whipped cream.

1 cup heavy cream
1 tablespoon confectioners' sugar
½ teaspoon pure vanilla extract
Kosher salt

In the bowl of a stand mixer fitted with the whisk attachment or using a hand mixer, combine the cream, sugar, vanilla extract, and a pinch of salt. Whisk the ingredients together, gently at first and then increasing the speed, until you can lift out the stopped whisk and leave behind peaks just shy of firm. Be careful not to overbeat, however, or you'll get very sweet butter.

MAKE AHEAD: *This is best made just before serving, but it will keep refrigerated for a few hours; give it a quick whisk before using.*

Chocolate Mousse

Made with more yolks than egg whites, this mousse is very rich, and a little goes a long way. Although I like deep, dark chocolate for eating out of hand, this recipe works best with semisweet. Bittersweet, which tends to have a higher ratio of cocoa solids, can make the mousse less smooth. (See the photo on page 290.)

¼ cup plus 1 tablespoon sugar

1 large egg

3 large egg yolks

6 ounces semisweet chocolate, chopped (I like Valrhona)

1 cup plus 1 tablespoon heavy cream
   Additional whipped cream for garnish (optional)
   Fresh raspberries (optional)

Heat the sugar in a small saucepan over high heat with 2 tablespoons water, stirring, until the sugar dissolves.

Whisk the egg and egg yolks together in the bowl of a stand mixer fitted with the whisk attachment or using a hand mixer until light in color. Carefully and slowly pour the sugar syrup into the bowl with the eggs while the mixer is on medium speed. Be careful that the syrup goes into the eggs and does not spatter on the sides of the bowl. Continue to whisk on medium speed until the mixture is completely cool, pale yellow, and quadrupled in volume and clings to the whisk when lifted from the bowl, 10 to 15 minutes.

Melt the chocolate in a small bowl set in a larger pan with boiling water over low heat, stirring until smooth; transfer to a large bowl.

In another bowl, with a clean whisk or beaters, whip the cream to soft peaks. Fold about a quarter of the cream into the melted chocolate and then fold in the rest. Fold the cooled egg and sugar mixture into the chocolate, too, and continue folding until no streaks remain. Divide among eight serving bowls or glasses and refrigerate to cool and set for at least 2 hours. To serve, top the mousse with a little whipped cream and some raspberries.

MAKE AHEAD: *You can make the mousse up to 2 days ahead; just be sure to cover it in plastic wrap before refrigerating.*

Oeufs à la Neige with Strawberries and Vanilla Crème Anglaise

This is a modern version of the classic French dessert featuring islands of cooked meringue floating in custard sauce. The meringue is baked instead of poached. (The final shape is admittedly not very oeuflike, but I like the old-fashioned sound of that name, and the light-as-air texture is very similar.) Though the portions are large, the meringue practically disappears on your tongue and is not at all filling. You can serve the meringue as is or, even better, lightly brown it.

You will need two baking sheets. A kitchen torch is also useful for browning the meringues. If you would rather broil them, slice them first and then broil, transferring them to the custard as they brown.

1½ cups egg whites (from about 12 large eggs; save 6 of the yolks
    to make the crème anglaise)
¾ cup sugar, plus more for the strawberries
1 pint strawberries, hulled and sliced to yield about 2 cups,
    or a mix of your favorite berries
Vanilla Crème Anglaise (recipe follows)

Heat the oven to 250°F. Line a 9-x-13-inch baking pan with parchment paper and spray it lightly with cooking spray. Have ready another baking pan of the same size and lightly spray it with cooking spray.

In the bowl of a stand mixer fitted with the whisk attachment or using a hand mixer, whisk the egg whites on medium-high speed until very frothy. Gradually add the sugar and continue to whisk until stiff peaks form. (When you lift the stopped whisk, there should be peaks with no drooping.) With a large flexible spatula, scrape the whipped whites into the parchment-lined pan and gently spread them to an even thickness. Invert the other pan on top to act as a cover. Place this in a larger baking pan and fill the baking pan with water until it comes halfway up the sides of the baking pan that holds the egg whites.

Bake until the whites are set, about 25 minutes. Take the pan out of the oven, remove the top pan, and cool to room temperature in the baking pan. If not serving right away, remove from the water bath and refrigerate.

A few hours before serving, toss the berries with 2 to 3 tablespoons sugar, depending on their sweetness, and let them macerate in the refrigerator. They should macerate for at least an hour and up to a day before serving.

To serve, pour about ¼ cup of the crème anglaise into each of eight wide bowls or large plates.

Slice the meringue into large squares or use a large round cookie cutter to cut out circles. (Don't worry about any residual liquid in the bottom of the pan; just leave it behind.) "Float" 1 or 2 meringues per serving over the custard. Brown the top of the meringues by sweeping a kitchen torch across the surface; if you are browning the meringue under the broiler, slice and broil first, then place the meringue on the custard. Top with some of the berries and a little of their juice and serve.

MAKE AHEAD:

▌ *You can make the meringues up to a day ahead and refrigerate, loosely covered with plastic wrap. Serve them cool but not super-cold.*

▌ *The longer the berries sit in the sugar, the softer they become; don't hold them for more than a day before serving.*

Vanilla Crème Anglaise
MAKES ABOUT 3 CUPS

Crème anglaise is the most delicious way to dress up dessert.

2	cups whole milk
	Kosher salt
1	vanilla bean or 1 teaspoon pure vanilla extract
6	large egg yolks
½	cup sugar

Put the milk and a pinch of salt in a medium saucepan. If using a vanilla bean, split the pod lengthwise and scrape out the seeds into the milk. Add the pod to the pan as well. Bring to a simmer over medium-high heat. Remove from the heat and let the vanilla bean steep for 10 minutes or so. (If using vanilla extract, skip this step.) Remove the pod and discard it.

Meanwhile, whisk the egg yolks with the sugar until the mixture turns pale yellow and thickens a bit.

Have ready a fine-mesh strainer set over a bowl or a large liquid measuring cup.

Reheat (or heat, if using vanilla extract) the milk over medium-low heat until hot but without any bubbles on the surface. (You don't want it to boil at this point.) Whisk about 1/2 cup of the hot milk into the egg yolks to temper them, then whisk the egg yolk mixture into the milk. Continue to cook the custard over medium-low to low heat, stirring constantly with a flexible, heatproof spatula, until the sauce feels as if it has more body and looks shinier and slightly thicker, 3 to 5 minutes. Take the sauce off the heat immediately, stir it for a minute off the heat so that it safely thickens a bit more, and pour it through the fine-mesh strainer into the waiting bowl.

If using vanilla extract, add it now and stir to combine. To chill, place the bowl of crème anglaise in a larger bowl filled with ice and water and stir until cold. Cover with plastic and refrigerate.

MAKE AHEAD: *The crème anglaise will keep for up to 3 days, covered and refrigerated.*

Yogurt Panna Cotta

Serve the cold panna cottas garnished with fresh seasonal fruit or your favorite compote or confiture.

1½ cups heavy cream
2   cups full-fat Greek-style yogurt, such as Fage Total
⅓   cup sugar
½   teaspoon pure vanilla extract
    Kosher salt
2   teaspoons powdered gelatin

In a medium saucepan, combine the cream, yogurt, sugar, vanilla extract, and a pinch of salt over medium heat just to dissolve the sugar.

Sprinkle the gelatin over ¼ cup cold water in a small saucepan and let it sit for 5 minutes to soften, then heat it over low heat until it becomes a clear liquid. Whisk this into the cream mixture and pour through a fine-mesh strainer.

Divide among eight 4- to 5-ounce ramekins or parfait glasses, cover with plastic wrap, and refrigerate until set, at least 4 hours, preferably overnight.

MAKE AHEAD: *These will hold, refrigerated and covered with plastic wrap, for 2 days.*

Butter Cookies

Delicious on their own with a cup of tea, these buttery cookies go well with fruit desserts like Peaches and Cream (page 310). Or serve alongside sliced fresh strawberries in summer for a gratifying treat.

10	tablespoons (1¼ sticks) unsalted butter, at room temperature
½	cup plus 2 tablespoons sugar
3	large egg yolks
1½	cups all-purpose flour
¼	teaspoon baking powder

In the bowl of a stand mixer fitted with the paddle attachment or using a hand mixer, whip the butter and sugar together on medium speed until light and fluffy, 3 to 4 minutes. Add the egg yolks one at a time, incorporating each one into the mixture before adding the next. Stop the mixer occasionally to scrape down the sides of the mixing bowl. Add the flour and baking powder and mix on low speed to combine. Lay a large piece of plastic wrap down on your work surface and scrape the dough out of the bowl onto the plastic wrap. Fold the plastic over the top and push down to flatten and shape the dough into a disk about ¾ inch thick. Refrigerate for at least 6 hours.

To bake the cookies, line two baking sheets with parchment paper. On a lightly floured surface, roll out the dough until it is about ¼ inch thick. Use a sharp knife or cookie cutter to cut the dough into your desired cookie shape. (Reroll and cut the scraps, too.) Transfer the cookies to the prepared baking sheets, leaving 1½ inches between them; these cookies will spread. Refrigerate the cookies on the sheets for 15 to 20 minutes. Meanwhile, heat the oven to 325°F, with racks in the center and upper third. Bake the cookies until golden, 15 to 20 minutes, switching the position of the sheets from the top to the center rack and vice versa halfway through baking. Transfer the cookies to a cooling rack. Once completely cool, the cookies can be stored in an airtight container at room temperature.

MAKE AHEAD: *You can make and chill the dough up to 3 days ahead of baking the cookies. The dough also freezes well. Let it thaw overnight in the refrigerator before rolling it out. The baked cookies will keep, stored in an airtight container when they are completely cooled, for a few days.*

My Favorite Chocolate Cookies

MAKES ABOUT
8 DOZEN COOKIES,
DEPENDING ON SIZE

Deeply chocolaty, these cookies have a surprising hint of sea salt. I keep a log of the dough in the freezer so I can bake some whenever the mood strikes, which is often. This recipe is a cross between French pastry chef Pierre Hermé's Korova Cookies (made famous by cookbook author Dorie Greenspan) and Cape Cod baker Terri Horn's addictively salty chocolate oatmeal cookies, which are finished with a sprinkle of sea salt. My cookie includes a touch of cinnamon and melted chocolate as well as cocoa powder for an intense flavor.

2½	cups all-purpose flour
¾	cup plus 1 tablespoon cocoa powder
1	tablespoon baking soda
1	tablespoon ground cinnamon
1	cup coarsely chopped bittersweet chocolate (preferably 85% cacao), plus 1 cup finely chopped bittersweet chocolate
11	ounces (2 sticks plus 6 tablespoons) unsalted butter, at room temperature
1½	cups sugar
1	teaspoon kosher salt
1	teaspoon pure vanilla extract
	Fleur de sel

In a medium bowl, whisk together the flour, cocoa powder, baking soda, and cinnamon.

Melt the coarsely chopped chocolate in a small bowl set in a larger saucepan of boiling water over low heat.

In the bowl of a stand mixer fitted with the paddle attachment or using a hand mixer, cream the butter on medium speed until soft and creamy. Add the sugar, salt, and vanilla extract and beat until incorporated, about another minute.

Reduce the mixer speed to low and add the dry ingredients in a few additions, mixing until incorporated; the dough will look crumbly. With the mixer still on, add the melted chocolate in a steady stream. Add the finely chopped chocolate and mix until just combined.

Turn the dough out onto a smooth work surface; divide it into 4 pieces for easier handling. Working with 1 piece at a time, shape the pieces into logs 1 to 2 inches in diameter. Wrap each log in plastic wrap and chill them for at least 1 hour (and up to 48 hours) to firm them up for easier slicing.

When ready to bake, heat the oven to 325°F, with racks in the center and upper third. Line two baking sheets with parchment paper.

Using a sharp chef's knife, slice the logs into rounds between ¼ and ⅓ inch thick. Because of the chips and because the dough is on the dry side, the cookies may crumble at times. If they do, just piece them back together on the baking sheet. Put the slices on the baking sheets with about 1 inch between them and sprinkle with a pinch of fleur de sel. Bake for 10 to 12 minutes, switching the position of the pans from the top to the center rack and vice versa after about 5 minutes. The cookies will not change much in appearance; they will set as they cool. Do not overbake. Let cool on a rack for a few minutes before removing the cookies from the baking sheets.

MAKE AHEAD:

▮ *Wrapped airtight, the unbaked logs can be refrigerated for up to 2 days or frozen for 1 month. You don't have to defrost the logs before baking. Just slice and bake the cookies for 1 minute longer.*

▮ *Packed airtight, the baked cookies will keep at room temperature for up to 3 days; they can be frozen for up to 1 month.*

Homemade Apple Butter Tart

This tart has the pure flavors of home: apple, butter, sugar, and cinnamon. Essentially an apple puree spread on a golden brown rectangle of puff pastry, the tart comes together quickly. I like it topped with thinly sliced apples that have been caramelized like a crème brûlée. I usually cut two-bite pieces and serve the tart as a little treat with coffee at the end of dinner, but you can definitely cut larger pieces for a more substantial dessert. Whether you include a scoop of ice cream with it is up to you.

FOR THE APPLE BUTTER

2	Granny Smith apples, peeled, quartered, and cored
2	tablespoons sugar
	Kosher salt
1	tablespoon unsalted butter
1	cup apple cider
1	tablespoon fresh lemon juice

FOR THE TART SHELL

	All-purpose flour for rolling
1	sheet frozen puff pastry, preferably all-butter (see page 9), defrosted

FOR THE CARAMELIZED APPLE TOPPING

5	tablespoons sugar, preferably superfine
1	teaspoon ground cinnamon
3–4	Granny Smith apples

FOR SERVING

Confectioners' sugar or ice cream (optional)

TO MAKE THE APPLE BUTTER: Heat the oven to 375°F. Toss the quartered apples with the sugar and a pinch of salt. Melt the butter in a medium saucepan over medium heat. Once the butter begins to bubble, add the apples and cook, stirring occasionally, until lightly caramelized, about 5 minutes. Add the apple cider and simmer until the apples are very tender and the liquid is almost evaporated, about 15 minutes. Remove the apples from the pan and puree until smooth in a blender or food processor. Stir in the lemon juice. Set aside to cool.

TO MAKE THE TART SHELL: On a lightly floured surface, roll out the puff pastry ⅛ inch thick. Line a baking sheet with parchment paper and put the puff pastry on it. Cover the puff pastry with another piece of parchment and then weigh it down with another baking sheet. Bake until golden brown—you'll have to sneak a peek—12 to 15 minutes. Remove from the oven, take the top sheet and parchment off, then slide the puff pastry onto a rack to cool.

TO PREPARE THE APPLE TOPPING: Line a baking sheet with a Silpat or other silicone liner. Combine the sugar with the cinnamon. Thinly slice the apples ⅛ inch thick. Even better, slice the apples on a mandoline using a gaufrette blade (the one used to make waffle fries), stopping when you hit the core. Spread the apple slices out on the Silpat and sprinkle evenly with the cinnamon sugar. If you have a kitchen torch, use it with a gentle sweeping motion to heat the sugar until it browns and bubbles. Let cool. If you don't have a torch, continue with the recipe as directed below.

TO SERVE THE TART: Heat the oven to 325°F. Spread the cooled apple puree over the cooled puff pastry. Lay the apple slices over the puree. Warm the pastry in the oven for about 5 minutes. If the apples are not already caramelized, briefly broil the tart, watching closely so the pastry does not burn. Remove from the oven and cut into pieces. If you like, serve smaller pieces dusted with confectioners' sugar and larger pieces with a scoop of ice cream.

MAKE AHEAD:

▎ *You can make the apple puree up to 2 days ahead and keep it refrigerated, covered with plastic wrap.*

▎ *You can assemble the entire tart up to 2 hours ahead of serving it; leave it at room temperature.*

Winter Citrus with Cumin Meringue and Whipped Crème Fraîche

SERVES 4   Fresh-tasting citrus segments are poached in a sweet syrup made with star anise, cinnamon, and cardamom pods for a slightly exotic touch. The compote is topped with crispy, light-as-air meringues flavored ever so subtly with cumin. Its earthiness grounds the overt sweetness of the meringues and complements the other spices. For the fruit, I like to use a combination of six different varieties: a Cara Cara orange, a satsuma, a tangerine, a Meyer lemon, a ruby red grapefruit, and a blood orange. You don't have to use that exact combination, but do use three or four different kinds of citrus.

FOR THE CITRUS

1/2	cup sugar
2	whole star anise or 2 teaspoons pieces
1	cinnamon stick
2	teaspoons whole cardamom pods (green or white)
6	assorted citrus fruit (see headnote), peeled and segmented (see page 187; squeeze juice left in pulp and reserve that, too, for about 1 1/2 cups juice)

FOR THE MERINGUES

3	large egg whites
1/8	teaspoon cream of tartar
1/8	teaspoon ground cumin
1/8	teaspoon kosher salt
1	cup sugar

FOR SERVING

3/4	cup crème fraîche

TO MAKE THE CITRUS: In a medium saucepan, combine the sugar, 1/2 cup water, star anise, cinnamon stick, and cardamom pods. Bring to a simmer and cook until the sugar has dissolved and the spices have infused their flavor, about 10 minutes. Add the reserved citrus juice and return to a simmer over medium-low heat until mixture has reduced by about half and is syrupy, about 1/2 hour. Strain and reserve the liquid. (Discard the spices.) If not using right away, refrigerate the fruit and the liquid, covered.

TO MAKE THE MERINGUES: Heat the oven to 200°F and line a baking sheet with a Silpat or with parchment paper. In a bowl, with an electric mixer, beat the egg whites on

medium speed until frothy. Add the cream of tartar, cumin, and salt. Gradually add the sugar, and continue to beat until stiff peaks form.

Using a large spoon, put dollops of the egg whites, each about the size of a large lime, on the baking sheet, leaving about 1½ inches of room around each; you will make about 20 meringues.

Bake the meringues until completely dry and crisp, about 4 hours. Ideally the crisps should not color or should color only slightly. (To test for doneness, take one out, let cool briefly, and bite into it.) Cool the meringues completely on a rack before storing them in an airtight container. (If they are even slightly warm when stored, they can get soft and sticky.)

To serve, beat the crème fraîche to medium peaks. Put a dollop on each of four rimmed plates or shallow bowls. Divide the citrus among the plates, being sure to include a few slices of each kind. Spoon the reduced citrus liquid over and around the fruit. Garnish with a couple of meringues (you will have extra).

MAKE AHEAD:

▌ *The meringues can be made up to 3 days ahead. Let them cool completely before storing them in an airtight container in a cool, dry place.*

▌ *The fruit and reduced sauce can be refrigerated for 2 days before serving, covered with plastic wrap.*

Peaches and Cream

I love the pure simplicity of this dessert: fragrant summertime peaches cooked in a wine-and-sugar syrup and served with sweetened creamy mascarpone. I often serve a crisp butter cookie, like the one on page 301, alongside, but the cookie is not vital; this is really all about the peach. Quick to make, this dessert is a knockout both in flavor and in looks; wait till you see the color of the cooking liquid, especially against the white mascarpone—it's just beautiful. I sometimes add a couple of extra peaches, because they're so delicious to eat right out of the fridge.

1	cup sugar
1	cup dry white wine, preferably Muscat or Riesling
3	just-ripe peaches, sliced in half, pits removed
1½	cups mascarpone
2	tablespoons confectioners' sugar
1	teaspoon pure vanilla extract
	Kosher salt

Combine the sugar and wine in a saucepan or deep skillet large enough to hold the peach halves in a single layer. Heat over medium heat until the sugar dissolves. Add the peaches cut side down in a single layer and cook gently for about 10 minutes. Flip the peaches over and continue to cook until tender (pierce them with a metal skewer to see), about another 10 minutes; you want the peaches to be tender but hold their shape. They will continue to cook a little as they cool. Take the pan off the heat and allow the peaches to cool in the syrup. Once cooled, you can easily slip off the skins, but you may serve them either way (skin on or skin off). Refrigerate the peaches in the syrup until ready to serve.

To make the cream, combine the mascarpone, confectioners' sugar, vanilla, and a pinch of salt in a medium bowl and whisk until the mixture increases in volume and thickens. Refrigerate until ready to serve.

To serve, put a large dollop of the mascarpone cream on each of six dishes or bowls. Remove the peaches from the syrup (but reserve the syrup) and place a peach half cut side down on top of the cream. Drizzle the syrup over and around the plate.

MAKE AHEAD: *Stored in their syrup and refrigerated, covered with plastic wrap, the peaches will keep for at least 3 or 4 days.*

Notes

index

Note: Page references in *italics* refer to photographs.

A

agnolotti, cheese, with butter sauce, celery, apple,
　　and prosciutto, 140–42, *141*
aïoli
　　lemon, 47
　　lemon, spicy, 47
　　saffron, 184
　　truffle, 20
almonds
　　Bibb lettuce with creamy Parmesan dressing
　　　　and cheese crisps, 62–64, *63*
　　spinach amandine, 282
anchovies
　　cauliflower, and pistachios, orecchiette with,
　　　　123, *124*
　　ricotta-stuffed heirloom tomatoes with black
　　　　olive vinaigrette and saffron croutons,
　　　　30–32, *31*
　　roasted eggplant with golden raisin–pine nut
　　　　vinaigrette and feta, *74*, 75–76
antipasto spread, preparing, 11
appetizers. *See* starters and small bites
apple(s)
　　caramelized, celery, and spiced walnuts,
　　　　pork chops with, 249–51, *250*
　　celery, prosciutto, and butter sauce, cheese
　　　　agnolotti with, 140–42, *141*
　　homemade apple butter tart, 304–6, *305*
arugula and tomato risotto with prosciutto,
　　166–67

asparagus

    soup with saffron croutons, 84

    steam-roasted, with fresh herb vinaigrette, 268

A-9 steak sauce, 243

avocados, slicing, 87

B

bacon and blue cheese dressing, iceberg wedges
    with, 65

baked cheese and tomatoes with black olive crisps,
    4, 5–6

barley and sweet potatoes, lamb stew with, 253–54

basil

    pesto, 126

    tomato tarte tatin, 26–28, *29*

bean(s)

    cannellini, and spicy sausage, rigatoni with,
        135–36, *137*

    spicy clam stew, 194

    torn pasta fagioli with shrimp polpettini,
        132, 133–34

    white, and spinach, seared salmon with, 185, *186*

    white, cooked, 195

    white, soup with sage and hazelnuts, 98–99, *99*

bean(s), green

    fennel, and cucumber salad with roasted
        potatoes and creamy yogurt, 72–73, *73*

    fritto misto with caramello sauce, 188–89, *190*

    pasta with potatoes and pesto, 126–27

    and roasted fennel, *274*, 275

    and seared shrimp salad with spicy curry
        vinaigrette, 77–78

beef. *See also* veal

    grass-fed, buying, 235

    seared steaks with cheese sauce and roasted
        onions, *234*, 244–45

    short ribs, buying, 248

    short ribs, red wine–braised, 246–47

    short ribs, trimming, 248

    steak cooking directions, 238

    tartare, butcher shop, *17*, 18

    tenderloin, slow-roasted, with thyme, 236

beet(s)

    and frisée salad with blue cheese, 66–67

    harvest salad, 69–70

Ben's wild rice salad, 287

berries. *See* strawberries

B&G coleslaw, 264, *265*

B&G pickles, *266*, 267

Bibb lettuce with creamy Parmesan dressing and
    cheese crisps, 62–64, *63*

bisque, creamy chestnut, 96–97

black olive(s)

    creamy leek and potato soup with bay scallops,
        93, *95*

    and fresh ricotta, brioche pizza with, 51

    paste, 6

    potato chips, 94, *95*

    slicing, into slivers, 95

    Taleggio-stuffed prosciutto-wrapped chicken
        with tomato and olive salad, 210–12, *211*

    vinaigrette, 33

    blini, corn, 271

blue cheese

    beet and frisée salad with, 66–67

    butter, 242

blue cheese (*cont.*)

    dressing and bacon, iceberg wedges with, 65

    Gorgonzola fondue, *36*, 37

Bolognese, butcher shop, 121–22, *122*

braised chicken thighs with rosemary and garlic, 213

braised lamb shanks with winter root vegetables,

    255–56, *258*

braised Tuscan kale, 276

bread crumbs, panko, 209

bread pudding, creamy vanilla, 292–93, *293*

bread(s). *See also* brioche pizza

    brioche, 55

    brioche rolls, 55

    crumbs, panko, notes about, 209

    saffron croutons, 32

    salad, toasted, with tomatoes and cucumber, 71

brioche bread, 55

brioche pizza

    with black olives and fresh ricotta, 51

    dough, 54–55

    with fried pistachios and honey, *49*, 50

    notes about, 48

    with roasted potatoes and rosemary, 52–53

brioche rolls, 55

broccoli

    fritto misto with caramello sauce, 188–89, *190*

butcher shop beef tartare, *17*, 18

butcher shop Bolognese, 121–22, *122*

butter cookies, 301

butters, flavored

    blue cheese, 242

    fresh herb, 239

    wild mushroom, 240, *241*

C

cabbage

    B&G coleslaw, 264, *265*

    chicken and vegetable soup with caraway

        gnocchi, 104–6, *105*

calamari, spicy, with spicy lemon aïoli, 45

caramel sauce, creamy, 294–95

caraway gnocchi, 106–7

carrots

    ginger-glazed, 269

    harvest salad, 69–70

    olive oil–glazed baby vegetables, 272, *273*

cauliflower

    anchovies, and pistachios, orecchiette with,

        123, *124*

    chaud-froid, 22–24, *23*

caviar

    cauliflower *chaud-froid*, 22–24, *23*

celery

    caramelized apples, and spiced walnuts,

        pork chops with, 249–51, *250*

    emulsion, 25

    leaves, cooking with, 25

celery root, pureed, and scallop gratinée, 196–97, *197*

chantilly cream, 295

cheese. *See also* ricotta

    agnolotti with butter sauce, celery, apple,

        and prosciutto, 140–42, *141*

    in antipasto spread, 11

    baked, and tomatoes with black olive crisps,

        4, 5–6

    Ben's wild rice salad, 287

    blue, beet and frisée salad with, 66–67

blue, butter, 242

blue, dressing and bacon, iceberg wedges with, 65

crisps and creamy Parmesan dressing,
    Bibb lettuce with, 62–64, *63*

crispy grilled, spicy tomato soup with, *90*, 91–92

Epoisses, notes about, 142

feta and golden raisin–pine nut vinaigrette,
    roasted eggplant with, *74*, 75–76

fontina- and mushroom-stuffed crespelles with
    brown butter–sage sauce, 170–72

Gorgonzola fondue, *36*, 37

grating, with Microplane, 21

and ham puff-pastry bites with honey mustard,
    7–8, *9*

mascarpone polenta, creamy, *221*, 286

mascarpone raviolini, 100

Mimolette, notes about, 165

pasta with potatoes and pesto, 126–27

peaches and cream, 310

risotto, 164

sauce and roasted onions, seared steaks with,
    234, 244–45

Taleggio-stuffed prosciutto-wrapped chicken
    with tomato and olive salad, 210–12, *211*

cheesecloth sachet, how to tie, 224

cherries, spiced, seared duck breasts with, 222–24, *223*

chestnut bisque, creamy, 96–97

chicken

    buying, 207

    consommé, 101–3

    cutlets, lemony breaded, 208–9

    cutting up, 219

    jus, 150–51

    meatball lasagnettes, *146*, 147–48

meatballs, 149–50

poulet au pain, *214*, 215–16, *217*

roasted, stock, 108

Taleggio-stuffed prosciutto-wrapped, with
    tomato and olive salad, 210–12, *211*

thighs, braised, with rosemary and garlic, 213

and vegetable soup with caraway gnocchi,
    104–6, *105*

chicken liver(s)

    butcher shop Bolognese, 121–22, *122*

    pâté, quick, 15, *16*

chilled tomato consommé, 86–87

chinois (sieve), notes about, 85

chocolate

    cookies, my favorite, 302–3

    grating, with Microplane, 21

    mousse, *290*, 296

chorizo and clam ragout, pan-fried cod with,
    180–81, *181*

citrus. *See also* grapefruit; lemon(s); limes; oranges

    -cured salmon, 41–42

    grating, with Microplane, 21

    segmenting, 187

    winter, with cumin meringue and whipped crème
        fraîche, 307–9, *308*

clam(s)

    and chorizo ragout, pan-fried cod with, 180–81, *181*

    fresh, storing, 179

    sauce, spicy, linguine with, 128–29

    slow-roasted, with spicy tomato sauce, 38

    stew, spicy, 194

classic shrimp cocktail, 43

cocktail sauce, 44

cod, pan-fried, chorizo and clam ragout, 180–81, *181*

coleslaw, B&G, 264, *265*

condiments

    in antipasto spread, 11

    black olive paste, 6

    cocktail sauce, 44

    honey mustard, 7

    lemon aïoli, 47

    olive-lemon relish, 187

    pesto, 126

    pickled onions, 13

    saffron aïoli, 184

    spiced prunes, 12

    spicy lemon aïoli, 47

    tomato confit, 28–29

    tomato jam, 284

    tomato syrup, 19

    truffle aïoli, 20

confit

    duck, 225–26, *227*

    duck, crisped, with kumquat marmalade, 228

    tomato, 28–29

consommé

    chicken, 101–3

    chilled tomato, 86–87

cooked white beans, 195

cookies

    butter, 301

    chocolate, my favorite, 302–3

cool corn soup with mushrooms, scallion, and lemon,

    82, 88–89

corn

    blini, 271

    off the cob, 270

    soup, cool, with mushrooms, scallion, and lemon,

        82, 88–89

    and tomato, roasted, lasagnettes, 143–45

Cornish game hen(s)

    cacciatore with creamy mascarpone polenta,

        218–19, *220*

    cutting up, 219

cornmeal. *See* polenta

crab(s)

    fresh, storing, 179

    Maine, lemon, and zucchini blossom risotto,

        168–69

cream, whipped

    adding to risotto, 167

    chantilly cream, 295

creamy caramel sauce, 294–95

creamy chestnut bisque, 96–97

creamy leek and potato soup with bay scallops, 93, 95

creamy vanilla bread pudding, 292–93, *293*

crème anglaise, vanilla, 298–99

crème fraîche

    saffron-steamed mussels with, *191*, 192–93

    whipped, and cumin meringue, winter citrus with,

        307–9, *308*

crepes, Italian, 170–72

crespelles, mushroom- and fontina-stuffed, with brown

    butter–sage sauce, 170–72

crisped duck confit with kumquat marmalade, 228

croutons, saffron, 32

cucumber(s)

    B&G pickles, *266*, 267

    fennel, and green bean salad with roasted

        potatoes and creamy yogurt, 72–73, *73*

    and tomatoes, toasted bread salad with, 71

curry vinaigrette, spicy, green bean and seared
    shrimp salad with, 77–78

D

deep-frying
    tips for, 46
    vegetables and fish (*fritto misto* with caramello
        sauce), 188–89, *190*
desserts
    butter cookies, 301
    chocolate mousse, *290, 296*
    creamy caramel sauce, 294–95
    creamy vanilla bread pudding, 292–93, *293*
    fresh fig sauce, 294
    homemade apple butter tart, 304–6, *305*
    my favorite chocolate cookies, 302–3
    oeufs à la neige with strawberries and vanilla
        crème anglaise, 297–98, *299*
    peaches and cream, 310
    vanilla crème anglaise, 298–99
    winter citrus with cumin meringue and
        whipped crème fraîche, 307–9, *308*
    yogurt panna cotta, 300
dips and spreads
    baked cheese and tomatoes with black olive
        crisps, *4,* 5–6
    black olive paste, 6
    cocktail sauce, 44
    fritto misto with caramello sauce, 188–89, *190*
    Gorgonzola fondue, *36,* 37
    homemade ricotta, easy, 35
    honey mustard, 7
    lemon aïoli, 47

olive-lemon relish, 187
pesto, 126
pickled onions, 13
quick chicken liver pâté, 15, *16*
saffron aïoli, 184
spiced prunes, 12
spicy lemon aïoli, 47
tomato jam, 284
tomato syrup, 19
truffle aïoli, 20
dough, fresh pasta, 115–18, *119*
duck. *See also* foie gras
    breasts, seared, with spiced cherries, 222–24, *223*
    confit, 225–26, *227*
    confit, crisped, with kumquat marmalade, 228
    confit, serving ideas, 227
dumplings
    caraway gnocchi, 106–7
    gnocchi, 154–56
    prune-stuffed gnocchi with foie gras sauce,
        125, 159–62
    ricotta gnudi, *152,* 153
    tomato gnocchi, 156
    truffled gnocchi, 156
    truffled gnocchi with peas and mushrooms, 157

E

easy homemade ricotta, 35
eggplant
    roasted, with golden raisin–pine nut vinaigrette
        and feta, *74,* 75–76
    salmon with roasted ratatouille and saffron aïoli,
        182–83

eggs
    harvest salad, 69–70
    oeufs à la neige with strawberries and vanilla
        crème anglaise, 297–98, *299*
    winter citrus with cumin meringue and whipped
        crème fraîche, 307–9, *308*
Epoisses cheese
    cheese agnolotti with butter sauce, celery, apple,
        and prosciutto, 140–42, *141*
    notes about, 142

F

fagioli, torn pasta, with shrimp polpettini, *132*, 133–34
fennel
    cucumber, and green bean salad with roasted
        potatoes and creamy yogurt, 72–73, *73*
    harvest salad, 69–70
    olive oil–glazed baby vegetables, *272*, *273*
    roasted, and green beans, *274*, 275
    toasted bread salad with tomatoes and
        cucumber, 71
feta cheese
    Ben's wild rice salad, 287
    and golden raisin–pine nut vinaigrette, roasted
        eggplant with, *74*, 75–76
fig
    fresh, sauce, 294
    ricotta, and prosciutto tartines, 10
first courses
    asparagus soup with saffron croutons, 84
    baked cheese and tomatoes with black olive crisps,
        4, 5–6
    beet and frisée salad with blue cheese, 66–67
    Bibb lettuce with creamy Parmesan dressing and
        cheese crisps, 62–64, *63*
    cauliflower *chaud-froid*, 22–24, *23*
    cheese risotto, 164
    chicken consommé, 101–3
    chicken meatball lasagnettes, *146*, 147–48
    chilled tomato consommé, 86–87
    citrus-cured salmon, 41–42
    cool corn soup with mushrooms, scallion,
        and lemon, *82*, 88–89
    creamy chestnut bisque, 96–97
    creamy leek and potato soup with bay scallops,
        93, *95*
    crisped duck confit with kumquat marmalade, 228
    fennel, cucumber, and green bean salad with
        roasted potatoes and creamy yogurt,
        72–73, *73*
    harvest salad, 69–70
    iceberg wedges with blue cheese dressing and
        bacon, 65
    lobster with toasted scallion–mushroom
        vinaigrette, 202–3
    mixed greens with fresh herbs, 60
    mushroom- and fontina-stuffed crespelles with
        brown butter–sage sauce, 170–72
    ricotta-stuffed heirloom tomatoes with black olive
        vinaigrette and saffron croutons, 30–32, *31*
    roasted corn and tomato lasagnettes, 143–45
    roasted eggplant with golden raisin–pine nut
        vinaigrette and feta, *74*, 75–76
    slow-roasted clams with spicy tomato sauce, 38
    toasted bread salad with tomatoes and
        cucumber, 71
    tomato tarte tatin, 26–28, *29*

STIR   MIXING IT UP IN THE ITALIAN TRADITION

white bean soup with sage and hazelnuts,
98–99, *99*

fish. *See also* anchovies; caviar; shellfish

cod, pan-fried, with chorizo and clam ragout,
180–81, *181*

fresh, buying and storing, 179

fritto misto with caramello sauce, 188–89, *190*

preparing and cooking, 177

salmon, citrus-cured, 41–42

salmon, seared, with white beans and spinach,
185, *186*

salmon with roasted ratatouille and saffron
aïoli, 182–83

sea bass, seared, with spicy soffrito, *176*, 178–79

foie gras

buying, 163

grades of, 163

sauce, prune-stuffed gnocchi with, *125*, 159–62

trimming, 163

fondue, Gorgonzola, *36*, 37

fontina- and mushroom-stuffed crespelles with
brown butter–sage sauce, 170–72

fresh fig sauce, 294

fresh herb butter, 239

fresh herb salads, preparing, 254

fresh pasta dough, 115–18, *119*

fried calamari with spicy lemon aïoli, 45

frisée and beet salad with blue cheese, 66–67

fritto misto with caramello sauce, 188–89, *190*

fruit. *See also* specific fruits

citrus, grating, with Microplane, 21

citrus, segmenting, 187

winter citrus with cumin meringue and whipped
crème fraîche, 307–9, *308*

G

ginger-glazed carrots, 269

gnocchi, 154–56

caraway, 106–7

gnocchi boards for, 158

prune-stuffed, with foie gras sauce, *125*, 159–62

tomato, 156

truffled, 156

truffled, with peas and mushrooms, 157

goose, spice-rubbed roast, 229–30

Gorgonzola fondue, *36*, 37

grains

Ben's wild rice salad, 287

cheese risotto, 164

creamy mascarpone polenta, *221*, 286

lamb stew with sweet potatoes and barley,
253–54

Maine crab, lemon, and zucchini blossom
risotto, 168–69

tomato and arugula risotto with prosciutto,
166–67

grapefruit

segmenting, 187

winter citrus with cumin meringue and
whipped crème fraîche, 307–9, *308*

graters, Microplane, 21

green bean(s)

fennel, and cucumber salad with roasted
potatoes and creamy yogurt, 72–73, *73*

fritto misto with caramello sauce, 188–89, *190*

pasta with potatoes and pesto, 126–27

and roasted fennel, *274*, 275

and seared shrimp salad with spicy curry
vinaigrette, 77–78

greens
  beet and frisée salad with blue cheese, 66–67
  Bibb lettuce with creamy Parmesan dressing and
    cheese crisps, 62–64, *63*
  braised Tuscan kale, 276
  iceberg wedges with blue cheese dressing and
    bacon, 65
  mesclun mix, note about, 59
  mixed, with fresh herbs, 60
  seared salmon with white beans and spinach,
    185, *186*
  spinach amandine, 282
  tomato and arugula risotto with prosciutto,
    166–67
  washing and storing, 61
gremolata, fresh mint, rack of lamb with, 252

320

H

ham. *See also* prosciutto
  and cheese puff-pastry bites with honey
    mustard, 7–8, *9*
harvest salad, 69–70
hazelnuts
  green bean and seared shrimp salad with spicy
    curry vinaigrette, 77–78
  and sage, white bean soup with, 98–99, *99*
  toasted, and sauce verte, seared sea scallops
    with, 198–99
herb(s). *See also* basil; mint; rosemary
  fresh, butter, 239
  fresh, mixed greens with, 60
  fresh, salads, preparing, 254

fresh, vinaigrette, steam-roasted asparagus with,
  268
seared sea scallops with sauce verte and
  toasted hazelnuts, 198–99
washing and storing, 61
homemade apple butter tart, 304–6, *305*
homemade potato chips, 267
honey
  and fried pistachios, brioche pizza with, *49*, 50
  mustard, 7
hors d'oeuvres. See starters and small bites
horseradish
  cauliflower *chaud-froid*, 22–24, *23*
  cocktail sauce, 44

I

iceberg wedges with blue cheese dressing and
  bacon, 65

J

jam, tomato, 284
jus, chicken, 150–51

K

kale, braised Tuscan, 276
ketchup (store-bought)
  A-9 steak sauce, 243
  cocktail sauce, 44
kumquat marmalade, crisped duck confit with, 228

L

lamb
    butcher shop Bolognese, 121–22, *122*
    Gorgonzola fondue, *36, 37*
    rack of, with fresh mint gremolata, 252
    shanks, braised, with winter root vegetables, 255–56, *258*
    shanks, frenching, 257
    stew with sweet potatoes and barley, 253–54
lasagnas, little (lasagnettes)
    chicken meatball, *146*, 147–48
    roasted corn and tomato, 143–45
leek and potato soup, creamy, with bay scallops, 93, *95*
lemon(s)
    aïoli, 47
    aïoli, spicy, 47
    aïoli lobster rolls, 200–201, *201*
    citrus-cured salmon, 41–42
    lemony breaded chicken cutlets, 208–9
    -olive relish, 187
    segmenting, 187
    winter citrus with cumin meringue and whipped crème fraîche, 307–9, *308*
limes
    citrus-cured salmon, 41–42
    segmenting, 187
linguine with spicy clam sauce, 128–29
liver, chicken
    butcher shop Bolognese, 121–22, *122*
    pâté, quick, 15, *16*
liver, duck. *See* foie gras
lobster(s)
    Bolognese, spicy, 130–31
    fresh, storing, 179
    rolls, lemon aïoli, 200–201, *201*
    with toasted scallion–mushroom vinaigrette, 202–3

M

main dishes (meat)
    braised lamb shanks with winter root vegetables, 255–56, *258*
    lamb stew with sweet potatoes and barley, 253–54
    pork chops with caramelized apples, celery, and spiced walnuts, 249–51, *250*
    rack of lamb with fresh mint gremolata, 252
    red wine–braised short ribs, 246–47
    seared steaks with cheese sauce and roasted onions, *234*, 244–45
    slow-roasted beef tenderloin with thyme, 236
main dishes (pasta and pizza)
    brioche pizza with roasted potatoes and rosemary, 52–53
    cheese agnolotti with butter sauce, celery, apple, and prosciutto, 140–42, *141*
    chicken meatball lasagnettes, *146*, 147–48
    gnocchi, 154–56
    linguine with spicy clam sauce, 128–29
    mushroom- and fontina-stuffed crespelles with brown butter–sage sauce, 170–72
    orecchiette with cauliflower, anchovies, and pistachios, 123, 124
    pappardelle with tangy veal ragu, 138–39
    pasta with potatoes and pesto, 126–27
    prune-stuffed gnocchi with foie gras sauce, *125*, 159–62

main dishes (pasta and pizza) (*cont.*)

ricotta gnudi, *152*, 153

rigatoni with spicy sausage and cannellini beans, 135–36, *137*

spicy lobster Bolognese, 130–31

tomato gnocchi, 156

torn pasta fagioli with shrimp polpettini, *132*, 133–34

truffled gnocchi, 156

truffled gnocchi with peas and mushrooms, 157

main dishes (poultry)

braised chicken thighs with rosemary and garlic, 213

Cornish game hen cacciatore with creamy mascarpone polenta, 218–19, *220*

crisped duck confit with kumquat marmalade, 228

duck confit, 225–26, *227*

lemony breaded chicken cutlets, 208–9

poulet au pain, *214*, 215–16, *217*

seared duck breasts with spiced cherries, 222–24, *223*

spice-rubbed roast goose, 229–30

Taleggio-stuffed prosciutto-wrapped chicken with tomato and olive salad, 210–12, *211*

main dishes (seafood)

fritto misto with caramello sauce, 188–89, *190*

lemon aïoli lobster rolls, 200–201, *201*

lobster with toasted scallion–mushroom vinaigrette, 202–3

pan-fried cod with chorizo and clam ragout, 180–81, *181*

saffron-steamed mussels with crème fraîche, *191*, 192–93

salmon with roasted ratatouille and saffron aïoli, 182–83

scallop and pureed celery root gratinée, 196–97, *197*

seared salmon with white beans and spinach, 185, *186*

seared sea bass with spicy soffrito, *176*, 178–79

seared sea scallops with sauce verte and toasted hazelnuts, 198–99

spicy clam stew, 194

main dishes (soups, salads, and risotto)

cheese risotto, 164

chicken and vegetable soup with caraway gnocchi, 104–6, *105*

green bean and seared shrimp salad with spicy curry vinaigrette, 77–78

Maine crab, lemon, and zucchini blossom risotto, 168–69

spicy tomato soup with crispy grilled cheese, *90*, 91–92

tomato and arugula risotto with prosciutto, 166–67

Maine crab, lemon, and zucchini blossom risotto, 168–69

maple syrup and sage cream, roasted winter squash with, 283

marinara, Odd Fellow, 120

marmalade, kumquat, crisped duck confit with, 228

mascarpone

peaches and cream, 310

polenta, creamy, *221*, 286

raviolini, 100

meat. *See also* beef; lamb; pork; veal

butcher shop Bolognese, 121–22, *122*

buying, notes about, 235

meatball, chicken, lasagnettes, *146*, 147–48

meatballs, chicken, 149–50

meringue, cumin, and whipped crème fraîche,
winter citrus with, 307–9, *308*

Microplane graters, 21

Mimolette cheese
cheese risotto, 164
notes about, 165

mint, fresh, gremolata, rack of lamb with, 252

mixed greens with fresh herbs, 60

mousse, chocolate, *290*, 296

mushroom(s)
and fontina-stuffed crespelles with brown
butter–sage sauce, 170–72
and peas, truffled gnocchi with, 157
scallion, and lemon, cool corn soup with, *82*,
88–89
seared steaks with cheese sauce and roasted
onions, *234*, 244–45
–toasted scallion vinaigrette, 202
wild, butter, 240, *241*

mussels
fresh, storing, 179
saffron-steamed, with crème fraîche, *191*, 192–93

mustard, honey, 7

my favorite chocolate cookies, 302–3

N

nonstick cooking mats, 64

nuts. *See also* hazelnuts; pine nut(s)
Bibb lettuce with creamy Parmesan dressing
and cheese crisps, 62–64, *63*

brioche pizza with fried pistachios and honey,
49, 50

creamy chestnut bisque, 96–97

orecchiette with cauliflower, anchovies, and
pistachios, 123, *124*

spiced walnuts, 251

spinach amandine, 282

O

Odd Fellow marinara, 120
oeufs à la neige with strawberries and vanilla
crème anglaise, 297–98, *299*

olive oil–glazed baby vegetables, 272, *273*

olive(s)
black, and fresh ricotta, brioche pizza with, 51
black, paste, 6
black, potato chips, 94, *95*
black, vinaigrette, 33
creamy leek and potato soup with bay scallops,
93, *95*
-lemon relish, 187
slicing, into slivers, 95
and tomato salad, Taleggio-stuffed prosciutto-
wrapped chicken with, 210–12, *211*

onions
honey mustard, 7
pearl, au gratin, 277
pickled, 13
roasted, and cheese sauce, seared steaks with,
234, 244–45

oranges
Ben's wild rice salad, 287
citrus-cured salmon, 41–42

oranges (*cont.*)

    segmenting, 187

    winter citrus with cumin meringue and
        whipped crème fraîche, 307–9, *308*

orecchiette with cauliflower, anchovies, and
    pistachios, 123, *124*

oysters

    cauliflower *chaud-froid*, 22–24, *23*

    fresh, storing, 179

    on the half shell with sparkling mignonette, 39

    shucking, 40

P

pancakes. *See* blini

pan-fried cod with chorizo and clam ragout, 180–81, *181*

panko, notes about, 209

panna cotta, yogurt, 300

pappardelle with tangy veal ragu, 138–39

Parmesan

    in antipasto spread, 11

    cheese agnolotti with butter sauce, celery, apple,
        and prosciutto, 140–42, *141*

    dressing, creamy, and cheese crisps, Bibb lettuce
        with, 62–64, *63*

    pasta with potatoes and pesto, 126–27

pasta. *See also* gnocchi

    agnolotti, cheese, with butter sauce, celery, apple,
        and prosciutto, 140–42, *141*

    Bolognese, butcher shop, 121–22, *122*

    chicken meatball lasagnettes, *146*, 147–48

    crespelles, mushroom- and fontina-stuffed,
        with brown butter–sage sauce, 170–72

    dough, fresh, 115–18, *119*

fagioli, torn, with shrimp polpettini, *132*, 133–34

gnudi, ricotta, *152*, 153

linguine with spicy clam sauce, 128–29

lobster Bolognese, spicy, 130–31

marinara, Odd Fellow, 120

orecchiette with cauliflower, anchovies,
    and pistachios, 123, *124*

pappardelle with tangy veal ragu, 138–39

with potatoes and pesto, 126–27

raviolini, mascarpone, 100

rigatoni with spicy sausage and cannellini beans,
    135–36, *137*

roasted corn and tomato lasagnettes, 143–45

pâté, quick chicken liver, 15, *16*

peaches and cream, 310

pearl onions au gratin, 277

peas and mushrooms, truffled gnocchi with, 157

pepper(s)

    Cornish game hen cacciatore with creamy
        mascarpone polenta, 218–19, *220*

    seared sea bass with spicy soffrito, *176*, 178–79

    yellow and red bell, agrodolce, 14

pesto and potatoes, pasta with, 126–27

pickled onions, 13

pickles, B&G, *266*, 267

pine nut(s)

    Ben's wild rice salad, 287

    –golden raisin vinaigrette and feta, roasted
        eggplant with, *74*, 75–76

    pesto, 126

    rack of lamb with fresh mint gremolata, 252

pistachios

    cauliflower, and anchovies, orecchiette with,
        123, *124*

fried, and honey, brioche pizza with, *49*, 50

pizza, brioche

    with black olives and fresh ricotta, 51

    with fried pistachios and honey, *49*, 50

    with roasted potatoes and rosemary, 52–53

polenta, creamy mascarpone, *221*, 286

pommes frites, 262, 280

pommes puree, 278

pork. *See also* bacon; ham; prosciutto

    butcher shop Bolognese, 121–22, *122*

    chops with caramelized apples, celery, and spiced

        walnuts, 249–51, *250*

    pan-fried cod with chorizo and clam ragout,

        180–81, *181*

    rigatoni with spicy sausage and cannellini beans,

        135–36, *137*

    sausages, in antipasto spread, 11

potato(es)

    chips, black olive, 94, *95*

    chips, homemade, 267

    corn blini, 271

    gnocchi, caraway, 106–7

    gnocchi, prune-stuffed, with foie gras sauce,

        125, 159–62

    gnocchi, tomato, 156

    gnocchi, truffled, 156

    gnocchi, truffled, with peas and mushrooms, 157

    and leek soup, creamy, with bay scallops, 93, 95

    mousseline, 279

    and pesto, pasta with, 126–27

    pommes frites, *262*, 280

    pommes puree, 278

    roasted, and creamy yogurt, fennel, cucumber,

        and green bean salad with, 72–73, *73*

roasted, and rosemary, brioche pizza with, 52–53

spice-rubbed roast goose, 229–30

sweet, and barley, lamb stew with, 253–54

potato ricers, 156

poulet au pain, *214*, 215–16, *217*

poultry. *See also* chicken

    buying, 207

    Cornish game hen, cutting up, 219

    Cornish game hen cacciatore with creamy

        mascarpone polenta, 218–19, *220*

    crisped duck confit with kumquat marmalade, 228

    duck confit, 225–26, *227*

    seared duck breasts with spiced cherries,

        222–24, *223*

    spice-rubbed roast goose, 229–30

prosciutto

    in antipasto spread, 11

    celery, apple, and butter sauce, cheese agnolotti

        with, 140–42, *141*

    fig, and ricotta tartines, 10

    tomato and arugula risotto with, 166–67

    -wrapped Taleggio-stuffed chicken with tomato

        and olive salad, 210–12, *211*

prune(s)

    spiced, 12

    -stuffed gnocchi with foie gras sauce, *125*, 159–62

pudding, bread, creamy vanilla, 292–93, *293*

puff pastry

    all-butter, buying, 9

    bites, ham and cheese, with honey mustard, 7–8, *9*

    homemade apple butter tart, 304–6, *305*

    tomato tarte tatin, 26–28, *29*

Q

quick chicken liver pâté, 15, *16*

R

rack of lamb with fresh mint gremolata, 252

radishes

harvest salad, 69–70

ricotta-stuffed heirloom tomatoes with black
olive vinaigrette and saffron croutons,
30–32, *31*

raisin(s)

Ben's wild rice salad, 287

golden, –pine nut vinaigrette and feta, roasted
eggplant with, *74*, 75–76

rack of lamb with fresh mint gremolata, 252

yellow and red bell pepper agrodolce, 14

ratatouille, roasted, and saffron aïoli, salmon with,
182–83

raviolini, mascarpone, 100

red wine–braised short ribs, 246–47

red wine sauce, 237

relish, olive-lemon, 187

rice

cheese risotto, 164

Maine crab, lemon, and zucchini blossom risotto,
168–69

tomato and arugula risotto with prosciutto,
166–67

wild, salad, Ben's, 287

ricotta

brioche pizza with fried pistachios and honey,
49, 50

fig, and prosciutto tartines, 10

fresh, and black olives, brioche pizza with, 51

fresh, buying, 34

gnudi, *152*, 153

homemade, easy, 35

-stuffed heirloom tomatoes with black olive
vinaigrette and saffron croutons,
30–32, *31*

rigatoni with spicy sausage and cannellini beans,
135–36, *137*

risotto

adding whipped cream to, 167

cheese, 164

Maine crab, lemon, and zucchini blossom, 168–69

making ahead, 169

tomato and arugula, with prosciutto, 166–67

roasted chicken stock, 108

roasted corn and tomato lasagnettes, 143–45

roasted eggplant with golden raisin–pine nut
vinaigrette and feta, *74*, 75–76

roasted fennel and green beans, *274*, 275

roasted winter squash with maple syrup and sage
cream, 283

rolls, brioche, 55

rosemary

and garlic, braised chicken thighs with, 213

and roasted potatoes, brioche pizza with, 52–53

S

saffron

aïoli, 184

croutons, 32

-steamed mussels with crème fraîche, *191*, 192–93

salads
    beet and frisée, with blue cheese, 66–67
    B&G coleslaw, 264, *265*
    Bibb lettuce with creamy Parmesan dressing and
        cheese crisps, 62–64, *63*
    fennel, cucumber, and green bean, with roasted
        potatoes and creamy yogurt, 72–73, *73*
    fresh herb, preparing, 254
    green bean and seared shrimp, with spicy curry
        vinaigrette, 77–78
    harvest, 69–70
    iceberg wedges with blue cheese dressing
        and bacon, 65
    mixed greens with fresh herbs, 60
    roasted eggplant with golden raisin–pine nut
        vinaigrette and feta, *74*, 75–76
    serving, notes about, 59
    toasted bread, with tomatoes and cucumber, 71
    tomato and olive, 210–12
    wild rice, Ben's, 287
salmon
    citrus-cured, 41–42
    with roasted ratatouille and saffron aïoli, 182–83
    seared, with white beans and spinach, 185, *186*
salting food, xv
sandwiches
    crispy grilled cheese, spicy tomato soup with,
        90, 91–92
    lemon aïoli lobster rolls, 200–201, *201*
sauces. *See also* butters, flavored
    brown butter–sage, mushroom- and fontina-
        stuffed crespelles with, 170–72
    butcher shop Bolognese, 121–22, *122*
    caramel, creamy, 294–95

caramello, *fritto misto* with, 188–89, *190*
    cheese, and roasted onions, seared steaks with,
        234, 244–45
    clam, spicy, linguine with, 128–29
    cocktail, 44
    foie gras, prune-stuffed gnocchi with, *125*, 159–62
    fresh fig, 294
    Odd Fellow marinara, 120
    pesto, 126
    red wine, 237
    steak, A-9, 243
    tomato, spicy, slow-roasted clams with, 38
    vanilla crème anglaise, 298–99
    verte and toasted hazelnuts, seared sea scallops
        with, 198–99
sausage(s)
    in antipasto spread, 11
    pan-fried cod with chorizo and clam ragout,
        180–81, *181*
    spicy, and cannellini beans, rigatoni with,
        135–36, *137*
scallion, toasted, –mushroom vinaigrette, 202
scallop(s)
    bay, creamy leek and potato soup with, 93, *95*
    buying, 199
    and pureed celery root gratinée, 196–97, *197*
    sea, seared, with sauce verte and toasted
        hazelnuts, 198–99
sea bass, seared, with spicy soffrito, *176*, 178–79
seafood, buying and storing, 179
seared duck breasts with spiced cherries, 222–24, *223*
seared salmon with white beans and spinach,
    185, *186*
seared sea bass with spicy soffrito, *176*, 178–79

seared sea scallops with sauce verte and
toasted hazelnuts, 198–99

seared steaks with cheese sauce and roasted onions,
234, 244–45

seasoning food, xv

shellfish
calamari, fried, with spicy lemon aïoli, 45
clam and chorizo ragout, pan-fried cod with,
180–81, *181*
clams, slow-roasted, with spicy tomato sauce, 38
clam sauce, spicy, linguine with, 128–29
clam stew, spicy, 194
fresh, buying and storing, 179
lobster Bolognese, spicy, 130–31
lobster rolls, lemon aïoli, 200–201, *201*
lobster with toasted scallion–mushroom
vinaigrette, 202–3
Maine crab, lemon, and zucchini blossom risotto,
168–69
mussels, saffron-steamed, with crème fraîche,
191, 192–93
oysters, shucking, 40
scallop and pureed celery root gratinée, 196–97,
197
scallops, bay, creamy leek and potato soup with,
93, 95
scallops, buying, 199
scallops, sea, seared, with sauce verte and
toasted hazelnuts, 198–99
shrimp, seared, and green bean salad with spicy
curry vinaigrette, 77–78
shrimp cocktail, classic, 43
shrimp polpettini, torn pasta fagioli with,
132, 133–34

shrimp
cocktail, classic, 43
polpettini, torn pasta fagioli with, *132*, 133–34
seared, and green bean salad with spicy curry
vinaigrette, 77–78

side dishes. *See also* salads
B&G coleslaw, 264, *265*
B&G pickles, *266*, 267
braised Tuscan kale, 276
corn blini, 271
corn off the cob, 270
creamy mascarpone polenta, *221*, 286
ginger-glazed carrots, 269
gnocchi, 154–56
homemade potato chips, 267
mascarpone raviolini, 100
olive oil–glazed baby vegetables, 272, *273*
pearl onions au gratin, 277
pommes frites, *262*, 280
pommes puree, 278
potatoes mousseline, 279
ricotta gnudi, *152*, 153
roasted corn and tomato lasagnettes, 143–45
roasted fennel and green beans, *274*, 275
roasted winter squash with maple syrup and
sage cream, 283
spinach amandine, 282
steam-roasted asparagus with fresh herb
vinaigrette, 268
tomato gnocchi, 156
tomato jam, 284
truffled gnocchi, 156
truffled gnocchi with peas and mushrooms, 157
turnip puree, 285

sieve, fine-mesh, about, 85

Silpat mats, 64

slow-roasted beef tenderloin with thyme, 236

slow-roasted clams with spicy tomato sauce, 38

soffrito, spicy, seared sea bass with, *176*, 178–79

soups. *See also* stews

    asparagus, with saffron croutons, 84

    chicken and vegetable, with caraway gnocchi,
        104–6, *105*

    chicken consommé, 101–3

    chilled tomato consommé, 86–87

    corn, cool, with mushrooms, scallion, and lemon,
        82, 88–89

    creamy chestnut bisque, 96–97

    leek and potato, creamy, with bay scallops, 93, 95

    roasted chicken stock, 108

    tomato, spicy, with crispy grilled cheese, *90*, 91–92

    white bean, with sage and hazelnuts, 98–99, *99*

spiced prunes, 12

spiced walnuts, 251

spice-rubbed roast goose, 229–30

spicy clam stew, 194

spicy lobster Bolognese, 130–31

spicy tomato soup with crispy grilled cheese,
    90, 91–92

spinach

    amandine, 282

    and white beans, seared salmon with, 185, *186*

squash

    Maine crab, lemon, and zucchini blossom risotto,
        168–69

    olive oil–glazed baby vegetables, 272, *273*

    salmon with roasted ratatouille and saffron aïoli,
        182–83

    winter, roasted, with maple syrup and sage
        cream, 283

squid. *See* calamari

starters and small bites

    antipasto spread, preparing, 11

    baked cheese and tomatoes with black olive
        crisps, *4*, 5–6

    brioche pizza with black olives and fresh ricotta, 51

    brioche pizza with fried pistachios and honey,
        49, 50

    brioche pizza with roasted potatoes and
        rosemary, 52–53

    butcher shop beef tartare, *17*, 18

    cauliflower *chaud-froid*, 22–24, *23*

    citrus-cured salmon, 41–42

    classic shrimp cocktail, 43

    corn blini, 271

    fig, ricotta, and prosciutto tartines, 10

    fried calamari with spicy lemon aïoli, 45

    Gorgonzola fondue, *36*, 37

    ham and cheese puff-pastry bites with honey
        mustard, 7–8, *9*

    oysters on the half shell with sparkling
        mignonette, 39

    pickled onions, 13

    quick chicken liver pâté, 15, *16*

    ricotta-stuffed heirloom tomatoes with black
        olive vinaigrette and saffron croutons,
        30–32, *31*

    slow-roasted clams with spicy tomato sauce, 38

    spiced prunes, 12

    spicy tomato soup with crispy grilled cheese,
        90, 91–92

    tomato tarte tatin, 26–28, *29*

starters and small bites (*cont.*)

  yellow and red bell pepper agrodolce, 14

steak sauce, A-9, 243

steam-roasted asparagus with fresh herb

  vinaigrette, 268

stews

  clam, spicy, 194

  lamb, with sweet potatoes and barley, 253–54

stock, roasted chicken, 108

strainers, fine-mesh, or sieves, 85

strawberries and vanilla crème anglaise, oeufs à

  la neige with, 297–98, *299*

sweet potatoes and barley, lamb stew with, 253–54

T

Taleggio-stuffed prosciutto-wrapped chicken with

  tomato and olive salad, 210–12, *211*

tartare, butcher shop beef, *17*, 18

tarts

  fig, ricotta, and prosciutto tartines, 10

  homemade apple butter, 304–6, *305*

  tomato tarte tatin, 26–28, *29*

toasted bread salad with tomatoes and cucumber, 71

tomato(es)

  and arugula risotto with prosciutto, 166–67

  and baked cheese with black olive crisps, *4*, 5–6

  confit, 28–29

  consommé, chilled, 86–87

  and corn, roasted, lasagnettes, 143–45

  Cornish game hen cacciatore with creamy

    mascarpone polenta, 218–19, *220*

  and cucumber, toasted bread salad with, 71

  gnocchi, 156

heirloom, ricotta-stuffed, with black olive

  vinaigrette and saffron croutons,

    30–32, *31*

jam, 284

Odd Fellow marinara, 120

and olive salad, Taleggio-stuffed prosciutto-

  wrapped chicken with, 210–12, *211*

pappardelle with tangy veal ragu, 138–39

peeling skin from, 6

rigatoni with spicy sausage and cannellini beans,

  135–36, *137*

salmon with roasted ratatouille and saffron aïoli,

  182–83

sauce, spicy, slow-roasted clams with, 38

soup, spicy, with crispy grilled cheese, *90*, 91–92

spicy clam stew, 194

spicy lobster Bolognese, 130–31

syrup, 19

tarte tatin, 26–28, *29*

tongs, notes about, 183

torn pasta fagioli with shrimp polpettini, *132*, 133–34

truffle(d)

  aïoli, 20

  gnocchi, 156

  gnocchi with peas and mushrooms, 157

turnip(s)

  harvest salad, 69–70

  puree, 285

Tuscan kale, braised, 276

V

vanilla
  bread pudding, creamy, 292–93, *293*
  crème anglaise, 298–99
veal
  butcher shop Bolognese, 121–22, *122*
  ragu, tangy, pappardelle with, 138–39
vegetable(s). *See also specific vegetables*
  baby, olive oil–glazed, 272, *273*
  and chicken soup with caraway gnocchi,
      104–6, *105*
  fritto misto with caramello sauce, 188–89, *190*
  harvest salad, 69–70
  winter root, braised lamb shanks with, 255–56,
      258
vinaigrettes
  black olive, 33
  curry, spicy, green bean and seared shrimp salad
      with, 77–78
  fresh herb, steam-roasted asparagus with, 268
  golden raisin–pine nut, and feta, roasted
      eggplant with, 74, 75–76
  toasted scallion–mushroom, 202

W

walnuts, spiced, 251
whipped cream
  adding to risotto, 167
  chantilly cream, 295
white bean(s)
  cooked, 195
  rigatoni with spicy sausage and cannellini beans,
      135–36, 137
  soup with sage and hazelnuts, 98–99, *99*
  spicy clam stew, 194
  and spinach, seared salmon with, 185, 186
  torn pasta fagioli with shrimp polpettini, 132,
      133–34
wild mushroom butter, 240, 241
wild rice salad, Ben's, 287
winter citrus with cumin meringue and whipped
      crème fraîche, 307–9, *308*

Y

yellow and red bell pepper agrodolce, 14
yogurt
  creamy, and roasted potatoes, fennel, cucumber,
      and green bean salad with, 72–73, *73*
  panna cotta, 300

Z

zucchini
  blossom, Maine crab, and lemon risotto, 168–69
  olive oil–glazed baby vegetables, 272, 273
  salmon with roasted ratatouille and saffron aïoli,
      182–83

Notes

Notes

Notes

Notes

STIR   READ   COOK   GATHER   GIVE